WRITING THE FIRST PERSON

Literature, History, and Autobiography in Modern Kerala

WRITING THE FIRST PERSON

Literature, History, and Autobiography in Modern Kerala

UDAYA KUMAR

permanent black

and

ashoka UNIVERSITY

Published by

PERMANENT BLACK

'Himalayana', Mall Road, Ranikhet Cantt,
Ranikhet 263645

perblack@gmail.com

and

Indian Institute of Advanced Study, Shimla

and

ashoka
UNIVERSITY

Distributed by

ORIENT BLACKSWAN PRIVATE LTD

Bangalore Bhopal Bhubaneshwar Chandigarh Chennai
Ernakulam Guwahati Hyderabad Jaipur Kolkata
Lucknow Mumbai New Delhi Patna
www.orientblackswan.com

ISBN 978-81-7824-520-1

Typeset in Adobe Garamond Pro
by Guru Typograph Technology, Ghaziabad 201009
Printed and bound by Manipal Technologies Limited, Manipal

MIX
Paper | Supporting responsible forestry
FSC™ C043100
FSC www.fsc.org

for

B. RAJEEVAN
in friendship

Contents

Acknowledgements

OVER ITS UNUSUALLY LONG period of gestation, this book has accumulated debts far too numerous to acknowledge adequately. Its origins were in a research project I worked on as a Fellow at the Indian Institute of Advanced Study, Shimla, almost two decades ago. Initially proposed as an enquiry into the development of autobiographical writing in Malayalam, the project developed into a study of idioms of self-articulation through several genres of writing from the late-nineteenth and early-twentieth century in Kerala.

A first draft of the manuscript was submitted to the Institute in 1998 and was soon accepted for publication. However, I felt that more research and thinking were needed. For a variety of personal and intellectual circumstances, the process took longer than expected. Much of my research and writing over the past years has been closely linked to the issues I began grappling with in Shimla; this has helped in developing my initial ideas more clearly, in greater detail, and in new directions. I would like to thank Professor Mrinal Miri, who was Director of the Indian Institute of Advanced Study during my fellowship, and Professor Chetan Singh, the present Director, for their warm and generous support in making this book and its publication possible.

In addition to the Indian Institute of Advanced Study, several institutions have supported my work on this book and I am indebted to them all. I wish to thank the University of Delhi, where I taught at the English Department for the major part of the past two decades; the Centre for Studies in Social Sciences (CSSSC), Calcutta, where I worked as a faculty member for three years; Newcastle University, which hosted me on a Leverhulme Visiting Professorship; and the Nehru Memorial Museum and Library (NMML), where a Senior Fellowship enabled me to complete this manuscript as well as do some new research. Friends, colleagues, and students at these institutions have played a tremendously important role in shaping this book. Many of them read earlier versions of the chapters, and their responses helped correct misconceptions and opened new directions of thinking. Partha Chatterjee and Mahesh Rangarajan—then directors of the CSSSC and the NMML, respectively—were unstinting in their support.

Earlier versions of some arguments developed in this book have appeared elsewhere. Parts of the analyses in chapters 2 and 3 were published in *Studies in History*; some ideas in chapters 4 and 5 were initially formulated for a contribution to the volume *Early Novels in India* edited by Meenakshi Mukherjee; initial versions of the analyses in chapter 6 were published in *History in the Vernacular* edited by Raziuddin Aquil and Partha Chatterjee, and in *Different Types of History* edited by Bharati Ray.

The intellectual friendship of G. Arunima, Sibaji Bandyopadhyay, Prathama Banerjee, Baidik Bhattacharya, Rimli Bhattacharya, Howard Caygill, Partha Chatterjee, Dipesh Chakrabarty, Pradip Datta, J. Devika, Oommen George, Aniket Jaaware, Ritty Lukose, Dilip Menon, Tilottama Misra, Udayon Misra, Sanal Mohan, Navaneetha Mokkil, Meenakshi Mukherjee, Janaki Nair, Francesca Orsini, Ayyappa Paniker, Rochelle Pinto, Ratheesh Radhakrishnan, Manas Ray, V. Sanil, K. Satchidanandan, Sambudha Sen, Suresh Sharma, Tridip Suhrud, Rajeswari Sunder Rajan, Milind Wakankar, and A.R. Venkatachalapathy have been invaluable for my thinking, and conversations with them have helped hugely. I have also been fortunate in my close personal friends—Anu, Jayan, Jose, Marcus, Maya, Nilofer, PK, Ritty, Sambudha, Sangeetha, Satheesh, Savithri,

Sebastian, Venu and many others—whose affection has been an unfailing source of sustenance during these past years.

My thanks to Veena are difficult to express; without her, this book, like so much else in my life, would remain unthinkable.

I owe a special note of thanks to Rukun Advani and Anuradha Roy of Permanent Black for accepting this as a manuscript. The book has gained a lot in clarity and coherence from Rukun's attentive, extraordinarily caring editing.

Thanks to Shibu Natesan's warmth and generosity, the jacket shows an image of his 'Kumarasan', a painting I admire for its rare beauty and force. I am very grateful for his permission to use it.

B. Rajeevan's work, as well as his personal and intellectual friendship, have been enormously important for my thinking, and this book bears indelible traces of his proximity. In affectionate acknowledgement, I dedicate this book to him.

UDAYA KUMAR
New Delhi, February 2016

1

Conditions of Self-Writing

This book began as an attempt to understand the beginnings of autobiographical writing in Malayalam, the major language of Kerala in South India. As in most Indian languages, autobiographies began to make their appearance in Malayalam in the nineteenth century.[1] Some of these were written in the context of Protestant Christian missionary activity and testified to experiences of religious conversion; others were authored by persons of some public standing.

The documentation of one's own life was not always undertaken with the aim of later publishing it; the beginnings frequently suggest an intent more modest and informal. For instance, when K. Kannan Nair, a well-known figure in the Nayar reform movement, decided to write his autobiography in 1939, he assured his readers that his account was based on a diary he had kept continuously for almost fifty years.[2] Kannan Nair was introduced to diary writing in

[1] Vaikathu Pachu Moothathu's *Atmakatha,* written in 1875, was for a long time regarded as the first modern autobiography in Malayalam. The rediscovery of Yakob Ramavarman's personal narrative has altered this: Ramavarman's account appears to precede Moothathu's by nineteen years. See Moothathu, 'Atmakatha'; Ramavarman, 'Yakob Ramavarman'.

[2] Kannan Nair was one of the founders of the Changanassery Nayar Samajam, an early initiative to organize the Nayars and initiate reforms in

school by a teacher called Selvanayakam, who considered it 'a good means of literary training on an easy subject matter.'[3] Short essays in periodicals, many of which had just begun to appear, offered another form in which idioms of first-person writing were forged. Entertaining anecdotes and ordinary experiences from the everyday formed an important part of these pieces.

In the twentieth century, autobiographical writing in Kerala stabilized as a literary genre and developed a canon. Narratives of personal life, set against a background of changing times, acquired prominence and came to shape the genre's principal features. In these texts, a narrative about one's own life—a self-narrative—became the means of documenting a world rapidly receding into the past, and for recording personal testimonies of social change. Autobiography became an important form for the writing of histories outside the professional or academic domain. Several dimensions of social and individual life, which often do not find much room in scholarly histories of the period, managed ample space in these personal narratives. Experiences of embodiment and social inhabitation, which relate a subject not only to the world but also to one's own identity, found at times their strongest articulation in them. These oblique pulsations of history in the timbre of the first-person voice raise some fertile questions.

Practices of personal narration in the late-nineteenth and twentieth centuries indicate an important moment in the discursive history of the 'subject'—understood here as the point where ideas of personhood, agency, and capacity for experience converge—in modern Kerala. Choosing one's life for narrative elaboration has

their customs and practices. He was the founder editor of the journal *Nayar*, published from Changanassery in 1903 and *Nayar Samudaya Parishkarini* from Kollam in 1904. See G. Priyadarshan, *Adyakalamasikakal*, 44–8. Later organizational initiatives in Nayar social reform are mentioned below. See also Jeffrey 212–21.

[3] K. Kannan Nair, *Karuthodi Kannan Nayarude Atmakatha*, v. All translations from Malayalam texts are mine, unless otherwise indicated.

often been seen as a distinctive marker of modernity. What would a nebulous, polyvalent term like 'modernity' effectively mean if one were to look at it through the lens offered by these narratives? How did the autobiographical subject appear in Malayalam writing? What can we learn about the nature of this moment of narrative inception? Where did self-narratives find the resources for their conception, for their processes of imagination? How did they forge their idioms of narration? These questions were in my mind when I began work on this book.

However, to address them even obliquely I had to shift gear and engage with a larger body of writing, a wider range of questions. This was primarily because autobiography is everywhere a deeply heteronomous genre, connected in all manner of ways with other genres of writing. Self-narratives do not fashion their idioms in isolation; they draw heavily on resources shaped elsewhere. Nor do autobiographies hold a monopoly in the domain of self-articulation: they share the space of first-person enunciation with novels and poetry, and, more importantly, with non-literary writings. Social, governmental, and historical prose played an important role in forging the language of self-writing in Kerala; so did translation, travel, and discursive bricolage. So, although I began this book as an inquiry into autobiography, I found it soon turning into a wider study of the emergence of new idioms of self-articulation in Malayalam from around the 1880s to the middle of the twentieth century.

In Kerala, as in many parts of India, the end of the nineteenth century witnessed new ways of imagining collective and individual belonging; family, caste, and gender were reconceived with new significations. Historians and social scientists have studied aspects of these transformations: for example, changes in matrilineal kinship, economic relations, political structures, caste organizations, and marital arrangements.[4]

[4] See, for instance, Arunima, *There Comes Papa*; Devika, *Engendering Individuals*; Kodoth, 'Courting Legitimacy'; Dilip M. Menon, *Caste, Nationalism and Communism*; K.N. Panikkar, *Against Lord and State.*

Caste (*jati*) functioned as perhaps the most prominent grid for social differentiation in early-nineteenth-century Kerala. While pervasively dominant in Hindu society, caste differences were also apparent among, and reproduced by, the Christians and Muslims of the region. The age-old Syrian Christian community, it has been noted, enjoyed rights and privileges commensurate with some of the upper Hindu castes. Clothing, jewellery, hairstyles, naming, food—all worked as part of an elaborate apparatus of signs which had its basis in a system of caste differentiation.[5] The appearance of the body was replete with, even shaped by, caste markers. People's movement in public spaces was normatively, and often practically, regulated through the practice of distance pollution. Separate spaces of sacredness and bodily purity were maintained through restrictions on proximity and access to other bodies—in terms of visibility, touch, hearing, and clearly specified distances. This was no doubt violated at times, especially for the convenience of men from the higher castes, as in sexual relations, followed by ritual acts of purification. Markers of individual differentiation, such as the personal name, foregrounded a person's caste status more than individual identity. Clothing and jewellery were among the most visible signs of caste on the body of the individual, and were instrumental in preventing or identifying infringements to a severe system of distance pollution.

The semiological status of attire is evident in nineteenth-century controversies around the conversion of lower-caste women to Christianity. Channar women from southern Travancore who converted in the 1850s began wearing blouses, and thin cotton shawls (*melmundu*, literally upper dhoti) across their shoulders.[6] Among upper-caste Hindus this form of dress was, at the time, meant for special occasions. A royal proclamation of 1829 had allowed Channar converts the right to follow Syrian Christian women in wearing a long white jacket. Worn by the new converts, the *melmundu* seemed to upper-caste Hindus

[5] See, for detailed discussion and documentation on this, Unni, *Pathonpatham Noottandile Keralam* (hereafter Unni).

[6] Ibid., 31–4, 743–51. See also Cohn, *Colonialism and Its Forms of Knowledge*.

an insult to their own caste status. The Channar *lahala* (rebellion) of 1858 was an explosion of these tensions. A royal proclamation in the year following, responding to the situation, declared that while there was no legal objection to Channar women clothing themselves in the *melmundu*, they should not emulate the attire of upper-caste women to the degree of obliterating all difference.[7]

There were riots around jewellery and naming. Until the royal proclamation of 944 ME (CE 1768/1769), and even till much later, there were restrictions in Travancore on the form of gold and silver jewellery that women from the Sudra castes could wear.[8] Nine decades after the proclamation, there were reports of a nose-ring being wrenched from the nose of a lower-caste woman in Pandalam in Central Travancore.[9] These examples may suggest that the hostility was only to lower-caste sartorial adoptions of high-caste dressing traditions. But there was more to it. A counter-example—which strengthens the notion that clothing and jewellery can be looked at through the lens of semiotics—can be seen in the Nayar–Pulaya confrontations of the early decades of the twentieth century. In 1915, the Sadhujana Paripalana Sangham, an organization of the Pulayas founded by Ayyankali, began a campaign of reform.[10] A leader of this movement, Gopaldas, argued that the red stone necklaces worn by Pulaya women were signs of primitiveness. Many Pulaya women followed his advice and relinquished their ornaments—only to invite the wrath of the Nayars, who began insisting that Pulaya women wear them again. Riots followed. Subsequently, some sort of reconciliation was effected at a public rally in Kollam, addressed by members of both castes, at the end of which Pulaya women discarded their traditional jewellery and piled them in a heap in front

[7] *Therenjedutha Rajakiya Vilambarangal*, 301–2; Unni, 743, 750.

[8] Unni, 751. A royal proclamation of 1818 removed the requirement for prior permission from the state, but maintained the restrictions on the kinds of ornaments that various castes could wear. See Balakrishnan, ed., *Sree Narayana Guru*, 40.

[9] Unni, 751.

[10] Ibid., 753.

of the dais. Ayyankali, who rushed to Kollam in the wake of these incidents, spoke at the rally in a conciliatory way on the virtues that his community should cultivate—including 'theistic faith, civilized attire, and obedience to the Nayars'—while also warning the Nayars in a less placatory tone of the difficulties they would face were they to fall out with the Pulayas.[11]

The sign system of caste differences was not an inverted pyramid, with the largest number of caste markers assigned to the highest caste, and the least to the lowest. Elements of the system, by their presence or absence, could function as caste markers, and the acquiring or relinquishing of items of attire or jewellery by any caste could invite the wrath of the higher castes. Such elements could include personal names as well. The addition of 'Amma' to the names of Ezhava women, 'Panikkar' to Ezhava men, and the dropping of self-deprecating diminutives (such as 'Kunju' and 'Kutty') by the lower castes—none of these changes, be it the adoption or rejection of any element that could serve as a caste marker, was allowed a smooth, unchallenged passage.[12] Potheri Kunjambu, the first lower-caste novelist in Malayalam, made his Brahmin protagonist Kuberan Nambutiri cite slokas from the *Manusmrti* to expound the law of personal names: 'The first part of a Brahmin's name should indicate auspiciousness and the second part prosperity; . . . the first part of a Sudra's name should indicate contempt and the second servitude.'[13] The Nambutiri is here shown expressing his displeasure at the pretensions implicit in his Nayar servant's name; the Nayars gave vent to similar displeasure at Pulaya and Paraya adopted names which lacked the signs of self-humbling.

The last decades of the nineteenth century saw new articulations of caste identities and the emergence of novel forms of agency in the social and political domains. Various non-Brahmin castes began

[11] *Mitavadi*, vol. 4, no. 1 (January 1916), 19. See, for a detailed discussion on Ayyankali's interventions, Ramadas, *Ayyankalikku Adarattode*.

[12] Unni, 751, 752.

[13] Kunjambu, *Saraswativijayam*, 70.

organizing themselves to campaign for their rights. The Sree Narayana Dharma Paripalana (SNDP) Yogam was founded by the Ezhavas, a lower caste, in 1903, followed by an organization of the Nayars, the Nayar Samajam, in 1906 (it became the Nair Service Society in 1914). The Sadhujana Paripalana Sangham of the untouchable Pulayas, some of whose activities we saw above, was founded in 1907. Soon the Brahmins followed suit: the Nambutiri Yogakshema Sabha, a forum for voicing the concerns of Nambutiri Brahmins, was formed in 1908. The actions, ideas, and ways of speaking generated by these organizations suggested new conceptions of collectivity and caste identity, signified by the wide currency of the word *samudayam* (community). In debates between the proponents and antagonists of caste reform, both parties used emergent notions of identity, even though these were at times announced as authentically traditional.

My account of these social changes contains no surprises and is in tune with studies on the transformation of caste identities in several parts of India over this period. Colonial governance, it has been argued, had largely to do with the formulation and application of rules and regulations to the country's various communities, in the construction and regulation of which technologies of enumeration—such as the census—played a crucial role.[14] This was supplemented by extensive ethnography, which gave anthropological substance to the existence of distinctions within castes and religious communities.[15] Myths of origin, occupational profiles, customary practices, and physiognomic features all became instruments of governance and knowledge making. But they worked also as vital components in the construction of new community identities, such consolidations in Kerala often replicating the two-pronged thrust—the enumerative and the ethnographic—of colonial discourse. In 1891 a petition, endorsed by more than ten thousand signatories from various

[14] See Cohn, 'The Census, Social Structure'; Samarendra, 'Anthropological Knowledge'.

[15] See, for examples relevant to Kerala, Thurston, *Castes and Tribes of Southern India*; Fawcett, *Nambutiris*; Fawcett, *Nayars*.

non-Brahmin castes, was submitted to the Dewan of Travancore. Known as the Malayali Memorial, this plea cited statistics from recent census data to point out anomalies between on the one hand the proportion of various communities within the total population, and on the other their proportion in government employment. The petition began in the ritual language of respectful prayer to a sovereign, but moved on to make its case in a distinctively modern idiom informed by a new conception of the social.[16] It was prepared by English-educated members of the Nayar elite, including the novelist C.V. Raman Pillai and the lawyer P.K. Sankara Menon, with advice from eminent lawyers in Madras. Then, in 1896, an 'Ezhava Memorial', drafted by a Dr P. Palpu and signed by thirteen thousand members of the community, showed even more vividly the newly formulaic combination of ceremonial submission to the king and the fresh idiom of petitioning. The pleaders portrayed themselves as 'humble subjects weeping before their affectionate sovereign, as children do before their mother', yet made veiled threats to the effect that, should their grievances fail to be remedied, they might have no option but to leave 'our sovereign's religion, which is our own religion', and consider converting to Christianity.[17]

Numerical arguments were supplemented by others that Kerala's communities used in order to define themselves. Chattampi Swamikal's *Pracheena Malayalam* (Ancient Kerala), in its arguments against Brahminic-mythic accounts of the origin of Kerala, used as 'evidence' not only the Puranas and old palm-leaf manuscripts in *vattezhuthu* (a very old writing system used for Malayalam and Tamil), but also European travel accounts.[18] Swamikal contested Brahmin narratives—found in eighteenth-century texts such as *Keralappazhama* and *Keralolpathi*—which linked the origin of Kerala with a reclamation of land from the sea by a mythical figure, Parasurama. Swamikal's

[16] For the full text of the petition submitted to the king, see Unni, 756–65.

[17] See Panikkassery, *Do. Palpu*, 44.

[18] Chattampi Swamikal, *Pracheena Malayalam*, 303–460.

alternative history claimed that Kerala belonged originally to the Nayars. Comparable histories appear to have been produced by the Nayars in other parts of Kerala: *Vidyavinodini*, a journal from Trissur, published a series of essays on 'Adikeralacharitram' (the early history of Kerala), proposing similar arguments.[19]

Dr P. Palpu, the third signatory of the Malayali Memorial and the author of the Ezhava Memorial, in his correspondence with colonial officials in the 1920s, worked up an entire mythography and served it up as his history of caste in Kerala.[20] He believed Kerala had been at the centre of a transoceanic Buddhist empire which extended from Mexico to China. Ezhavas were the descendants of these Buddhists, who had lost their social status after the Brahminical usurpation of power and the creation of a caste society in Kerala. Like Jyotirao Phule in Maharashtra, Palpu produced a reading of Hindu mythology, especially the ten incarnations of Vishnu, interpreting them as cryptic records of the defeat of Buddhism at the hands of Brahmins.[21]

Community histories written in the early decades of the twentieth century echoed these arguments or put forward similar claims, often making partial and unorthodox use of scholarly literature to establish fanciful connections between historical phenomena. Etymological arguments—mostly speculative assertions—were commonly deployed, sometimes to suggest eccentric links and conclusions. Palpu, for instance, cited the Greek word 'therapy' as evidence in support of his arguments for a Buddhist history of Kerala: this word, he claimed, derived from *theraputra*, which in Pali, he said, referred to a Buddhist monk. Such monks, in Palpu's account, had travelled from Kerala to

[19] 'Adikeralacharitram'. For a discussion of this text, see Nambiar, 'Print, Communities and the Novel', 18–25.

[20] For a detailed discussion, see Kumar, 'Dr Palpu's Petition Writings'.

[21] Phule, 'Slavery', 22–99. See, for a discussion of these arguments, O'Hanlon, *Caste, Conflict and Ideology*, 137–73, especially 143–6. For Palpu's correspondence, see Dr Palpu Papers. For a detailed discussion, see Kumar, 'Dr Palpu's Petition Writings', especially 20–6.

Greece and, being renowned as medical practitioners, left their traces in words associated with medical care.[22]

Variars, an upper-caste group associated with temple occupations, were, according to one community enthusiast, originally a warlike race that protected Brahmins. In his concoction European visitors, impressed by the heroism of Kerala's Variars, carried the name back and used it in their language to denote all soldiers: this was the origin of the English word 'warriors'![23] At times the etymological method was even pushed towards morphologies of the body: Palpu claimed that the medieval Chinese custom of styling hair into a tuft indicated an earlier domination of China by Kerala.[24] These outlandish flights of the imagination were not only dreams of power, they were also acts of mimicry and inversion that had their distant originals in modern scholarship of Western provenance.

For our purposes, it is more important to notice how, towards the end of the nineteenth century in Kerala, these arguments illustrate the diverse moves through which several communities began fashioning a language of identities. Colonial discourse, we saw, combined enumeration with ethnography, often mapping on to the colony metropolitan schemata relating to racial and other social categories. In the new discourses of the region's communities, this dual structure reappeared as a dovetailing of the empirical and the mythographic. It is easy to mistake the effort as a deft negotiation between tradition and modernity; on a closer look it appears less a matter of the old and the new, for the empirical and the mythographic discourses both appear to have emerged from an encounter with colonial governance and scholarship. The language of community identities of the time seems to parallel the curious combination of governmental and sovereign vocabularies of power and subjection under colonial rule.[25]

22 Ibid., pp. 27–8.

23 P.S. Variar, *Varianmarude Purvacaritra Samkshepam*, 8.

24 Palpu, 'Memorandum: Some Additional Notes'.

25 For a discussion of multiple sovereignties in colonial rule and its implications for postcolonial India, see Hansen, 'Sovereigns beyond the State'.

My book is, among other things, an exploration of this ambivalent discursivity.

The sense of ambivalence is not unique to caste identities. We also find it in the formulation of new gender identities. Projects to redefine femininity in relation to newly emergent domestic spaces drew not only from modern Western values, but also from idioms found in tradition: in the epics, the Puranas, and ancient history. Projections of the 'new woman' as the true inheritor of time-honoured values entailed a rearticulation of tropes and scripts from antiquity in the terms of a new patriarchy. The body and mind of the new woman, her desires and her pleasures, derived simultaneously from hoary custom and contemporary arguments about gender within and outside India. This was accompanied by a disavowal of certain practices—such as the puberty ritual *tirandukalyanam* and the widespread form of marital alliance known as *sambandham*—as primitive or promiscuous. Feminist historians of Kerala have shown how early women writers expressed themselves in the language of this new patriarchy, even as they contested it.[26]

Alongside the discursive redefinition of women's identities, we find less eloquent and indirect expressions of change within ideas of masculinity; it may be too simple to see these solely as a reaction to the former. Transformations in notions of masculine identities have not received the incisive critical attention they deserve. Some of the chapters in the present book consider certain registers in which the self-identities of Malayali men found redefinition: asceticism, sexual desire, military prowess, loyalty, authority within and outside the family, and the memory of national and community histories being some.

Caste and gender identities were not merely external to or background noise against these new discursive reformulations of the individual subject. By inhabiting these identities the individual was being styled as a locus of feeling, self-reflection, bodily experiences,

[26] See Devika, *Engendering Individuals*; Devika, ed., *Her-Self*.

and collective solidarities. Gender and caste did not, in other words, appear to an unmarked originary individual and impose specific determinations. Even if identities are seen as having been cast in antique moulds, individuation involves distinctive ways of inhabiting such moulds. This holds true also for attempts to erase ascribed identities and recover a primal ground of species existence, as in Sree Narayanan's thought; such ground had to be produced. His identification with humankind was not only an ontological insight, but also a task to be accomplished through newly invented individual and collective practices. This book is less interested in analysing identities as stable figures than in tracking styles of inhabitation as they surface in self-narration.

II

Theoretical discussions of autobiography have been riddled with paradoxes: the genre is seen as the modern individual's medium of expression, yet its history is also traced back a very long way; its truth claims invoke the immediacy of self-intuition and the privileges of a first-person account, but it is often aimed at convincing a public through strategies of persuasion; it refers to an interior realm inaccessible to others, yet one that is constructed in a language commonly shared. The generic regularities of autobiography, on a closer look, turn out to be anything but stable. Readers who search self-narratives for a literal, verifiable correspondence to reality are bound to be disappointed; yet, self-narration invariably makes some sort of claim to truth, even if in the end it reveals only the truth of deception.

Autobiography's association with the individual has acquired a sort of paradigmatic status in most of the scholarly writing on the genre. The late emergence of autobiographies in India has often been explained as the consequence of a civilizational absence of 'the individual' before the colonial encounter. Historians have disputed this claim in recent times, pointing to the existence of individuals and personal narratives in earlier periods. This debate, valuable as social history, has distracted attention from an issue that seems more urgent to the literary historian: what is the relationship between the individual and autobiographical expression? Are personal narratives to be seen as the necessary discursive choice of a pre-existent form of social and political life, namely the individual? Or, conversely, is the very capacity for autobiography—i.e. the ability to turn one's life into an object of narrative elaboration——constitutive of what we recognize as the individual? Must modern autobiographical acts be necessarily manifest in genres of self-narration that are recognizable as having long existed through history?

There could be another approach to this problem: rather than treat the relation between the individual and autobiography as a causal one, we may look more closely at the varied nature of autobiographical practice. The question then becomes: under what conditions does one occupy the position of the subject in relation to self-narration? What enables the insertion of oneself into a discourse whose theme is one's own life? There is no single universally valid answer to these questions. Even canonical histories of autobiography in the West show that the situations under which St Augustine and St Teresa wrote their lives were markedly different from those of, say, Rousseau and Mill. In India too, self-narrations—first-person statements about one's own life—have been created within very diverse conditions and situations, and show a range of motivations. Devotional enthusiasm, spiritual and ethical practices, testimonies in law courts, administrative documentation, political participation, and historical witnessing were perhaps the most obvious driving forces. Can we probe these various activities from the traces they leave behind in autobiographical texts in order to attempt a genealogy of the subject of self-narration? Would such an inquiry take us beyond the familiar history of the autobiographical genre and its paradigmatic presupposition, the individual?

The student of self-narratives in India is likely to be struck by two features which resist the analytical assumptions of modern autobiography studies. Indian autobiographies from the nineteenth and twentieth centuries, especially those written by men, rarely speak of private interiorities: self-narration in them is seldom confessional intimacy. Second, the distinctiveness of the individual life is not the focal point of most such texts. It is, in fact, as if the author's distinctive life were a pretext for revealing something more typical or larger. As we shall see in chapter 6, historical changes during the narrator's lifetime represented an important reason for personal life-narratives making their appearance. What, then, of the inner world of intimate experiences and affective living? If they did not directly figure in most autobiographies, where did they find the discursive laboratory for fashioning their expressive forms?

Once again, we may need to ignore the generic boundaries of autobiography and look at adjacent domains: it was in the novel, in new genres of lyric and monologic poetry, and in forms of reflective and spiritual writing that a language of feeling and inner deliberation developed in nineteenth-century Kerala. The fictional and metaphysical orientation of these genres made it easier to explore personal experiences that did not find room in autobiographical accounts. In poetry and fiction we see the arrival of characters who can be depicted in their private moments, alone or in intimate interaction with other characters. Interestingly, through an apparent negation of the speaker's singularity, metaphysical and spiritual writing allowed the appearing of a first-person relationship to one's own body and to the experience of one's worldly existence. It is important to see these genres as more than mere resources for the fuller discourse of autobiography; some strands of self-narration found articulation in them. So it is necessary to consider these diverse forms as part of a composite history of self-articulation.

These genres do not always privilege a narrative unfolding of events: lyric poetry seldom tells us stories; monologic forms often subordinate the narrativization of external events to emotional experiences and inner deliberation. The metaphysical or spiritual genres we shall discuss do not re-narrate puranic stories; in the main, they adopt the form of a structured explanation of reality, or an analytical delineation of stages of phenomenal experience. Devotional poetry too was not always narrative in orientation, and invocations of events associated with the deity were subordinated to expressions of fervent worship and prayer. We shall see in chapter 2 that devotional poetry often staged dramatic scenes out of an inner metaphysical drama. Temptation and revulsion, fear and despair, and the ecstasy of union were invoked through graphic descriptions in which the devotee appeared as the experiencing first-person locus of intensities. Such scenarios were not usually allowed to develop into extended narratives; they appeared as moments in a sequence of impassioned devotional states.

Autobiography studies have arguably valorized structures of narration over the non-narrative modes. This has been partly because the genre of autobiography, especially in the nineteenth century, saw itself as primarily telling a story. A more important conceptual reason may be found in the belief that autobiographies are essentially expressions of individual agentiveness. Narrative has been regarded as the privileged medium of human agency.[27] Bringing into focus forms of writing with a strong non-narrative dimension allows us to reconsider the identification of self-articulation with the capacity for individual action.

The concept of agency is in itself complex and calls for careful handling. Etymologically linked to *agere*, the word for action in Latin, 'agent', denotes the one who 'acts or exerts power'—as distinct from 'patient' and 'instrument'.[28] This sense has been dominant in contemporary social and cultural theory, where its use often implies a sovereign originary source of actions. But the word can also mean exactly the opposite: when it refers to 'one who acts for another, a deputy, steward, factor, substitute, representative, or emissary.'[29] The second usage, in referring to authorized performers—rather than to

[27] Mascuch, *Origins of the Individualist Self*, 21 and 22.

[28] *Oxford English Dictionary*, 2nd edn. For a penetrating discussion of agency and its use in modern scholarship, see Asad, 'Thinking About Agency and Pain', 67–99.

[29] *Oxford English Dictionary*, 2nd edn.

real originators—of action, helps us see the link between agency (as the capacity to carry out actions) and authority (as the power of the originating intent to authorize their execution). This insight might be relevant for thinking about autobiographical agency: rather than extend the scope of *autos* to cover the author's originary self, it might be useful to explore structures of authorization in autobiographies. Under what authority does one gain the right to speak about one's life, write one's autobiography?

A nuanced notion of agency may also enable a better estimation of 'passivity' in self-narration. This is not merely a question of the autobiographical subject splitting itself into an active, writing pole, and a passive pole that merely observes what is being written. Self-narratives are not solely about one's actions in the world; they also present oneself as an experiencing subject, in an attitude of receptivity. Self-narration requires the writer to capture a passive dimension of one's selfhood, even as the act of such self-capture involves an active stance. At an even more fundamental level, the very possibility of autobiography may be seen as premised on our capacity to be affected by our own presence. The experience of being affected by ourselves—where we are simultaneously active and passive—is a necessary condition for self-representation. This convergence of agency and passivity is possibly intrinsic to the modern conception of the subject. Kant famously argued, in relation to inner intuition, that 'we intuit ourselves only as we are inwardly *affected* by ourselves', leading to the paradox that 'we should then have to be in a passive relation . . . to ourselves.'[30] Kant's discussion of 'auto-affection' has elicited significant philosophical discussion.[31]

Giorgio Agamben's analysis of holocaust testimonies led him to examine the configuration of the subject in auto-affection. 'Passivity

[30] Kant, *Critique of Pure Reason*, 166. For a discussion, see Agamben, *Remnants of Auschwitz*, 109.

[31] See, for instance, Heidegger, *Kant and the Problem of Metaphysics*, esp. 132–6; Agamben, *Remnants of Auschwitz*, 109–12; also Derrida, *Of Grammatology*, passim.

does not simply mean receptivity,' Agamben argued, 'the mere fact of being affected by an external active principle. Since everything takes place here inside the subject, activity and passivity must coincide. The passive subject must be active with respect to its own passivity.' In the experience of shame, a recurrent affect in holocaust testimonies, Agamben found an analogue to Kant's account of auto-affection. Drawing on Emmanuel Levinas' characterization of shame as 'the fact of being riveted to oneself, the radical impossibility of fleeing oneself to hide oneself from oneself, the unalterably binding presence of the I to itself,' Agamben argued that 'to be ashamed means to be consigned to something that cannot be assumed.'[32] It is not an external entity that cannot be assumed here, but 'what is most intimate in us': 'the "I" is overcome by its own passivity, its ownmost sensibility; yet this . . . is also an extreme and irreducible presence of the "I" to itself.'[33]

The insistent appearance of humiliation in Dalit self-narratives from contemporary India has brought the trope of passivity into discussions of autobiographical enunciation.[34] By recounting experiences of humiliation, Dalit autobiographies make a public claim regarding the norms that govern the treatment of each other in society. However, the force of Dalit autobiographies arises more often from the intensity of the affect produced in such experiences. In situations of humiliation, as in shame, the subject is in an unassumable relation to itself. The paradigmatic instance of such humiliation is perhaps found in stripping or forced nudity, which places the subject in a situation where it is unable to inhabit its body or escape from it. The radical contribution of Dalit autobiographies—and more generally Dalit literature—to idioms of self-writing in India arguably derives

[32] Levinas, *On Escape*, 64; Agamben, *Remnants of Auschwitz*, 105.

[33] Agamben, *Remnants of Auschwitz*, 105–6.

[34] For an excellent discussion of the trope of impossibility in Dalit writing, see Tharu, 'The Impossible Subject'. A theoretical discussion on humiliation and shame in relation to Dalit autobiographies may be found in Kumar, 'Consciousness, Agency and Humiliation'.

from the ability to foreground instances of impossible inhabitation where agency and passivity are difficult to separate.

These discussions may help us revisit the relations between subjectivity, agency, and figures of passivity in self-narration. Even in autobiographies presented as products of autonomous agency, other figures of the subject fleetingly appear. In non-narrative genres we find a more detailed engagement with these structures of passivity, but even in autobiographical narratives they sometimes announce their subdued presence in vital 'slippages' that silently or fleetingly disrupt the dominant telling. Such dissonances redeem early autobiographies in Kerala from being simple narratives of modernity using a linear and progressivist conception of time. The normative structures they foreground are at times belied by less prominent signs of disorientation. If autobiographies possess a vital link to history, it is not to be sought solely in the rich documentation of the times unfolding through the events; one may sense the presence of history perhaps even more vitally via fleeting or sudden moments of an opening within the narrative—or 'slippages'—through which we can glimpse a different landscape of the subject and its inhabitation of the world. Leaving instances of this to a longer discussion in chapter 6, I shall here merely indicate some consequences of this for our understanding of modernity.

A sense of its modernity is prominent in contemporary Kerala's self-consciousness. This often finds expression in exceptionalist claims about the region's progressive polity, social development, cultural superiority, and cosmopolitanism in ideas and art. Social reform, lower-caste movements, democratic political mobilization, and egalitarian left politics are frequently cited in this narrative of Kerala's life. The nineteenth century features in this story as the critical watershed, and as the horizon of contemporary Kerala's historical imagination. The all-too-frequent valorization of social reform in Kerala is often also a suppression of the memory of norms and practices of earlier times, a refusal to recognize their continued existence. Autobiographical genres developed here from the cusp of changes in normative structures—in order to speak about them. The authors of the texts we examine in chapter 6 not only lived through this period of change but also took active part in reform initiatives. Most of their autobiographies are narratives of progress and freedom, open endorsements of enlightened modern values. The grip of the past, however, is not so easily loosened; it retains some of its claims, deflecting the privileged narrative of progress and autonomy. This appears in autobiographical narration, contrary to authorial plan, in the shape of slippages in the subject's inhabitation of new identities. In such unavowed moments, self-narratives demonstrate what may be considered a less easily narrativizable dimension of the subject's embeddedness in time, or the historicality of the subject. The past sticks invisibly to the narrator's body, movements, and utterances despite its conscious rejection, and despite the narrative itself being in the main an account of its overcoming. Can we call this form of existence of the past, its survival, after Marcel Mauss' celebrated study of techniques of the body, a literary form of 'habitus'?[35] Autobiography's vital link with history is not just its documentation of life and society in a lived past; even more importantly, it is revealed in the lack of fit between narrative and subjectivity.

This is true not only of autobiographies; novels too have their moments of slippage. Unlike in self-narratives, however, in fiction such slippage becomes a structural principle, and in many early novels determines their aesthetic—as distinct from their narrative—form. While celebrating their enchantment with the modern world, many such novels produce—through description and detailing, and through their way of looking at things—a perceptual economy that finds itself in opposition to the general run of values endorsed in the narrative. When these novels turn away from realism to draw on protocols of description more commonly found in poetic traditions, or deviate from the norms of verisimilitude, they fleetingly reveal the 'non-narrativizable' presence of the literary habitus of the times. Intimate tensions between avowable histories and disowned inheritances are nowhere more pronounced than in historical novels. They shape the

[35] Mauss, 'Techniques of the Body'.

aesthetic and the perceptual economy of the work, which works as the condition for imagining characters in their sometimes very different or contradictory moments of action and passion.

Our discussion has stayed at a distance from the apparent anchoring of autobiographies in individual interiorities. As we saw, early Indian examples of this genre were neither intimately confessional nor deeply introspective. Self-narration in them was part of a public exercise, not an activity carried out in hermetic solitude. So, even if theoretical discussions of autobiography have privileged the relationship between the text and its author-protagonist, self-narratives must also be seen as resolutely public utterances.

Is it possible to develop an account of autobiographical practice which sees its public dimension as fundamental? Resources for an enquiry in this direction are scattered within recent theoretical enquiries into subjectivity and political existence. Hannah Arendt called politics the domain where human beings exhibit themselves to one another through actions and utterances. She noted the inseparability of political existence from appearance: to be and to appear are one and the same thing there.[36] Following this line of thought, Adrianna Cavarero suggested that what is revealed in self-narratives is a desire for exteriority—the desire to appear in the narrative of another as its object: at the heart of autobiography, for Cavarero, was the biographical desire to hear one's story being told by another.[37] Judith Butler, drawing on Cavarero, argued that the core of one's singular existence consists in one's 'exposedness' to others; what human beings share in common is their constitutive exposedness.[38]

These insights open up the possibility of developing a vocabulary for analysing the public, exterior dimension of self-narration. Instead of seeing the autobiographical act as a movement from the inner domain to the outer, we may see it as located from the outset in a

[36] Arendt, *The Life of the Mind, One: Thinking*, chapter 1: 'Appearance'; idem, *The Human Condition*.

[37] Cavarero, *Relating Narratives*.

[38] Butler, *Giving an Account of Oneself*, 34.

public, exhibitionary space. This means shifting our attention from introspection to the outer, to gestures of extrospection. The thematic of shame I referred to earlier offers an account of the subject in a rigorously exteriorized frame of exposure. A focus on exteriority may help us see autobiographical utterances as performances. By this I do not mean to suggest a distinction between inner selves and their outer dissimulations; we need to consider the inner world itself as inscribed on the surface of things, as produced through actions and utterances in a field of mutual exposure and unevenly shared visibility.

The approach has a special burden in locations like Kerala, where the very existence of a commonly shared field of visibility was in doubt till the nineteenth century. Distance pollution treated not only touch, but even the act of seeing as contaminating. Vision was considered in this scheme a form of contact akin to touch, as something which had the power to affect another, as the bearer of a force that could be benign or violent. Like the shared field of visibility, the common space for public utterances began emerging in Kerala in the nineteenth century. This space was shared unevenly—large sections of the population had little access to it. Yet an idea of the public as an entity which could potentially, or at least hypothetically, include most, if not all—and therefore also as an arena threatened with division and strife—seems to have come into being at this time.

The texts discussed in the ensuing chapters presuppose, and also work to create, the idea of a shared public. Literature was the principal activity within which this new publicness of utterances was imagined. This was a consequence, and also a precondition, of the democratization of literature. The status of literature as an art of special enjoyment exclusive to the traditional elite began to change; especially in prose forms, it addressed a much larger public with widely varied backgrounds and competences. Literature in its modern form emerged in Kerala when it came to stand, synecdochially, for the idea of an inclusive, contestatory space of public utterances—a status it possesses in Kerala even today.

III

The preceding discussion suggested that we approach autobiographical writing as public utterance rather than as the expression of pre-existing 'private' selves. In this view, the private domain does not possess any ontological primacy in relation to the public domain. We shall encounter, in the following chapters, changes in the significance of both privacy and publicness, and shifts in the borders of these concepts. The spatial or topographical idioms in which the private and the public are conceived of as distinct areas may be seen as the work of what Ranciere calls a 'partitioning of the sensible' ('sensible' here in the sense of 'that which can be sensed'), of configuring the world of experience.[39] Or, more radically, the public–private distinction is one of the modes of partitioning the sensible, of establishing distinct norms of access and behaviour for specified locations, activities, and contexts. The institutional dimension of these distinctions has been noted both in Western and postcolonial contexts. Habermas famously linked the emergence of new forms of public enunciation in Europe with the spread of print and new locations of interaction. The trajectories taken by publicness in modern India have been studied in their postcolonial specificity. Arundhati Roy has suggested that the word 'public' ought in the Indian context to be recognized as a vernacular word signifying opposition to 'sarkar', the word for the state in many Indian languages.[40] 'Public' here denotes 'the people', as separate from the state, indicating a situation of political existence. The drawing of the line that carves out the public as a distinguishable, thinkable entity is always a political act. It demarcates the shared space of exposure in which utterances are made and received.

We noted that early autobiographies in India, particularly by men, possessed a strong public dimension. Many autobiographers in the early twentieth century saw their destinies as tied to the changing

[39] See Ranciere, *Dissensus*, especially 'Ten Theses on Politics', 27–44.

[40] Roy, *Public Power in the Age of Empire*, 6.

life of their nation or community. The emergence of a new sense of individuation from a deep involvement in nationalism has prompted some to see the relationship between autobiographical selves and the nation in homological or allegorical terms. Philip Holden found in nationalist autobiographies, especially from the postcolonial world, parallels between the individual and the emerging nation, arguing that these narratives of growth towards emancipation imagined the nation less as a community than as an individual.[41] Similar analogies have been observed in prison autobiographies written by nationalist leaders: the prison is regarded as a metaphoric counterpart to the nation's servitude, and self-disciplining, especially in relation to the senses, reflects the disciplining of the crowd by nationalist movements.[42]

While these parallels may find resonance in self-narratives written by pan-Indian and cosmopolitan nationalist leaders, they may not work smoothly in autobiographies considered later in this book. Governmental and mythographic constructions of community, more than nationalist identification, appear to shape autobiographical narration in them. Their 'vernacular' character indicates their difference not only from professional historiography but also from nationalist self-imaginings.[43] The language in which personal narratives negotiated their public dimension drew from several contemporary genres of public articulation. Before we proceed further, we need to get a sense of the public field of writing in Kerala in which the genres of self-articulation we discuss in the ensuing chapters made their appearance.

The second half of the nineteenth century, its last decades in particular, saw the emergence of a new print-public sphere in Kerala. Interestingly, many figures central to this moment were from outside Kerala. Benjamin Bailey of the Church Missionary Society,

[41] Holden, 'Other Modernities'. See also his *Autobiography and Decolonization.*

[42] Arnold, 'The Self and the Cell'.

[43] See Aquil and Chatterjee, 'Introduction', in idem, ed., *History in the Vernacular.*

Hermann Gundert of the Basel Mission, a Gujarati merchant Devji Bhimji, and Kalahastiyappa Mutaliar are important names in the early history of printing and publishing in the region.[44] Among the Malayalis, important contributions to the early development of print came from Christians like Kunnamkulathu Ittuppu, Maliyammavil Kunjuvarithu, and especially Kandathil Varghese Mappila, who edited a number of seminal publications: *Keralamitram*, *Malayala Manorama*, and *Bhashaposhini*. Varghese Mappila played a crucial role in creating a literary public sphere that cut across caste and religious divisions and regions.[45] His regular columns for poetry and *samasyapuranam* (competition in composing a stanza which concludes with a line announced in advance by the editors) offered room for many lower-caste writers to publish their first work. Paravur Kesavan Asan published a newspaper called *Sujananandini*, perhaps the first initiative in this direction from the lower caste of Ezhavas.[46] Friendships spawned by this new realm of public exchanges could cross boundaries of region, caste, and religion.

The word 'public' does not translate easily into the Malayalam language, which has no counterpart of the various senses of the word in English. 'Public' as an English word became familiar in Kerala through governmental usage; phrases such as 'public road' became key political terms in the 1920s, when the lower castes waged sustained campaigns for their right to use roads around temples. A public works department was set up in Travancore in the mid-nineteenth

[44] For a brief discussion of some of these figures in the context of early print history, see Aiyer, *Kerala Sahityacharitram*, vol. 4, 284–9. For the impact of print on Kerala culture, see Ramakrishnan, '*Varthamanappathrangaludeyum Achadiyanthrangaludeyum*'. On early newspapers in Kerala, see Priyadarshan, *Kerala Patrapravarthanam: Suvarnadhyangal.*

[45] For a biography, see Harisharma, *Kandathil Varghese Mappila*. A collection of Varghese Mappila's editorials on several topics, including the Malayalam language, may be found in *Kerala Navothhanam*. For a discussion of some of his ideas on language, see Arunima, 'Imagining Communities'.

[46] Pravur Kesavan Asan began publishing the newspaper *Sujananandini* in 1892; after an interruption, it was revived in 1903 and published till 1907.

century. 'Public works' is usually translated into Malayalam as '*pothumaramathu*'. The prefix (*pothu-*) has the sense of 'general', or 'something that pertains to all'. This prefix was added to the word '*janam*' (people) to create '*pothujanam*', the Malayalam word for 'the public' as a collectivity. *Swadeshabbhimani*'s editor, K. Ramakrishna Pillai, the first writer from Kerala to reflect extensively on the idea of the public, used the words '*pothujanam*' and '*janasamanyam*' (again, *samanyam* signifies a similar idea of generality) interchangeably for the new idea of the public that he proposed in his writings. The English word 'public' also appears in some of his Malayalam writings, where it refers, in the main, to social spaces that can be contrasted with domestic interiors. For example, elite women emerging from their houses into the open to watch a royal procession are described as 'appearing in public'.[47] This usage underlines the importance of access and exposure in defining notions of the public.

I shall focus briefly on Ramakrishna Pillai's engagement with the concept of the public, as it highlights some of the formative tensions of this domain in early-twentieth-century Kerala. In 1903, in the opening editorial of his newspaper *Keralapanchika*, Ramakrishna Pillai reflected on the duties of newspapers. 'Newspapers have, in the main, two duties,' he wrote. 'First, to form public opinion, and second, to obey public opinion.' He argued that in 'our country' the first of these duties had greater importance, as 'here, people have not really grasped the nature of the relationship between the State (*rajyam*) and the public (*pothujanam*).'[48] There is a tension—or, if one were to push the argument, a paradox—inherent in the nature of the address to be performed by newspapers: they were to represent a public which did not as yet exist; the public was constituted through the very act of address.

This project of forming public opinion may appear at first sight as

[47] See Ramakrishna Pillai's editorial '*Garhyamaya Nadatta*' (Reprehensible Conduct), in *Swadeshabbhimani*, 24 August 1910, quoted in Kamalamma, ed., *Swadeshabbhimaniyude Sahitya Sapraya*, 187.

[48] Editorial in *Keralapanchika*, 22 April 1901, quoted in Bhaskara Pillai, *Swadeshabbhimani*, 47.

a move towards an abstract and more universal subject, and towards grounds of greater universality for politics. However, this is belied by Ramakrishna Pillai's journalistic practice. He used scandal writing as a powerful form of political criticism, especially in his attacks on the Travancore dewan, P. Rajagopalachari. This eventually led to Pillai's expulsion from Travancore in 1910. I use the word 'scandal' to refer to Ramakrishna Pillai's mode of journalism on account of the twin senses of the word: it refers both to (scandalous) events that cause public outrage and to malicious (scandalizing) representations of people's private lives. Pillai's use of scandal as a tool for political publicity had elements of both these meanings: while some of his criticisms were directed at the public functioning of Rajagopalachari, and of other high officials in the palace, others concerned events from their private lives.

The mode of scandal writing oscillates between the explicit and the suggestive. Sometimes details, dates, etc. are mentioned and the persons involved identified; at other times, the reports adopt the language of hints directed at an implied knowledge already possessed by the public. The public is regarded here as a formless, amorphous entity; few members of this undefined group—perhaps none of them—actually possessed the information alluded to in the report. The imprecise network of gossip and the untraceable transfer of information through hearsay give the individual reader the sense that everyone else is in the know, or at least some people are in the know. The reader is interpellated into this group by the tacit offer of sharing a body of non-explicit knowledge. Such information acquires the status of public knowledge through its appearance in a printed newspaper; this confers political value on the information and turns it into a potential object of public moral outrage.

The truth claims made by the journalism of political scandal thus involve an imprecise but convincing sense of public knowledge. This leads to an attenuation of the usual demarcation between gossip and reporting, and between on the one hand private information possessed by individuals, and on the other public knowledge shared and used by all as grounds of moral indictment. Scandal reporting pushes the boundaries of legitimate representation in newspapers, dragging out for the public gaze sordid details from the private lives of powerful individuals. For Ramakrishna Pillai, people in public office were not entitled to claim immunity from moral scrutiny for a violated private life.

Ramakrishna Pillai's use of scandal writing, with its oblique suggestions and imprecise details, had consequences both for the nature of the public being constituted as the addressee of the newspaper, and for the nature of what was being constituted as public opinion. It was through his interpellation into the universe of whispers and murmurs, of hearsay and gossip, that the subject came to occupy the public field of political criticism. The truth of public opinion was arrived at and articulated through the rhetoric of a non-public arena of opinion and rumour.

This also complicated the distinction between the domains of news and fiction. In the early years of the public uses of print, a newly emergent body of readers negotiated such distinctions in markedly different ways from what is professionally mandated in academic disciplines. In her study of early print culture in Goa, Rochelle Pinto demonstrated the difficulty of establishing sharp differences in use between various print genres such as government notifications, news writing, pamphleteering, and fiction.[49] Scandal reporting as a form of political criticism raises a similar problem. Even when readers regard lapses in the private lives of high officials as scandalous, the appearance of such unseemly information in newspapers may embarrass them: use of the form ran the risk of violating the sense of decorum commonly associated with the public domain. This explains the obliqueness and suggestiveness of the reports, which gesture towards preserving a sense of public decorum by 'de-realizing' or insufficiently specifying the details referred to.

While these strategies push news reporting closer to fictional writing, a converse movement is also seen: alongside Ramakrishna Pillai's journalism on public scandals, a genre of political fiction began to

[49] Pinto, *Between Empires*, esp. chapters 5–7.

emerge in Travancore in the first decade of the twentieth century. Pillai played an active role in this—as the author of two novels and as the publisher of some of the most controversial political novels of the time. Two fictional works that he published created much debate in Travancore—*Parappuram* and *Udayabhanu*—both written by his former teacher, K. Narayana Kurukkal. These contained thinly veiled representations of scandals surrounding the Travancore court, contrasting them with images of the high ideals needed for moral regeneration in the country. The novels suggested, without openly affirming, parallels between the characters in the story and public figures in Travancore. The method shows striking parallels to the representational techniques of scandal writing: these novels too appealed to an implicit public knowledge, a so-called 'open secret' that everyone was expected to recognize and no one to speak directly about.

Ramakrishna Pillai tried to turn the tables on those who accused him of slander by arguing that their views betrayed a lack of literary cultivation and an inner sense of guilt. 'Just as a thief thinks that everyone he meets is a police constable, some people have been struck by similarities between the conduct of certain characters in this novel and their own ways of living.'[50] Works of fiction, even if they emerge from the writer's experiences and observations, are ultimately products of the imagination. Ramakrishna Pillai used claims regarding the autonomy of the literary world as a device for protecting these novels from charges of libel.

This argument, and the way in which the genre of political satires worked in Travancore, imply two distinct notions of publicity. As interventions in the political field, these novels were indeed thinly disguised representations of people and events in the real world. However, since they were 'literary' works, one could not criticize them on the basis of such parallels. Literariness denied any close connection with the real world of politics, and, in that sense, marked

[50] Ramakrishna Pillai, 'Onnam Pathippinte Mukhavura' (Preface to the First Edition), in Kurukkal, *Parappuram,* iii.

its distance from the world of pamphlets and newspapers, claiming for its representations an aura of the ideal and typical. However, the literary work could indeed be made use of in the political field; events presented in the quasi-imaginary space of the novel might direct political, not literary, criticism at the real events to which they alluded. This was possible because a shared notion of the public informed both literature and politics: the readers of novels were also politically interested readers of newspapers.

Ramakrishna Pillai's negotiations with the public domain are instructive; they enable us to recognize the ambivalences that lay at the root of the literary arena in Malayalam. The early print history of literature in Malayalam did not work with a stable opposition between the imaginary and the real. The eighteenth chapter of *Indulekha*, widely regarded as the first 'proper' Malayalam novel, shows the ease with which elements from non-literary discourses could make their way into novels without much regard for the economy of storytelling. *Lakshmikesavam*, another novel written in the late nineteenth century, included a chapter comprising no more than an itemized summary of the provisions of the new Malabar Marriage Act. The political novels of Travancore in the 1900s and 1910s provide exacerbated instances of negotiating the borderline between the proper domain of fiction and reality.[51] C.V. Raman Pillai's 'social novel' (*samudayikakhyayika*), *Premamrtam* (1914), may be read as working with and transforming the representational strategies used in some of the more contentious political novels of Travancore.[52] We shall engage with some of these in later chapters.

Ramakrishna Pillai's arguments and interventions demonstrate the ways in which the domains of literary and political publicity overlapped in early-twentieth-century Kerala. The amphibious character

[51] See O. Chandu Menon, *Indulekha*; Padu Menon, *Lakshmikesavam*. See also Arunima, 'Glimpses from a Writer's World'; Kumar, '*Kazhchayum Vayanayum*'.

[52] For a discussion of some aspects of representation in this novel, see Kumar, 'Seeing and Reading'.

of public discourses is visible in the works of several writers. Figures like Kandathil Varghese Mappila, C.V. Kunjuraman, and Moorkothu Kumaran, who played a central role in the formation of a space of public discussion in Malayalam, worked with both a specific community locus as well as normative ideas of a larger public as their addressee. Their writings oscillate between a register addressed to their own community—engaged in contestations with other groups to gain dominance over the emergent public space—and another which assumes the existence of a domain where interactions normatively presume equality.

Ramakrishna Pillai's scandal writing and fictional allegories of Travancore politics point to two modes in which lives were rendered visible for political censure. In contrast to these critical strands, official discourses of life writing at the end of the nineteenth century were dominated by the registers of commemoration and veneration. The emulation of great lives was considered an important means of moral and historical education. A textbook committee set up in 1866 by the Travancore government commissioned a series of biographies called '*Mahacharitamala*' (The Garland of Great Lives). Early periodicals in Malayalam published several short biographies of religious and secular figures. The idioms of life writing developed in these texts had their own share of ambivalence. The protagonists of these life narratives are perceived both as characters operating in a fictional or mythical space as well as inhabiting a real historical field. Ramakrishna Pillai's own biography of Karl Marx combined a precise summary of the latter's political and economic arguments with a celebration of his life in the language of spiritual commemoration. His account of Marx's death is telling; in his narrative it follows on the footsteps of his wife's demise. Sitting in his chair, his visage showing contentment, Marx receives death: 'A smile played on his face at the time of death. This is how Marx the Maharishi (great sage) attained *samadhi*.'[53] The use of diverse registers in life writing had its

[53] Ramakrishna Pillai, *Karl Marx*, 76.

consequences for truth: the claims made by biographies did not always square with verifiability; they also drew on allegiance and belief. It was in this terrain, where utterances possessed an uncertain valence, that autobiographers began writing the stories of their lives.

IV

This book takes a close look at a few important moments in the development of a language of self-articulation in Kerala. The analyses offered do not add up to a comprehensive history of that process; the number of texts considered is small; and the discussion is mostly focused on the relations between language and figurations of the subject in order to understand the discursive economies within which these writings made sense. Even for the short timespan it deals with, this study is neither exhaustive in its coverage nor representative in its choice of texts. Most of the works I discuss were written by male authors from Hindu upper castes, or from the Ezhava low caste. My choice was determined to an extent by the nature of the public sphere of the times, by the dominant idioms of individuation and self-reflection which have come down to us from this period, and by the particular discursive trajectories that appeared to me to merit closer probing. I am concerned with a critical understanding of this seemingly well-known strand and its complex heritage. A recovery of other currents—suppressed or silenced—has been attempted in recent scholarship: necessary as it is and critically complementary as it would be to an inquiry of this kind, that has not been my aim here.

The chapters of this book do not necessarily follow a chronological or causal sequence. At an apparent level, each chapter is on a body of work held together under an author's signature or the coherence of a literary form, but those unities are not meant to be the mainstay of the book. Such discursive units, on closer examination, appear as sites of pluralization: an author or a literary form quickly turns into a multiplicity of concerns, tropes, and pulls. The proper name of an author or the seeming coherence of a genre often serves as a refracting prism that separates seemingly united strands and elements. The chapters that follow are attempts to reconfigure them into varieties of thought and enunciation. This enables other kinds of connections between chapters: tropes, issues, and themes introduced in one are taken up in another to introduce variations or mutations. This somewhat diminishes narrative continuity, but helps highlight continuities and breaks that the pressures and pleasures of storytelling often obscure. Within individual chapters I have also sometimes found it useful to work against the grain of the narrative: such interruption has allowed the isolation of elements which, in the arguments developed in this book, play a more vital role than is allowed in the stories within which they appear.

I begin by examining, in the next chapter, some of the writings of Sree Narayana Guru, the most significant social-reform figure to emerge in Kerala in the nineteenth century. His writings are varied in form and intent. They range from metaphysical and devotional compositions often closely tied to forms of spiritual practice, to texts such as 'Jatilakshanam' (The Signs of Caste) and 'Jatinirnayam' (The Determination of Caste)—which advanced philosophical arguments against the validity of *jati* (caste) as a category of thought—and on to instructions in prose pronounced in the context of new initiatives of community making. In spite of their diversity in objectives and audiences, Sree Narayanan's writings and actions are linked by the recurrence of certain concepts, tropes, patterns of thinking, and discursive organization. For instance, one of his arguments—that *jati* involves a false differentiation of the social body—deploys a form of argumentation used in his philosophical texts, which in turn drew on elements from Advaita, Saiva Siddhanta, and the writings of the Tamil Siddhars. Narayanan's instructional texts call for a reading that is sensitive to the relations between doctrines and practices: doctrines perform varied functions, including generating new practices and conferring fresh meanings on practices from the past. This has, by implication, consequences for our reading of his metaphysical texts as well.

My discussion of Sree Narayanan's writings takes the figure of the body as a strategic point of departure. As metaphor, and as all too real and physical—occupying the levels of the individual, the collective, and the species as a whole—the body is repeatedly foregrounded in his texts. The positions and postures of the subject in Sree Narayanan's spiritual writings, instructional texts, and practices appear connected in new ways when viewed from this angle. He lived and wrote during a period when bodily practices—those already noted as pertaining to dress and jewellery, marriage and sexuality, proximity to and distance from other bodies—were undergoing crucial changes in Kerala. It is reductive to suggest an easy determination of Sree Narayanan's thought by the popular landmarks of a materialist history. My aim is rather to track the emergence of a discursive space in Malayalam writing within which subjects of new bodily practices, with a new relationship to their bodily existence, could appear. I argue that Sree Narayanan's diverse and at times seemingly paradoxical investments in the body enabled corporeality to acquire a new valence in processes of thinking about the concept of difference at the levels of individuation, species identity, and social life. In denuding the body of caste markers and producing it as the site of the 'degree zero' of difference between human beings, a new discursivity around the body begins to emerge, whose elaborations I track in subsequent chapters.

This perceptual economy is also evident in the poetry of Sree Narayanan's prominent disciple Kumaran Asan, which forms the focus of chapter 3. Asan was an active participant and leader in the community reform movement inaugurated by Sree Narayanan. He is, however, best known as one of the most important poets in the history of Malayalam writing. His poetry marked a distinctive turn in literary sensibility, emblematized in his fashioning of a monologic discourse of meditation and self-relation. At the core of this shift was a new language of thoughts (*vicharabhasha*) through which the subject—often a female protagonist—made her inner self available to an interlocutor and, in the process, to herself. Even forms of dialogic exchange serve in Asan's poetry primarily as pretexts for introspection and self-revelation. The interlocutor is turned into a rhetorical device in order to facilitate monologic self-articulation. Mutual dependence and responsiveness, typical of a dialogic organization of discourses, are absent; even where one senses the presence of an impulse to dialogue, it stands in most cases for the play of inner differences within the soul of the protagonist. Asan's monologues appear primarily within contexts of deliberation in which the subject, after taking measure of divergent inner impulses, consolidates her position in decisiveness and action. *Chintavishtayaya Sita* (Sita Immersed in Thought) shows this in its most consummate form: after taking stock of her entire life, Sita reaches a state of readiness to relinquish her body.

Asan's new discourse of the mind raises important questions: what prompts the subject to enter into this active self-relation, and what initiates and sustains the inner action of deliberation and articulation? These turn our attention towards the economy of desire in his mature poetry. Asan's female protagonists often leave their domestic locations behind in pursuit of their intense, inexorable desires. The poetry which contains them establishes close connections between the realm of the inner, the experience of desire and moments of deliberation and action. Asan's valorization of the 'inner' involves, interestingly, a displacement of the body: erotic intensities, which presuppose embodiment, are in their ultimate manifestations not considered as bodily; they belong to the inner self. The ambivalent placement of the body in Asan's work involves a tense complicity between the restraint of bodily senses and the experience of intensities. This is crucial to the shift effected by Asan's poems in discourses of desire and erotic enjoyment in Malayalam. Gendered subjects, manifest in the figure of the woman, are placed at the core of this shift. Our discussion of Asan's poems will take forward some of the concerns introduced in the earlier chapter: if Sree Narayanan's work involved cleansing the body of caste semiology, Asan's poetry created a clearing in language whereby gender difference found articulation as inner experience, marking the subject's relationship to desire and speech.

Two later chapters turn to early novels in Malayalam: even as our engagement with the body persists, new issues come to the foreground. Central to chapter 4 is the novel's configuration of a world of objects and spaces. When novels began to be written in Malayalam in the late nineteenth century, many of them, including the famous *Indulekha* (1889), distinguished themselves from older genres of literary representation and claimed a lineage that came from 'English novel books'. The novel's ability to show its readers a plausible world was its strength; it was in equal measure a source of anxiety. Appu Nedungadi, the author of *Kundalata* (1887), set his story far away, in an imaginary kingdom called Kalingam, to ward off criticisms of his possible deviations from existing Keralan customs and conventions (*mathirikalum maryadakalum*).[54] A new conception of the literary public, not defined in terms of skills and training, but negatively, as lacking in special qualifications or preoccupations, began to take shape. The objective of the novel, for Nedungadi, was to 'provide harmless entertainment to people who [did] not know English, as well as to women who [did] not have much work and [found] it difficult to while away their time.'[55] Chandu Menon's *Indulekha* also aimed at 'entertaining the mind of the common man and imparting knowledge'; Menon defined the novel as a device of realistic representation, distinct from the improbable stylization used in traditional narrative forms.

Although the novel was announced as modelled on a Western form, the nature of the relationship remained unsettled. In their prefaces, the early novelists turned to metaphors of translation, retelling, and adaptation to describe their art. The discourse of the early novel reveals a complex and inconsistent picture. This is indicated in the tension between different modes of representing characters, some of which came from the English novel of the nineteenth century, and some from Malayalam or Sanskrit poetry, or local visual and performing arts. Chandu Menon, in his Preface to *Indulekha*, spoke of a shift in taste away from traditional representations which 'in defiance of all possible existence' depicted 'Vishnu as half man and half lion',

[54] Nedungadi, 'Preface', *Kundalata*, v.
[55] Ibid.

and the 'god Krishna, with his legs twisted and twined into postures in which no biped could stand and blowing a cowherd's horn', towards an appreciation of 'pictures, whether in oil or water colours, in which shall be delineated men, beasts, and things according to their true appearance.'[56] As we shall see, however, a close look at *Indulekha* reveals Menon's reliance on non-realistic and schematic forms of organization in his portrayal of characters. Such tensions are even more pronounced in novelists like Padu Menon and Chathu Nair.

Three major thematic strands are usually identified in early Malayalam novels. The first, loosely modelled on the liberal novel of ideas, addressed questions of education, reform, and issues in the civic sphere. Many of these novels came from Malabar, then directly under British rule, and were often written by Nayar writers worrying over issues raised by English education and the legitimacy of their caste practices within the colonial world. Debates around the validity of customary marital alliances (*sambandham*) among Nayar women and the proceedings of the Malabar Marriage Commission were central to the discourse of many of Nayar reform novels from Malabar.[57] Chandu Menon's *Indulekha* (1889) and *Sarada* (1892), Padu Menon's *Lakshmikesavam* (1892), and Cheruvalathu Chathu Nair's *Meenakshi* (1890) incorporate discussions on these issues. Romantic love and the choice of marital partners occupied the centre of plots and marked the new subject positions endorsed in these novels.

By contrast, in Travancore—a princely state under indirect rule by the British—C.V. Raman Pillai produced a trilogy of historical

[56] O. Chandu Menon, Preface to the First Edition, in *Indulekha,* 10. For an English translation, see O. Chandu Menon, *Indulekha,* tr. W. Dumergue, xiii–xiv; and *Indulekha,* tr. Anitha Devasia, Appendix I, 237–40.

[57] The Malabar Marriage Commission was appointed in 1891 by the Government of Madras to report on the customs of the Hindus of Malabar related to matrilineal inheritance, family structures, and marital practices. The novelist O. Chandu Menon was a member of the commission and submitted a note of dissent with the report.

romances around the royal court and its history. Even while placing kingship at the centre of their political and moral universe, these novels show a world corroded by deep instabilities, in which subjects face having to deal with, interpret, and unravel the obscure mysteries of an unreliable, deceptive environment. Sentimental love figures in this universe too, but is of secondary importance.

Nineteenth-century Kerala also saw the development of a third strand in novels about conversion, mainly written by lower-caste Christian converts and Christian missionaries in northern Kerala. Erotic desire and sentimental love did not figure prominently in the inner world of these novels, which were primarily concerned with practices of self-making and self-discipline demanded by the new faith. Education recurs as an implicit trope, often in order to transform the subject and show his or her earlier life as inauthentic and unethical. Reading the Bible converged with the idea of learning in some of them. Lower-caste social-reform novels, such as the anti-caste *Saraswativijayam* by Potheri Kunjambu, used a variant of this model. The struggle against caste involves education and a transformation of the subject by imparting new knowledge.

Our discussion tries to move away from these thematic taxonomies to look at the way early novels showed a new world of things and people. By organizing their fictional worlds as domains of varied visual experiences, these novels impelled a consideration of human beings as people who were engaged in acts of seeing and reading; conversely, being human in the world of the novel meant being viewed and interpreted by others. Therefore, questions of visibility and legibility—and the production of a field in which objects, spaces, and bodies appeared—are the central engagements of the chapter that deals with these fictions. I contend that the novel opened a space in discourse for new modes of visibility and new orders of subjectivity. The voice that emerged in this process was not only a subject of sensation—one affected by the world of objects, but also of exposedness—open to the gaze of the world. Caste and gender were not external entities merely referred to in the novel; they were produced not as categories but as living processes by the marking of human subjects in particular ways within the new perceptual field being configured by these novels.

C.V. Raman Pillai's (hereafter 'C.V.') fictions and political writings lead us in chapter 5 to explore in greater detail the links between perception and fiction, and their close kinship with questions of affect and memory. C.V.'s extensive use of modes of stylization serves as a useful point of departure. Drawing on performing art forms such as the Kathakali, he created a new language of exaggeration for the physiognomies, expressions, and gait of his characters. The fictional images in his novels constantly oscillate between the poles of realistic representation and schematic performance routines. I regard this oscillation as a key to the aesthetic-political form of historical recollection in his novels.

Although his trilogy of historical romances—*Martandavarma* (1891), *Dharmaraja* (1913), and *Ramaraja Bahadur* (1918–19)—presented celebratory accounts of two eighteenth-century kings of Travancore, i.e. Martandavarma (r. 1729–58) and Ramavarma (r. 1758–98), the novelist saw *Dharmaraja* and *Ramaraja Bahadur* as the first two volumes in a planned trilogy on the eighteenth-century Nayar dewan Kesava Pillai (1745–99), better known as 'Raja Kesavadas'. The shift in focus from the king to the Nayar minister may be seen as a screen that conceals an additional level of complexity, found in the recurrent and obsessive preoccupation in C.V.'s fiction with Kazhakkuttam house, a destroyed *taravad* (matrilineal family) of rebel Nayar chiefs (*madampimar*). They appear to rise from the ashes, novel after novel, to confront royal power anew. If C.V.'s novels celebrate images of Nayar loyalty, valour, and governance through the figure of Raja Kesavadas, they also manifest a powerful subterranean strain of heroic mourning for earlier forms of Nayar power destroyed by Martandavarma's consolidation of the Travancore state.

I argue that tensions between two configurations of sovereignty, two forms of political life, underlay C.V.'s fictional and political projects. Language and narration in his historical novels negotiate their opposed pulls through the invocation of a heroic register and the use of stylization and schematic performance routines; they bring together praise and mourning, ritualized royal acclamation and new forms of discursive restraint. The subject of historical memory in C.V.'s fiction is produced at the tense convergence of these conflicting elements.

The theme of memory leads to chapter 6, which engages with the discourse of remembrance in autobiographical writing. Personal narratives developed a special tone in Malayalam with the emergence of what may, somewhat crudely, be called 'reform autobiographies'. Their authors were people who took an active part in community reform movements in the early decades of the twentieth century, the autobiographies being written mainly in the middle of the twentieth century, after independence and the creation of Kerala as a state. I focus on the modes of self-articulation in these self-narratives and try to place them within a longer history of the genre in Malayalam.

The chapter begins with a discussion of two early autobiographies, by Yakob Ramavarman (1814–58) and Vaikkathu Pachu Moothathu (1815–83). Both texts invoke the divine as source of veridiction. Ramavarman's narrative introduces a new conception of time by privileging the moment of individual transformation and linking it to the subject revealing a hidden truth about himself.

The chapter juxtaposes these early narratives with autobiographies that have social reform and changes in social life as their primary points of reference. Personal narratives written by two Nambutiri Brahmin authors, Kanippayyur Sankaran Namboodiripad (1891–1981) and V.T. Bhattatiripad (1896–1982; hereafter 'V.T.'), show us new idioms of temporal articulation. For Kanippayyur, autobiography was not the story of an individual's life: it was a recording of the customs and practices that had disappeared from his society, but which could be conjured through personal recollection, in the mode of an auto-ethnography of the past. V.T., by contrast, used his autobiography to critique conservative practices among Nambutiri Brahmins and to affirm the pleasures and desires of the new subjects produced by the reform movement. We find important moments of ambivalence in these texts: Kanippayyur, who praises the harmonious pre-modern ethos of caste societies, resorts to a modern understanding of caste in his historiography; V.T.'s affirmative new subject appears enmeshed in acts of betrayal when we take a closer look at his invocation of female figures.

Jeevitasamaram (1953–65)—the autobiography of C. Kesavan (1891–1969), an Ezhava leader who later became chief minister of the Travancore-Cochin state—shows the emergence of a different model of self-presentation. In this narrative a rebellious, 'natural' masculinity combines with a secular-modern desire to plan one's future. It also shows a powerful strand of popular memory at work, which often militates against the principles and ideals endorsed by the reform movement. This permits Kesavan's self-narrative to produce an ethnography of modernity which disrupts easy inhabitation of the norms avowed in the text.

I conclude with a brief discussion of a fragmentary autobiography written by Lalitambika Antarjanam, which makes the difficulty, even impossibility, of autobiographization determine the very form of self-narration. Lalitambika's account foregrounds the conditions of entry into the world of autobiographical eloquence. These conditions did not merely reflect or reproduce inequalities that existed in the 'real' world; they shaped the fabric of writing by determining who could speak under what signature, and what discursive manoeuvres allowed speech about oneself, one's life.

Self-narratives tend to provoke discussion of the author's conscious design: what sorts of events or details were selected for narration or suppressed, what self-image is projected, what pattern is meant to emerge from the story as a whole. However, we often find instances where what is drawn into self-narratives goes beyond the ambit of authorial control. Descriptive detail, narration, and conversation pull in resonances that are inadequately contained by authorially intended patterns or self-images. Autobiographical self-exhibition exceeds that which was meant to be exhibited. The very force of storytelling—the intoxication with the flow of elements from the world into one's story—may result in a breakdown or betrayal of control. If autobiographies have been a means for writing history, and not merely raw material to be processed by the discipline of history, the reason is their capacity for drawing in things that cannot be assimilated by the intended story.

A powerful instance of this is the anecdote: the memory work of autobiographies clears a space for this and draws it in. A good anecdote is not exhausted by its value as illustration. It possesses a memorable, compelling sense of detail, and often a quirkiness which fits with what is being said, but only to an extent, and without being submerged. A detail sticks out to outlive the purpose for which it was brought in, producing resonances that may go beyond, even against, what is being said. The anecdote 'speaks' of itself, independent of the author of the self-narrative, even if it originated in the personal experience of the author. The anecdote, like a rolling pebble, acquires its form through repeated recounting. It has a loose sense of contextual belonging: it shakes off the dust of the longer stories within which it has appeared to move into new tales. Anecdote, in a real sense, is not answerable to its author; its very mode is that of being retold by others. Its repetitions invoke and betray authority. Its links are to a less regulated popular realm of remembrance and recollection. A discussion of self-narratives is bound to remain flawed unless the work of the anecdote is taken on board. How do anecdotes impel us to reconsider the figure that appears in autobiographies as the subject of recollection and retelling? This question informs some of the discussion in chapter 6, but its consequences may be larger.

During work on this book, two concepts grew increasingly important. They have determined the analyses in it, often without marking the text's surface. These are the concepts of 'inhabitation' and 'style'. Both have been useful in probing the limits of self-identification, and in asking after elements that escape the table of self-descriptions and the calculus of identities. This is not always a matter of remainders, and we may need a different kind of question: closer to a 'how' than to a 'what'. 'Inhabitation' helps us ask after the 'how' of identities: how are identities lived or lived in, how are they inhabited? 'Style' is vital to identifying and differentiating the levels to which questions belong. I was drawn to 'style' initially because of its flexibility in comparison to more 'robust' concepts like 'representation', 'structure', and even 'imaginary'. Style suggests a movement best captured in the process of enunciatory unfolding. It is closer to the manner, the habits, the gestures of saying and telling, than to the story told. I have tried to focus on postures and movements which appear within acts of enunciation, but which may slide away from the apparent goals of what is said. Such slides show us snapshots of subjects in their imperfect inhabitation of narrativizable identities. I have used 'style' as a name for this plane of visibility.

2

The Degree Zero of Difference

Passages of the Body in Sree Narayana Guru's Writings

AT THE BEGINNING OF THE First World War, Sree Narayana Guru, renowned for his spiritual and social initiatives, is said to have advised his followers to pray for Britain's victory. 'The British are like our guru: it is they who gave us *sanyas*,' he observed, recalling the age-old denial of the right to ascetic practice to the lower castes in Hindu society.[1] These words, tinged with the wry humour typical of many of Sree Narayanan's observations, bring into relief the non-traditional authority behind his own ascetic career. A famous riposte attributed to him is revealing: when he founded the Siva temple at Aruvippuram in 1888—by consecrating a stone from the local river as idol—and his eligibility to perform such rituals was challenged by the upper castes, Sree Narayanan is said to have responded with disarming wit: 'What I installed is only an Ezhava Siva.'[2] The unauthorized character of his initiatives was important within Sree Narayanan's thoughts about his own practice. Till late in

[1] Sanu, *Narayanaguruswamy*, 306.

[2] Moorkothu Kumaran, *Sree Narayanaguruswamikalude Jeevacharitram*, 87. See also ibid., 123. For a critique of the apocryphal character of this statement, see Rajan and Reghu, 'Backwater Universalism', 66–7.

life he did not don the robes of a *sanyasi*.[3] His statements on religion suggested diverse and apparently contradictory positions. The nature of religious belief and identity, the relationship to tradition, and the founding presuppositions of community—all these remained live issues in his work and thought throughout his life.

Sree Narayanan was born in Chempazhanti near Trivandrum in 1856. After a spell of primary education he engaged in agriculture, his family's main occupation, until the age of seventeen. He went on to study Tamil spiritual texts in Trivandrum, and Sanskrit texts from Kummampilli Raman Pillai Asan, a scholar interested in Sanskrit as well as Tamil literature.[4] On his return to Chempazhanti in 1881, Narayanan set up a traditional elementary school (*pathasala*) where children of the untouchable castes were also taught. Around this time, probably on account of family pressure, he married a woman named Kalikkutty. He forsook conjugal life soon after and took to wandering as an *avadhuta* (a spiritual practitioner who has freed himself from social etiquettes) to engage in ascetic austerities. Around this time he met Chattampi Swamikal and Thycaud Ayya, two advanced practitioners of yoga, and was quite possibly trained by both. In 1888 Sree Narayanan founded a temple at Aruvippuram, following this up with consecrations of new temples at Ayiramthengu (1892), Kolathukara (1893), and Kayikkara (1893). He set up an organization around the Aruvippuram

[3] Sree Narayanan began wearing saffron robes at the insistence of some of his disciples before his journey to Ceylon in 1918, ten years before his death. He is reported to have said that saffron robes had the advantage that dust did not show on them. Sanu, *Narayanaguruswamy*, 352.

[4] Kummampilli Raman Pillai Asan (1845–1911) is said to have composed texts such as *Prabodhachandrodayam*, *Dasakumaracharitasamgraham*, and *Pattanattupillayar Pattu*. He had a school (*gurukulam*) in Puthuppally in Onattukara, where training was given to learners in the Sanskrit language, Kathakali, and Aksharaslokam—the intricate art of reciting quatrains in sequence—without discrimination against anyone on the basis of caste and religion. See Muthulekshmi, 'Samskrtabhashayude Navodhanasandarbham', 9.

temple called Vavoottu Yogam, and, with the help of Dr P. Palpu—an Ezhava doctor in the service of the Mysore government—founded the Sree Narayana Dharma Paripalana (SNDP) Yogam in 1903. His subsequent life is well documented. He authored several devotional and philosophical texts in Malayalam, Tamil, and Sanskrit. These form an important part of his work—alongside prescriptive writings, instructions, messages to the SNDP Yogam and to the ashrams he founded, as well as the records of his conversations with co-workers, visitors, and devotees. Located at the intersection of philosophical reflection, religious doctrine, and communitarian practice, Sree Narayanan's work combines diverse modalities of discourse to re-cite and re-signify tropes from a variety of traditions.

Sree Narayana Guru has been the object of widespread adulation, worship, and commemoration in Kerala, and across parts of the country. A visitor to the state cannot escape chancing upon some of the numerous statues of the Guru, erected by local branches of various Sree Narayana organizations, which punctuate the length and breadth of Kerala. Hundreds of institutions— schools, colleges, and hospitals, for instance—have been named after him. Beginning with Kumaran Asan's brief sketch in 1907, Narayanan's life has been written about in numerous biographies; anthologies of his compositions, scholarly studies of his work, and selections from contemporary writings on caste society also circulate well in Kerala.[5] The widest possible political spectrum—ranging from the far left to the right—shows Sree Narayana Guru being invoked as a commanding spiritual figure, modernizing social reformer, lower-

[5] Biographies of Sree Narayana Guru include those by K. Damodaran (1929), Moorkothu Kumaran (1930), Pandit K.K. Panikkar (1954), Swami Dharmanandaji (1965), and M.K. Sanu (1976). Notable among collections of studies on the Guru are P.K. Balakrishnan's *Sree Narayana Guru* (1954) and K.N. Shaji's *Narayanaguru: Jeevitam, Krtikal, Darsanam* (2002). Sree Narayanan's life has also been commemorated in novels and films: K. Surendran's *Guru* (1992) is an example of the former, and *Narayana Guru* (1985, dir. P.A. Backer) and *Yogapurushan* (2010, dir. R. Sukumaran) of the latter.

caste campaigner, and harbinger of the ideals of egalitarian democracy. This unanimous valorization has arguably limited the possibilities of interpretation—for instance, in relation to Sree Narayanan's legacy *vis-à-vis* contemporary critical thought—as well as reduced the arena for new idioms of engagement outside the registers of adulation and canonization.[6]

A strict separation between life and thought is difficult when viewing figures like Sree Narayanan. Biographical commemoration is an important means through which his heritage has been constructed, interpreted, and disseminated. Most accounts of his life use the techniques of charismatic biography and hagiography to construct the Guru as a source of authority for contemporary redefinitions of community identity.[7] Commemorative spiritual biographies often operate by the logic of the exemplum, interweaving human effort and superhuman agency in idioms that prevent easy distinction between the secular and the sacred. While many of Sree Narayanan's biographers regard him as an exceptionally great, spiritually enlightened individual, and as a privileged, emblematic sign of his times, popular hagiographical accounts in books and pamphlets give greater prominence to his *siddhis* (miraculous powers). They retain a strong residue of the popular estimation of Sree Narayanan in his time, found only with increasing difficulty in the more rational, secular, and disciplined constructions of his legacy. A critical engagement with the Guru's work needs to step outside these dominant frames of canonization and the divide between the secular and the sacred. Is his thought a singular event or does it acquire meaning only in historical narration? Is the newness of his thought to be sought in the doctrines he presented or in the context in which he invoked and deployed elements from tradition? Here I respond to these questions

[6] There are notable exceptions to this: see the essays by B. Rajeevan, reproduced in the section 'Sree Narayanante Rashtriyam', in *Vakkukalum Vasthukkalum*, 241–347; Reghu, 'Sree Narayana Prasthanam Keralattinte Yuvatvamanu'.

[7] For a discussion of these biographies, see Kumar, 'Writing the Life of the Guru'.

obliquely, by tracking the figures of the body, the species, and the community in Sree Narayana Guru's writings.

II

The bulk of modern scholarship considers Sree Narayana Guru an Advaitin thinker, a latter-day Sankara from a lower caste. Sree Narayanan drew on Advaita Vedanta arguments in prominent metaphysical writings such as 'Atmopadesa Satakam', 'Darsanamala', and 'Advaitadeepika'. Reading his texts for doctrinal consistency, however, raises important questions regarding the links between doctrines, thought-events, and practices. Advaitin arguments were invoked in a range of writings in nineteenth-century India in relation to worldly life and social action. The salience of these interventions is often found less in their strict adherence to Advaita doctrine than in its re-citation, in the way the later texts make the doctrine confront fresh experiences and authorize new discursive moves. It is over the course of this innovative repetition that the space of a new subject—of thought, articulation, and action—takes shape. This does not mean that the invocation of metaphysical arguments is instrumental or strategic. Authorizing doctrines appear as essential and indispensable to the 'work' performed by these texts, but collapsing all distinctions between them may be reductive. A productive reading requires moving away from doctrinal labels to track discursive events.

This is particularly important in the case of Sree Narayanan's writings, where Advaitin arguments at times appear influenced by other doctrinal and discursive lineages. Sree Narayanan, as we saw, was educated in Tamil as well as Sanskrit traditions. He is said to have received special lessons in yogic practice from Thycaud Ayya and Chattampi Swamikal. Both these thinkers, along with scholars such as P. Sundaram Pillai, were members of a group called Jnanaprajagaram, organized around Pettayil Raman Pillai Asan in Trivandrum, to discuss philosophy, literature, and spiritual matters.[8]

[8] See Paravur K. Gopala Pillai, *Paramabhattarashri Chattampi Swamikal Jeevacharitram.*

Sree Narayana Guru seems to have known these people well. Thycaud Ayya was a disciple of Vaikundaswamy (aka Ayya Vaikuntanathar) from Tirunelveli, a Dravidian sage with a millenarian, egalitarian vision.[9] Vaikundaswamy and Thycaud Ayya came from the strands of an anti-Brahmin spiritual practice of lower-caste provenance. They drew upon a Tamil intellectual and spiritual tradition which combined elements from Advaita Vedanta with Saiva Siddhanta and the practice of the Tamil Siddhars. Sree Narayanan is said to have travelled widely in southern Tamilnadu in the 1880s and to have interacted with practitioners of this spiritual tradition. He may be better understood in relation to these thinkers, who were part of a vernacular context of spiritual initiatives in southern Travancore in the second half of the nineteenth century.

Chattampi Swamikal, closely associated with Sree Narayanan during this period, had had a long-standing and intimate engagement with Sanskrit and Tamil traditions. He authored texts such as 'Advaitachintapaddhati' and 'Nijanandavialasam' to explicate Advaita Vedanta doctrines, as well as writings that maintained a close relationship to contemporary anti-Brahmin Dravidian thought—for example, 'Pracheena Malayalam', 'Vedadhikaranirupanam', and 'Adibhasha'. Some of his contemporaries recall his proficiency in the Advaitin and Saiva Siddhanta traditions: 'Although Chattampi Swamikal was a *sanyasi* in the Siddhanta tradition, he was a great rishi who had equal scholarship and experience in both the traditions [Saiva Siddhanta and Advaita Vedanta]. Therefore, with great independence, he disseminated an Advaita practice that combined both Vedanta and Siddhanta.'[10]

Chattampi Swamikal's reluctance to adopt the external attributes of a *sanyasi* was perceived as a sign of his connection with the tradition of

[9] For a discussion of Ayya Vaikuntanathar, see Pandian, 'Meanings of Colonialism and Nationalism'; P. Sundaram Swamikal and Ponnumani, *Ayya Vaikuntanathar*; Patrick, *Religion and Subaltern Agency*.

[10] Pandit C. Ramakrishnan Nair, 'Chattampi Swamikalum Trithapadasampradayavum', 70–1.

the Siddhars.[11] The confluence of elements from Advaitin and Siddhar traditions was also a feature of the intellectual and spiritual context within which Sree Narayanan's thought took shape. In some of his explicitly Advaitin texts, details of doctrine as well as metaphors used for illustrating arguments appear to have derived from Siddha or Saiva Siddhanta sources. Tamil Saivite saints such as Appar, Sambandhar, Sundarar, and Manikyavachakar are prominent in Narayanan's writings.[12] Advaitin arguments at times deflect in the direction of the traditions of Saiva Siddhanta or of the Siddhars, and arguments from texts in these traditions are recast in an Advaitin idiom.

Arivu and *jnanam*, two words for knowledge prominent in Siddhar texts, occur repeatedly in Narayanan's work. Kamil Zvelebil points out the predominance of *arivu* and its identification with God in the Siddha tradition: 'Civavakiar identifies *civam*, the Absolute, with *arivu*, knowledge. This is, of course, nothing new; again we may point back to Tirumular who says, "Those who say that knowledge and *civam* are two different things are ignorant."'[13] *Arivu* in Narayanan's writings often occupies a privileged structural space analogous to that of 'Brahman' in the philosophical discourse of Advaita.[14] It is seen as the sole essential reality, and the world and all lived experience are considered moments in *arivu*'s self-searching movement.

An early composition by Sree Narayanan, which begins '*Atu pampe!*' (Dance, snake, dance!), initially known as 'Pampattichintu' (the snake-charmer's song), is evidently modelled on a song composed by a major Siddha poet in Tamil known as 'Pampatti Siddhar' (the snake-charmer Siddha), and the refrain 'Dance, snake, dance!' is borrowed from his compositions. Later, Sree Narayanan's poem came to be known as 'Kundalinippattu' (Song of the Kundalini), after the

[11] Ibid., 73.

[12] See 'Anukampa Dasakam', in Narayana Guru, *Sreenarayanaguruvinte Sampurna Krtikal*, 519–21.

[13] Zvelebil, *The Smile of Murugan*, 230.

[14] See Narayana Guru, 'Arivu', *Sreenarayanaguruvinte Sampurna Krtikal*, 522–30; 'Atmopadesa Satakam', ibid., 339–40.

concept of the Kundalini, the source of energy in yogasastra, conceived in the form of a small snake resting in three and a half coils at the base of the spine. With yogic practices the Kundalini can be awakened and made to rise through the spinal column via a series of *chakras* towards the head, releasing the practitioner into a state of final, ecstatic liberation. Pampatti Siddhar's work too has invited yoga-sastric readings.[15] The word 'Kundalini' does not appear in Sree Naryanan's composition, and some commentators have disputed the identification of the snake in the poem with the Kundalini.[16] The poem moves between the worship of Siva in concrete, corporeal terms, and the ecstatic contemplation of a moment of realization which is beyond figural representation; the latter appears in the poem as the culminating sound and final effulgence that encompass the entire universe. Sree Narayanan used metaphors from yogasastra more directly in some of his other compositions, such as 'Atmopadesa Satakam'.

Presenting the body in intimate play serves as the nodal point for these eclectic processes of re-signification. Sree Narayanan's writings house numerous moments where phenomenal experience is regarded as lacking in ultimate validity. These moments exist alongside instances when the world is seen as Siva's body, suggesting a positive characterization of its ontological status. The dualism associated with the vision of Siddha and Saiva Siddhanta thinking allows differentiation of reality, though false differentiation is criticized and rejected.

Valorization of the world as Siva's body is paralleled by a positive evaluation of the human body. The Siddha texts often insisted that *uyir* (life force) does not exist without *utal* (body). Tirumular, one of the eighteen Siddhars, saw the body and its care as prerequisites for spiritual practice:

[15] See for instance, Heehs, ed., *Indian Religions*, 289.

[16] See T. Bhaskaran's commentary in Narayana Guru, *Sreenarayanaguruvinte Sampurna Krtikal*, 273–9. For a commentary with more explicitly Advaitin leanings, see Narayana Guru, *Sree Narayana Gurudeva Krtikal*, vol. 2, 614–65.

If the body perishes, Prana departs
Nor will the light of truth be reached;
I learned the way of preserving my body
And so doing, my Prana too.[17]

For Tirumular, despising the body is untenable: *porul* (essence, meaning) is discovered within *utal*. The body is the temple of God and its attentive preservation is the new task entrusted to the enlightened devotee.[18] In another verse, Tirumular characterizes the heart as the temple and body as the house.[19] All these tropes imply that the body is a site of positive practices.

However, in a strand of the classical yoga tradition, and in the work of some of the later Siddhars, the sensory body is denounced as a locus of decay and filth.[20] Some of Pattinattar's poems illustrate this.[21] One also finds criticism of bodily existence in Pampatti Siddhar, Kaduveli Siddhar, Bhogamuni, and even Tirumular. T.N. Ganpathy has argued that the 'negative attitude of some of the Tamil Siddhas towards the human body is explainable in the background of the positive attitude developed in the doctrine of *kayasadhana* (culture of the body) with a view to attaining *kayasiddhi* (perfection of the body).'[22] Thycaud Ayya, who instructed Sree Narayanan in yoga, is believed to have been an advanced practitioner of *kayasadhana*.[23] Narayanan's work draws

[17] Tirumular, *Tirumantiram*, v. 724.

[18] Ibid., v. 725.

[19] Ibid., v. 1823.

[20] Zvelebil, *Smile of Murugan*, 234–5.

[21] Kamil Zvelebil says: 'there is a very notable difference between Pattinattar and the early *cittar*: they liked their own body, they wanted to cherish and foster and preserve it, in order to use it for yogic techniques. Pattinattar, in this sense, is more of a "classical" yogi than a siddha: according to Patanjali (*Yogasutras*, II.40), physical purification produces disgust with one's own body, and cessation of contact with other bodies—a point at which "classical" yoga and the "magical", Siddha yoga differ significantly.' *Smile of Murugan*, 235.

[22] Ganapathy, *The Philosophy of the Tamil Siddhas*, 116.

[23] Some have even suggested that Chattampi Swamikal and Sree Narayanan moved away from Thycaud Ayya after the latter became engrossed

from both positive and negative attitudes to corporeality found in Siddha literature. This adds richness and complexity to the figure of the body in his writings.

Narayanan's early texts, such as 'Mananateetam' and 'Siva Satakam', include passages where the devotee-subject entreats Siva to rescue him from temptations of the flesh. The figure of the woman in these verses stands for the lower state of the body, entrapped in desires of the flesh. In diametrical contrast to sensuous descriptions of the female figure in Sanskrit and Malayalam poetic traditions, here the female body is imaged as disgusting, resembling a vast stinking waste-heap.[24] Women's breasts are compared to boils, and life with the woman is represented as an infernal ocean filled with blood and pus.[25] 'Mananateetam' oscillates frenetically between the opposed poles of fear and attraction. The female figure is viewed as an irresistible conqueror before whom the devotee is powerless without the support of Siva's grace. The soul is compared to a bird caught in a snare set by Kamadeva. Death and madness haunt the presence of the woman:

---

in a strand of Siddha practice similar to alchemy. T. Bhaskaran attributes this view to Sahodaran Ayyappan. Narayana Guru, *Sreenarayanaguruvinte Sampurna Krtikal*, 274. The oral reminiscence of Thycaud Ayya's second son and disciple Pazhani Velayya Swamikal suggests that Sree Narayanan and Chattampi Swamikal were initiated into alchemy (*rasavadam*) by Thycaud Ayya, but disputes that the latter was interested in making gold through this method for private use. See *Brahmashri Thycaud Ayya Swamikal*, 80. For a discussion of alchemy in Siddha practice in medieval India, see White, *The Alchemical Body*.

[24] Narayana Guru, 'Siva Satakam', v. 72, *Sreenarayanaguruvinte Sampurna Krtikal*, 205.

[25] Ibid., 205. Zvelebil cites passages from Pattinattar with similar imagery. '[H]e describes the female body as a bag of filth. The belly, compared by poets to a banian leaf, is a shaking screen of dirt and dregs; the breasts, compared to lotus-buds, are in fact two hanging dried-up pouches, parched and full of inner heat, scratched by the finger-nails of lusty men. The neck is full of sweat and dust and filth, and out of the hellish mouth spouts poison.' *Smile of Murugan*, 234–5.

the female body appears as a corpse, or the woman reveals herself as a raving lunatic in the midst of fervent embraces.[26] Fear of the female figure merges with the fear of mortality and unfreedom.

In these texts by Sree Narayanan, bodily senses appear as lacking any knowledge of what they can celebrate, what their legitimate enjoyments are. They are reminders of the proximity of death and the promiscuous trap of existence. They produce *jugupsa* (disgust); to escape the experience of revulsion, the senses have to be reinscribed in a new relation to the body and the self. Another poem by Narayanan, 'Indriya Vairagyam', tells us that the senses contain neither the problem nor the solution: the senses do not feel any suffering; it is the self that suffers.[27] The devotee perceives his body as being abused by the senses; the latter are inferior beings irredeemably engrossed in the sensible world. The devotee's only recourse is to pray to Siva to save him from the untruthful entrapment of the senses and make him embrace a new, uncorrupted body.[28] The conceptions of a pure body and its maintenance are articulated in terms that come from yogasastra.

Narayanan's most elaborate discourse of the doctrine of the self is to be found in 'Atmopadesa Satakam'.[29] Presumed to have been composed when he stayed at Aruvippuram, and initially circulated as 'Atmabodham', this text is believed to have reached its present form by 1897.[30] It is written in the mode of advice, and the title captures vital ambiguities: it could mean advice to oneself or advice on the doctrine of the self. Each stanza concludes by stressing the modality of instruction, evident in locutions such as 'may be uttered', 'may be

[26] Narayana Guru, 'Mananateetam', *Sreenarayanaguruvinte Sampurna Krtikal*, 270.

[27] Narayana Guru, 'Indriya Vairagyam', ibid., 225–6.

[28] Ibid., 230.

[29] Narayana Guru, 'Atmopadesa Satakam', *Sreenarayanaguruvinte Sampurna Krtikal*, 334–45.

[30] Ibid., 334. See also Narayana Guru, *Sree Narayana Gurudeva Krtikal*, vol. 1, 539.

remembered', and 'may be practised'. The guru and *sishya* both seem intermittently to be the enunciating subject; the speaking voice in the poem seems to oscillate between the two, becoming the subject as well as the object of advice. The text's performative mode is that of self-practice, comprising actions performed by the self on itself, effecting and recognizing moments of transformation. This is stressed by the appearance, several times in the text, of postures of the body, beginning with the *pranamam* in the opening verses and ending with the *amarcha* of the closing lines, presenting the condition of an active containment of energy.

'Atmopadesa Satakam' is widely read as Sree Narayanan's most important text on the Advaitin doctrine of the self, subtly extending its scope beyond the ambit of spiritual affairs. The poem also contains elements that resonate with the discourses of Saiva Siddhanta and the Tamil Siddhars.[31] The prominence given to *arivu* as the manifestation of God and the placing of the senses (*indriyam*), inner sense (*karanam*), the body (*kalebaram*), and the world (*jagat*) as its manifestations pick up elements from these traditions. The third verse, for example, describes the five elements as *vivartham* in the Advaitin tradition and as *vibhuti* in the Saiva Siddhanta way. While *vivartham* denotes the projection of an unreal figure onto a real object, as in mistaking a rope for a snake, *vibhuti* refers to the eight powers of Siva.[32] The verse introduces the metaphor of 'waves in the ocean', a trope which runs through several of Narayanan's texts. The ocean produces waves, but the waves are inseparable from the ocean: the image brings together apparent difference and underlying unity; it also presents difference as a result of creation, as the work of the ultimate.

The poem charts a phenomenology of *arivu*, seeking itself and going through a series of manifestations. The conception of the evolution of *prakrti* in the Saiva Siddhanta and Sankhya traditions underpins

[31] For a reading of 'Atmopadesa Satakam' that highlights its Advaitic orientation, see Nataraja Guru's commentary in Narayana Guru, *One Hundred Verses*.

[32] Narayana Guru, *Sreenarayanaguruvinte Sampurna Krtikal*, 338–9.

this narrative.[33] *Ahanta* (sense of the self) is seen as comprising skin, bones, excreta, and volatile inner thoughts (*anthakalakal*).[34] But *ahanta* is itself a moment in the differentiation of *arivu*.[35] Even time, the very modality of differentiation, is the play of *arivu*. The temporality of the body has an ambivalent status: even as it is a site of transience and decay, it is a moment in the narrative of the search for the self by *arivu*.

Narayanan describes the body as the shadow of the soul (*atmavu*), but the soul is presented as a lamp of which the senses form the container, *vasana* from earlier life the oil, and *vrtti* or the forms assumed by the inner sense the wick.[36] The metaphors of light and darkness make the body's positioning ambivalent. The image of the shadow suggests that the body, while unreal in itself, has its origin in something real and thus may serve to guide one's attention to a point where that reality may be grasped.[37] In other words, while the body's ontological status may be open to question, it may possess epistemological and axiological value in the search for self-realization.

The text's ambivalence in relation to the body is expressed more fully in verses 8 and 9 of the 'Satakam'. Verse 8 describes the body as a foul-smelling tube on which tantalizingly play the five birds of the senses, feeding on five distinct objects.[38] The use of the word *nalika* is interesting. *Sabdataravali*, Sreekanteswaram Padmanabha Pillai's canonical dictionary of the Malayalam language, defines *nalika* as a tube and *nalikam* as a gun.[39] *Nalikagulika* is a cannon ball, and *nalikarandhram* the apertures in forts for mounting cannons. Nataraja Guru and T. Bhaskaran take *nalika* to mean 'gun' in their

[33] See *Sankhya Karika*, especially xv–xvi and xxii–v, for a discussion of some differences between Sankhya and Saiva Siddhanta.

[34] Narayana Guru, *Sreenarayanaguruvinte Sampurna Krtikal*, 348.

[35] Ibid., 368.

[36] Ibid., 352.

[37] Ibid., 404.

[38] Ibid., 34. See Bhaskaran's commentary on this verse, ibid., 343–4.

[39] Sreekanteswaram Padmanabha Pillai, *Sabdataravali*, 1063.

commentaries on this verse. This is an unusual image in Sree Narayanan's writings, and, if we follow this reading, the relations between the senses and the body appear more complex. Does the image of the gun— associated with annihilation—suggest that the foul-smelling body in which the sense organs are located may also be used as a means for their destruction? The verse ends with a contrasting image of the body—that of a body of light or knowledge (*velivuru*). This new avatar of the body is the slayer of the birds of the senses. Two notions of the body appear here: one is presented as the subject of a self-practice, while the other is not only the object but in all probability also a means for carrying out this practice.

The juxtaposition is made possible by the availability of distinctions between various figurations of the body in yogasastra and Siddha practice—*sthula sariram* (gross body) and *sukshma sariram* (subtle body), for example. In fact, the next verse in 'Atmopadesa Satakam' offers a re-presentation of the body in terms of the yogic tradition. Verse 9 presents the image of a sage meditating under a tree, on the two sides of which climbs a creeper bearing six blossoms.[40] The tree has been read as a yogasastric diagram of the body, with the two sides of the creeper being *ida* and *pingala*, and the six flowers suggesting the six stations in the ascent of the Kundalini towards its final station of enlightenment, *sahasrara*. These verses also point to the complex intertextual universe behind Sree Narayanan's images. The image of the birds resonates with Pattinattar's description of the body as a cage with five birds inside.[41] Tirumular's writings also speak of the 'six birds in the house of five' and the 'hundred birds on top of the tree' and the seven steps that lead to the home.[42]

Sree Narayanan's writings of the self, in drawing on diverse strands of philosophical and spiritual practice, thus produce an ambivalent estimation of the body. We shall consider below the ways in which

[40] Narayana Guru, 'Atmopadesa Satakam', *Sreenarayanaguruvinte Sampurna Krtikal*, 344.

[41] Ibid.

[42] Tirumular, *Tirumantiram*, v. 2905.

his philosophical thought and his poetic imaginary connect with the arguments he developed on practices of worship and community identities. The reading proposed below seeks to stay away from two prominent tendencies in the scholarship on Sree Narayanan and other thinkers whose work straddles the distinction between the social and the spiritual. One approach involves treating philosophical arguments and doctrines as providing an interpretative key to the practice, while the other creates a sharp dichotomy between them, treating the doctrine and the practice as independent of each other in fundamental ways. From the first point of view, practices are expressions of metaphysical principles, while the second perspective considers doctrines rather like ideologies which make practices possible but obfuscate their real nature. The focus of this chapter is on the innovative moves and effects produced by the invocation of doctrines and discourses. One needs to track not only philosophical lines of argumentation but also the iteration and transformation of tropes and locutions. The discursive function of doctrines is not exhausted by their legible meanings; their performative and incantatory function also needs to be accounted for.

III

Sree Narayanan's interventions towards altering practices of worship have generally been seen as efforts to civilize Ezhava rituals and bring them in tune with upper-caste Hindu methods. An account of the Ezhavas in 1909 by the colonial anthropologist Edgar Thurston describes their popular religion as 'Bhadrakali' worship and animal sacrifice. By this Thurston meant the worship of indigenous deities like Chattan, Madan, and Kali prevalent in lower-caste shrines in nineteenth-century Kerala. Thurston noted that 'the Bhadrakali cult [was] gradually losing favour under the teaching of a Vedantic scholar and religious reformer named Nanan Asan' and that 'in many Central and South Travancore shrines, images of Subramania have been set up at his instance.'[43]

[43] Thurston, *Castes and Tribes of South India*, vol. II, 400.

Vivekodayam, the official journal of the SNDP Yogam, published reports of Sree Narayanan putting an end to animal sacrifices and the worship of Kali, Madan, and other deities, and instituting the worship of Subramanian, Sivan, and Devi. We find the following in a 1915 report:

> During the past month, Swamikal travelled to Kottar and Kadukkara and reformed the primitive forms of worship among the Ezhavas. In Kadukkara, in a Samadhi temple in an Ezhava street, Swami stopped rituals involving alcohol and meat and, following his command, devotees have started practising satvika forms of worship. The cruel act of killing animals in a Devi temple there has also been stopped. The people of this locality are very happy about all this. The horrifying (*bhayankara*) images kept in the Arumugham Pillayar temple in Kottar and in the street nearby were also removed.[44]

This is followed by a list of the images removed: 'Isakki (yakshi) idol (*vigraham*): 2; Madan's platform (*peedam*): 2; Poothathan platform: 1; Vankaramadan platform: 1; Chudalamadan platform: 1; Isakki platform: 1; Mallankarunkali platform: 1; Karuppan, Irulai, etc.: 21.' The report goes on to say that the young men of the locality were very enthusiastic about getting rid of these evil deities (*pisachukkal*), and as soon as the Swamikal issued his command, they destroyed the stone platforms of these deities with iron implements.[45]

There has been little discussion in historical scholarship on the impact of the removal of these ancient gods from the moral universe of lower-caste communities. What imaginary and ethical events were required for the transfiguration of these deities, which commanded worship for a long time, into 'horrifying' images? Was a sacrificial rite of passage necessary for entry into the idioms of the high Hindu community and secular history? Or do such moves require a different historical understanding? Roby Rajan and J. Reghu have proposed an interesting argument which regards the valorization of Sree

[44] *Vivekodayam* XII: 10 (1915), cited in Sanu, *Narayanaguruswamy*, 296–7.

[45] Ibid., 297.

Narayanan's installation of Siva at Aruvippuram as a response to this problem. '[W]ith the unseating of the old gods, the very substance-effect of Ezhava communality was suspended in a collective self-contraction. *Every attempt to historicize this contraction as a form of progressive secularization or Sanskritization must pass silently over the void that opened up between the departure of the old gods and the arrival of the new . . . This moment of extreme contraction which exceeds the grasp of historicization is what is memorialized in popular remembrance as the* Aruvippuram Pratishta.'[46] Rajan and Reghu are right to highlight the limits of historicist arguments in understanding these acts. We shall note the discursive moves which mark and negotiate this complex knot in temporality in Sree Narayanan's writings.

Narayanan's early prose text 'Daivachintanam' (Meditations on the Deity), written in 1881, argued against offerings to malignant deities (*durdevata*; *kshudradevata*) and recommended the worship of benevolent ones (*saddevata*). Interestingly, Sree Narayanan did not deny the existence and power of these deities.[47] 'Just as there are myriad varieties of living beings on earth, in the atmosphere (*vayulokam*)—which has the properties of heat and cold and smell—there are innumerable living beings. This is revealed at times through actions like the pelting of stones, their resolution through performance of magical rituals, and the miraculous deeds performed by persons possessed by deities.'[48] After admitting their existence, Narayanan listed the attributes of malevolent deities, and then forbade their worship, instead recommending *saddevatas* (benevolent gods). The cult of *durdevatas* was not the only practice Narayanan criticized in this text; he also castigated atheists and atomists who denied divine causation to the universe. Their worldviews, which he censured,

[46] Rajan and Reghu, 'Backwater Universalism', 75. Emphasis in the original.

[47] See 'Daivachintanam 1', written around 1881, arguing against the worship of malignant deities. Narayana Guru, *Sreenarayanaguruvinte Sampurna Krtikal*, 616–22.

[48] Ibid., 616.

resulted in death and destruction, while the worship of good deities, he said, leads to knowledge of the absolute (*brahmajnanam*) and liberation. Even if the law of karma compelled us to be reborn, we would go to the abode of the good deities at the end of each life, enjoy divine comforts, and then be born anew in propitious circumstances. A gradation of enlightenment, ranging from the primitive worship of malign forces to the ultimate attainment of *brahmajnanam* and liberation, is suggested: each of these stages possesses its own degree of reality.

Biographers, beginning with Kumaran Asan and Moorkothu Kumaran, have included in their accounts stories from popular memory in which Sree Narayanan performed supernatural acts, including expelling and banishing spirits and ghosts from persons and places haunted by them. Dharmanandaji, the author of a strongly hagiographical account of Sree Narayanan's life, writes of infertile women coming to the Guru, eating his leftovers, gaining fertility, and bearing children.[49] An incident narrated often in biographical accounts involves a Christian by the name of Pereira approaching Narayanan for protection from the attacks of a Kuttichathan, a mischievous imp-like spirit. Sree Narayanan asks Pereira if the Kuttichathan will defer to his intervention. Yes, Pereira reassures the Guru, he will. Narayana Guru gives Pereira a letter signed by him, addressed to the Kuttichathan, asking him to trouble Pereira no more.[50] The story is frequently cited as an example of Narayana Guru's humour and his ironic yet indulgent response to popular superstitions.[51] However, Dharmanandaji reads this as a true illustration of the Guru's magical powers. He notes that, following this intervention, the Kuttichathan stopped troubling Pereira, and that the letter—now

[49] Dharmanandaji, *Sree Narayana Gurudevan*, 359–63.

[50] Balakrishnan, ed., *Sree Narayana Guru*, 129–32.

[51] 'There are several stories about Swamy's compassionate, and at times humorous, responses to devotees who approached him for solutions to their problems. These stories have been recorded by many people with a veneer of the fantastic.' Sanu, *Narayanaguruswamy*, 127.

lost—was displayed as a talisman among the sacred objects in Pereira's house.[52] He recounts similar instances of Sree Narayanan performing acts of exorcism by verbal command, by letter, and by the sheer power of his thought.

It is difficult to determine the nature of these interventions: while they are marked by the compassionate irony characteristic of Narayanan's gestures towards worldly life, they are also celebrated in popular lore as magical feats that resonate with subaltern imaginations of sovereign power. Could Sree Narayanan's successful efforts at dislodging older, indigenous objects of Ezhava worship in favour of mainstream Hindu deities be the source of his magical power over inferior deities celebrated in these accounts?

The similarities between the new lower-caste devotional practices introduced by Sree Narayanan and upper-caste Hindu idioms of worship have provoked two opposed readings: while some see in them the logic of 'Sanskritization'—an emulation of upper-caste practices with a view to ameliorating one's social status—others read them as acts of appropriation by which dominant Brahminical religious practices are made to serve the ends of new social groups. Narayanan's comment about the idol he consecrated at Aruvippuram as an Ezhava Siva tantalizingly brought together these idioms: it may be read as a deft move by which the Ezhava could assume the powers of a Brahmin priest; it may equally be seen as a move by which Siva is turned into an Ezhava and brought outside the ambit of caste-Hindu protocols. B. Rajeevan has, in a series of essays, argued that Sree Narayanan's interventions need to be seen as involving a 'minorization' of Vedanta.[53] This invocation of the conception of the minor—as in Deleuze's argument that minor literature works by denuding a major language and making it stutter—is useful in understanding the discursive grammar of the new concept of Ezhava

[52] Dharmanandaji, *Sree Narayana Gurudevan*, 342–3.

[53] Rajeevan, 'Sree Narayanante Rashtriyam', esp. 'Sreenarayanaguruvum Vedantathinte Nyunapakshavatkaranavum' (Sree Narayana Guru and the Minorization of Vedanta), *Vakkukalum Vasthukkalum*, 249–53.

Siva.[54] It places Sree Narayanan's innovative acts at the confluence of idioms of sovereignty and minorizing subversion.

Sree Narayanan's writings make these gestures possible through a citation of the familiar reference in Vedanta to the two orders of perception: on the one hand there is the conception of Brahma, which is often identified as *arivu* in texts such as 'Atmopadesasatakam' and 'Arivu'; on the other there are specific Saivite deities such as Subramanian, Siva, Ganesa, and Devi to whom Sree Narayanan addressed most of his devotional writings.[55] The play between the two conceptions of the divine—one abstract and the other specific—is a feature of the Advaita tradition and prominent in Sankara's writings.

Narayanan's social interventions were inlaid with this dual perspective: the sage-reformer engages with different levels of perceived reality, as a *brahmajnani* and master working with the worldly consciousness of his followers. The new rituals he proposed relied less on metaphysical justification than everyday practical reasoning. When his followers sought Sree Narayanan's permission to institute an annual pilgrimage to Sivagiri and requested him to decide on the colour of the garments to be worn by the pilgrims, he suggested yellow: this was not only because the colour was dear to the Buddha and Krishna. Pilgrims could obtain yellow robes inexpensively: they just needed to dip their white clothes in turmeric, and after their pilgrimage the yellow could be washed off and the clothes would fit their *grahastha* lives again.[56]

Unlike many of the anti-caste spiritual reformers of the times, Sree Narayanan consecrated temples and installed idols. This was

[54] Deleuze and Guattari, *Kafka: Toward a Minor Literature*, 16. See also Kumar, 'Literature and Intensity', 123–35.

[55] Although Saivite deities figure prominently in Sree Narayanan's devotional writings, he also wrote some Vaishnavite compositions, e.g. 'Sree Vasudevashtakam'. Narayana Guru, *Sreenarayanaguruvinte Sampurna Krtikal*, 239–42.

[56] Balakrishnan, ed., *Sree Narayana Guru*, 149.

criticized by some of the other spiritual thinkers of the times, such as Brahmananda Sivayogi and Vagbhatanandan. Sivayogi's strong criticism of idol worship in texts such as *Mokshapradeepam* (1905) and *Vigraharadhana Khandanam* (1916) were perceived at times as directed against Sree Narayanan's practice. Vagbhatanandan directly questioned Sree Narayanan on idol worship but the Guru agreed with his interlocutor's criticism, while adding that he thought temples would help people practise cleanliness.[57] He once clarified that temples were founded in response to demands from Hindus, and he would be willing to found places of worship for people of other religions too if they so desired.[58] In 1917 he suggested that it might be better to found schools rather than temples as belief in temples was on the decline; and, contrary to his aims, temples had served to strengthen caste differences.[59] Most of the idols consecrated by Sree Narayanan were images of Siva, Subramanian, and Devi; he also installed a Vaishnavite Jagannatha idol at the temple in Tellicherry.

The less orthodox idols that Narayana Guru consecrated have attracted wider scholarly attention. He ordained lamps as objects of worship in Karamukku in 1920, and in Murukkumpuzha the following year. Towards the end of his life he installed mirrors with the inscription 'Om' in temples at Kalavamkodam and Vaikom in 1927. The installation of mirrors as idols has precedence in Vaikunta Swamikal's practices, and probably in the Tamil Jain tradition. The symbolic value of the mirror, signifying reflection, and the preoccupation with selfhood have been widely noted. In Narayanan's text of abstract meditation, 'Atmavilasam', the mirror appears as a prominent trope. The word *atmavilasam* may be translated as 'play of the self' (or the 'Self'), emphasizing the reflexive and substantive aspects of the phrase. The text presents the production of the real in terms of the mirror conceived as a reflective-optical machine. The

[57] Swami Brahmavratan, *Maharshi Vagbhatananda Gurudevar*, 69–70.

[58] Desabhimani, 15 July 1916, cited in Vaidyar, *Sree Narayana Guruvum Kumaran Asanum*, 6.

[59] Balakrishnan, ed., *Sree Narayana Guru*, 77.

visible plane of the mirror also contains a moment of blindness, as the opening indicates:

> Om! All this seems to be like a shadow that appears in a mirror placed before us. How amazing! The eye that sees everything—it is not seen by the eye. When we hold a mirror before the eye, the eye appears as a shadow in that mirror. Then the eye sees the mirror as well as the shadow. The shadow is lifeless (*jadam*). It does not have the power to see the eye. The eye does not have the power to look directly at itself. Thus, when the eye and its shadow are not visible in our eye, it is *we* who see the eye there. Similarly, we do not see the *we* who sees the eye.[60]

While the eye can see the external world, it cannot see itself except as a shadow that appears in the mirror. The viewer is divided between the blindness of the eye to itself and the visibility of the reflected shadow. The subject is available to its vision only as a shadow in an imagined mirror, which does not have the power to see and which cannot reciprocate its gaze. A second order of subjectivity becomes necessary in order for the first-person 'we' to be perceived. That is the position of the divine: 'O! This is truly astonishing! God has given space within himself for us as well as all that we see to appear as shadows. Besides, God sees all these. Thus God has become a divine mirror as well as an eye.'[61]

The play of this mirror is at the core of the human experience of exteriority. However, the subject also realizes that it was always located (as a shadow) in a divine mirror. 'Our God is none other than this mirror. We had not seen this earlier. Now it is visible to us without any concealment. We have become one with God. There is no room for articulation (*vyavaharikkuka*) any more for us. O, we are becoming one with God.'[62] This moment of inner perception of itself as a shadow in the divine mirror is a moment of dissolution for the subject. This shadow does not have an original any more. The

[60] Narayana Guru, 'Atmavilasam', *Sreenarayanaguruvinte Sampurna Krtikal*, 630. Italics mine.

[61] Ibid.

[62] Ibid., 633.

original, the mirror, the shadow, and the perceiving eye all coalesce in this final moment of disarticulation.

In Narayanan's phenomenology of perception, the 'real' world appears and disappears through a specular play that renders objects visible at the cost of the viewer's visibility to himself. Orders of reality are thus established through constitutive acts of vision and blindness. The sage-reformer figure oscillates between a final disarticulation of the self, and an exterior, specular engagement with the real. The play between these two orders of the real made a range of styles available to Sree Narayanan: devotion, irony, compassion, and the contrasting registers of the practical and the abstract. The importance of this becomes clearer when we turn to his arguments about the social, and his use of philosophical doctrines and discourses. This may enable us to revisit the challenge of a history of acts that exceeds historicism.

IV

Sree Narayanan wrote two texts that directly address the question of caste. One of them is titled 'Jatinirnayam' (The Determination of Caste), after a well-known anonymous Brahminical treatise on caste. Narayanan's text begins with a verse in Sanskrit, followed by four verses in Malayalam. The first, with the succinctness of a sutra, offers a philosophical definition of *jati* and the poem goes on to reject commonly used caste categories such as 'Brahmins'. The only *jati* of human kind is human-ness: as cow-ness is to cows, so human-ness is to humans. After defining *jati* as a natural kind, as that which differentiates man from other beings, Narayanan goes on to proclaim 'one caste, one religion, one God for man', a line which became a popular motto for the Sree Narayana movement as well as for the critique of caste divisions in Kerala. In its common, decontextualized use, this line is often understood as a programme for unifying and harmonizing castes and religions. However, in 'Jatinirnayam' it is firmly located in a discourse of natural kinds, as it is followed by the verse: 'men come from the same *yoni*, they have the same shape, there is no difference in any of this.' The text goes on to develop an argument about the unity of the human *jati* based on the natural logic of procreation—all human beings are born from the same *jati*, including Brahmins and Parayas. It was from a Paraya woman that Rishi Parasara was born; Vedavyasa was born of a fisherwoman. Narayanan's critique of caste here is based on the status of the human body as the common, natural endowment of the species. The act of procreation, with the human body as its locus as well as end, indicates that all human beings belong to the same caste. All this seems to be consistent with—and perhaps echoes—Buddhist arguments that the only valid meaning of *jati*, as far as living beings are concerned, is 'species'. However, Narayanan's meaning is not clear when he extends the scope of unity from *jati* to religion and to God, to announce: 'One caste, one religion, one God for humankind.' Is Sree Narayanan suggesting that religion and theistic belief are also universals which arise from the unity of the human species as a natural kind?

To engage this question, one needs to consider some of Narayanan's other texts and pronouncements. Firstly, let us turn to 'Jatilakshanam' (The Signs of Caste). Here too Narayanan uses the Buddhist argument that *jati* is a natural kind: the poem begins by suggesting that 'all beings that embrace and procreate with each other belong to the same kind (*inam*).' The argument echoes Siddhars like Siva Vakiar who exclaimed: 'What is caste? . . . What is it to sleep with a Brahmin woman or a Paraya woman?'[63] Except in the title, Narayanan does not use the word '*jati*' in this composition, using *inam* (kind) instead, emphasizing his philosophical argument on differentiation. We saw that 'Jatinirnayam' concluded with a rejection of caste categories such as Brahmin as valid principles of differentiation. 'Jatilakshanam' begins at this point by considering 'human kind' as a 'kind' and moves on to a meditation on the process of differentiation which gives rise to 'kinds' and the value that such differentiation may have. After stressing the importance of reproduction and mating as signs of belonging to

[63] See Zvelebil, *Smile of Murugan*, 229–30.

the same caste, Narayanan cites physiological features—body, voice, odour, taste, temperature, appearance—that members of the same natural kind share.

If this commonality establishes the genus, what would be the use of further, specific differentiation? Narayanan admits that there are valid marks that enable us to differentiate individuals within the species: signs indicating one's personal name (*peru*), place (*ooru*), and occupation (*thozhil*). These contrast with the logic of the body, which announces the generic commonality of human kind. Narayanan says that one may ask individuals for their names, places of origin, and occupations, but one cannot ask them for their *jati* since their bodies announce they belong to the human race. 'As *inam* takes the form of the body to announce itself, people with sight and intelligence will not ask after the *inam*.' Caste is a false principle of differentiation as it has no grounding in nature. This is revealed in the common propensity that people who believe in caste display in announcing to others that they belong to a higher caste: such dissimulation is possible because caste is not the 'kind' that the body announces. By contrast, sexual difference—the bodily mark of being a man or a woman—belongs to natural differentiation. It is sex and not caste that offers a case of naturally grounded differences within the human species.

Thus there are two sorts of difference. The one announced by the body has the status of natural kinds; the other, invisible to the naked eye, and not naturally given, but which may allow us to differentiate natural kinds further, pertains to names, places of origin, and occupation. These differences arise from human acts—naming, habitation, and work—and do not originate in nature. Caste, in its common usage, pretends to belong to the first kind of difference by claiming that it is naturally grounded, but is open to falsification and dissimulation. Believers in caste treat the second set of differences as signs of caste, mistaking their status and attributing to them a natural origin.

Naming, as we saw in the Introduction, was a performative act in the politics of caste in Kerala. Personal names, as well as signs of occupation and place of origin—as instruments of self-designation—were deeply embedded in the discursive politics of caste in Narayanan's time. Caste indicators in names were often signs appended to individual personal names to indicate place of origin or occupation. It was expected that Pulaya and Paraya names would include a prefix or suffix, such as *kutti* or *kunju*, indicating self-diminution. We saw that attempts by the lower castes to change practices of naming in the nineteenth century met with stiff resistance from upper-caste Nairs and Nambutiris. The use by Ezhavas of names such as 'Panikkar' and 'Amma'—traditionally used by Nairs—led to conflict in the early decades of the twentieth century, and some Ezhava writers even introduced a new 'second name' for themselves—'Saundikan'. In instances of defiance, names were not randomly chosen. Arguments are advanced about the appropriateness of the new second names, such as Saundikan, and these presuppose a community locus for the use of names. Narayanan did not propose alternative second names for use by Ezhava individuals: his point was that names indicate man-made individual differences within the human species, which means they have no natural foundation. By this argument, naming is a useful resource for identification universally available to all individuals within the human species. For Narayanan, naming was not the performative announcement of a new social or communitarian identity.

Occupations and place names were also caught in similar debates when Narayanan was writing. The Travancore government, in response to the Malayali Memorial of 1891, argued that 'Thiyyas . . . have largely been devoid of education, being satisfied with their own occupations such as agriculture, coir-making and toddy-tapping rather than going in for education which would make them eligible for jobs with the Government.'[64] This paved the way for Dr Palpu's campaign and the Ezhava Memorial submitted in 1896. It was against this background that Sree Narayanan presented occupation as a non-

[64] Balakrishnan, ed., *Sree Narayana Guru*, 50.

natural principle of differentiation freely chosen by individuals. Two other initiatives need to be placed next to this: Narayanan's appeal not to 'tap, drink or sell toddy', and his emphasis on agriculture, industry, and education as central to the Sree Narayana movement. One may see in these an attempt to rewrite the association between Ezhavas and their designated caste occupations. Sree Narayanan disagreed with Gandhi's endorsement of *varnashramadharma*, arguing for mobility and personal interest.[65]

Lastly, the place of one's origin was a hotly contested issue in the politics of Ezhava identity in the early decades of the twentieth century. Narratives of arrival were deeply entwined with arguments about the historical origins of caste in Kerala. Arguments were put forward to the effect that the Ezhavas had come to Kerala from Sri Lanka—that the caste name 'Thiyyan' is a corruption of 'Dweepan', indicating a connection with islands, and that the word 'Ezhava' came from 'Ilam', i.e. Sri Lanka. In proposing these arguments, C.V. Kunjuraman and other Ezhava intellectuals were trying to place Ezhavas outside the traditional caste structure of Kerala, as well as to trace a Buddhist lineage for them. Sree Narayanan neither endorsed nor contested these views directly. He is said to have argued against the use of the word 'Ezhava', saying that, if it indicated place of belonging, one should use 'Malayali' since Ezhavas had long been in Kerala; or 'Malayalam'—the word referred to the territory as well as the language.[66] Sree Narayanan's reluctance is marked by an attempt to set limits to the use of history in his arguments on the social domain. I examine this attitude later in the chapter.

Although 'Jatilakshanam' denies name, place, and occupation any fundamental value as natural kinds, they are given an important, positive status in the text. Enquiring after these attributes is a valid means for differentiating individuals, unlike enquiring after one's caste identity. If the human body announces its caste—that it belongs to the

[65] Moorkothu Kumaran, *Sree Narayanaguruswamikalude Jeevacharitram*, 219–20.

[66] Ibid.

human species—and this is the only meaning of *jati* which Narayanan allows, why do we need principles of further differentiation? The last three stanzas of 'Jatilakshanam' are about differentiation and its positive role.

The discussion of Sree Narayanan's philosophical works, such as 'Atmopadesa Satakam' and 'Arivu', showed that differentiation is an integral part of the manifestation of *arivu* or knowledge. This argument is repeated in 'Jatilakshanam': *inam* (kind) emerges from the ocean of knowledge. The water of this ocean comprises differentiated entities. The relation between *inam* and knowledge is similar to that between waves and the ocean. *Inam* is the mould in which the differentiated entity is cast; it is also the root that gives rise to all entities or kinds. The metaphor of 'casting' is repeated when Narayanan suggests that difference (*inam*) is the mould cast by the blacksmith called *arivu*.[67] The entire world of creation reappears incessantly, moulded in new forms. Differentiation, as in *arivu*, appears here as the very mode of temporality. 'Jatilakshanam' concludes by pointing to the link between difference (*inam*) and specificity or particularity (*innathu*). Without differentiation, there are no particulars; difference indeed has a positive function, giving rise to the world of creation and to the knowledge of particulars.

One may rightly feel that Narayanan is repeating an argument from the Advaitic tradition, accounting for the phenomenal world in terms of a process of differentiation. What interests us here is the use of this argument in his critique of caste, where it is employed not to reject difference but to stress a positive role for differentiation. The focus is not on the difference between a non-dualist apprehension of Brahma and a differentiated perception of the phenomenal world. The crucial distinction is between valid and invalid principles of differentiation. *Jati* as species is a valid principle of differentiation; but *jati* in the sense of 'Brahmin, etc.' is a false principle. Name, place, and occupation are valid categories of individual differentiation

[67] Narayana Guru, 'Jatilakshanam', *Sreenarayanaguruvinte Sampurna Krtikal*, 505.

when they are recognized as the product of human institution; they are false categories if seen as caste markers.

Designating the human body as the site of natural difference was central to Sree Narayanan's intervention in the politics of caste. We have already noted how attire, jewellery, and hairstyles served as physical markers of caste in nineteenth-century Kerala. In this scheme of things such marks are not separable from the body, they are borne by the body as a sort of natural extension and external manifestation. Clothes do not conceal the body; rather they 'visibilize' the caste body. Visibility is important where caste bodies are concerned, not merely on account of its role in preventing polluting touch; caste identities may be seen as a mode of political existence which works within a frame of intersubjective visibility and recognition. The practice of distance pollution presupposed a spatial frame for understanding caste bodies in which vision functioned as an attenuated form of touch; even the touch of shadows could result in pollution. Caste markers offer a semiological system through which the body was offered for perception in the social domain. Changes in this model at the end of the nineteenth century inflected the visual imaginary of literary works in Malayalam, as we shall see in later chapters.

It needs also to be recalled that, around this time, colonial discourses were trying to develop ways of 'naturalizing' caste by linking it to theories and debates on race in the imperial metropolis. Anthropometry was one of the means of this process, as the work of ethnologists like Thurston and Fawcett attests. Fawcett argued that the Nambutiri was 'perhaps, as his measures seem to prove, the truest Aryan in South India.'[68] This discourse may be seen as producing 'caste bodies' through racial inscription, visible physiognomically, and measured through the nasal index and other such ways.

Sree Narayanan's conception of the body militated against both these ways of 'materializing' caste bodies. By contrast with them, he adopted a strategy that privileged the human body's biological and

[68] Fawcett, *Nambutiris*, 33.

reproductive functions. This is the 'degree zero' of difference—the only difference inscribed in the body. The valorization of the body as a site of true difference was an important moment in Narayanan's writings on the social. He used it in order to initiate new moves in ethical thinking and propose fresh notions of religion and the community. It is to these arguments that we next turn.

V

What are the ethical consequences of taking the species body of the human, denuded of all social inscription, as a point of departure? Sree Narayanan's writings offer some pointers. An attempt to take the discussion of the human body to its own degree zero, its minimal origins, is found in the poem 'Pindanandi', which meditates on the body's first stage of formation—as a foetus in the mother's womb.[69] Earlier than the appearance of one's parents and relations, in absolute fragility, the formation and survival of the foetus is attributed entirely to Siva's compassion (*anpu*). Compassion as ethical orientation, coeval with creation, is thus prior not just to the social domain but to the originary human bonds that connect offspring to mother. Compassion exceeds the human coordinates within which it is practised; its provenance is in an anterior domain of fragile creatureliness which human beings share with all living entities. This sets a special task for humans: to devise their ethics under the sign of a compassion of non-human provenance.

In 1914 Sree Narayanan wrote two poems, 'Jivakarunya Panchakam' and 'Anukampa Dasakam', that had as their theme compassion in the context of human creatureliness. These texts were written at a time when he was actively campaigning to put an end to animal sacrifices in Ezhava shrines. A little later, Chattampi Swamikal wrote 'Jivakarunya Nirupanam', parts of which were initially published

[69] Narayana Guru, 'Pindanandi', *Sreenarayanaguruvinte Sampurna Krtikal*, 217–24. Bhaskaran suggests that the poem was composed between 1887 and 1897.

as essays and compiled posthumously as a book.[70] Sree Narayanan was not a strict vegetarian in his early years: there are stories of his eating fish with fisherfolk during his Avadhuta years.[71] His writings on compassion do however speak against the killing and eating of animals. This attitude comes up in his conversations as well: he is said to have recommended travelling by hand-pulled rickshaws rather than horse or bullock carts, for the rickshaw puller, unlike the animals, wants the traveller to use his vehicle.[72] The domesticated animal like the foetus is the proper site of compassion on account of its inarticulateness and lack of autonomy.

'Jivakarunya Panchakam' begins by suggesting that all creatures are our brothers and sisters (*atmasahodarar*) and concludes by identifying compassion as a distinctly human imperative:

> If he does not kill, he is a worthy human
> If he does, he is an animal's equal
> Even with all virtues
> The killer has refuge for none.[73]

The capacity for offering refuge (*saranyata*) is distinctively human; in its absence the distinction between the human and the animal is eradicated. 'Animal' here does not carry the pejorative connotation it often does in ordinary discourse: it is rather that not to kill is distinctive to human ethics; animals have no obligation not to kill. 'Anukampa Dasakam' develops this line of thought further: without compassion, man is just a degraded body, a bundle of 'bones, skin

[70] Chattampi Swamikal, 'Jivakarunya Nirupanam', in K. Maheswaran Nair, ed., *Chattampi Swamikal: Jivitavum Krtikalum*, 747–71. The text was written in 1918. R. Raman Nair and Sulochana Devi, *Chattampi Swamikal*, 441; for a discussion of the text, see 229–31.

[71] Kumaran, *Sree Narayanaguruswamikalude Jeevacharitram*, 75.

[72] Ibid., 218.

[73] Narayana Guru, 'Jivakarunya Panchakam', *Sreenarayanaguruvinte Sampurna Krtikal*, 514. A literal translation of the last two lines would be: 'even with all other virtues, the killer lacks the quality of offering refuge or protection [*saranyata*]'.

and nerves', and his life is wasted like water thrown on a desert or a flower without fragrance or fruit.[74] The highest praise is offered to the practitioner of compassion: he is compared to Krishna, Buddha, Sankara, Jesus, and Muhammad, and to the renowned *siddhas* from the Tamil tradition: Sambandhar, Appar, Manikyavachakar, and Nandanar.[75]

What is it that differentiates the human from the animal? We saw Sree Narayanan suggesting that the human body reveals the true caste of the human species. But unlike animals, human beings often do not recognize this. Sree Narayanan was fond of using this point of contrast: an animal can recognize its own *jati* by sight, human beings are inferior to animals in that they cannot recognize their own kind.[76] This places the human being in a paradoxical state: unable to recognize its own kind and commanded by its originary creaturely fragility to practice compassion towards all creatures. How is this ethical passage to be effected? What is the idiom in which the human being can recognize his own kind? Sree Narayanan's thoughts on *dharmam* and the social domain include efforts to chart this difficult passage.

His version of Advaita argues for the identity of the worldly and the spiritual aspects of existence. A prescriptive text, written around the time of the founding of the *math* at Sivagiri, and later published by Kumaran Asan under the title 'Advaita Jeevitam', illustrates this point well.[77] It begins by asserting that all human beings desire happiness, and that the human soul in general prefers eternal, spiritual happiness to that of a transient, sensory nature. Narayanan introduced a social dimension into this familiar argument in order to suggest that the internal reforms of diverse communities influence the extent to which such happiness is attained. This passage is worth quoting at length:

[74] Narayana Guru, 'Anukampa Dasakam', *Sreenarayanaguruvinte Sampurna Krtikal*, 517.

[75] 'Anukampa Dasakam', vv. 6–9, ibid., 519–21.

[76] Moorkothu Kumaran, *Sreenarayanaguruswamikalude Jeevacharitram*, 183.

[77] Narayana Guru, 'Advaita Jeevitam', *Sreenarayanaguruvinte Sampurna Krtikal*, 1.

> For a community to achieve prosperity of all sorts—related to the body, the mind and the soul—the religious and moral rectitude of its members could be a source of great help. Temples and places of worship may be useful for developing these qualities in everyone within the community. However, the economic prosperity of the community's members is equally essential. For this, we need to reform agriculture, trade and technical education, among other things.
>
> The worldly and the spiritual are not two separate things. In reality, both work with the same aim. The body enjoys happiness thanks to the harmonious functioning of all its parts. Similarly, the harmonious functioning of various spiritual and worldly arrangements is necessary for the human community to attain its ultimate goal of happiness.[78]

This passage displays two moves that Sree Narayanan's writings rehearse time and again. Firstly, there is a movement from the individual to the community and from the community to the species as a whole. Individual aspirations to well-being and the self-practices necessary in spiritual endeavours are used as a model for thinking about initiatives of social reform. Secondly, imaging the human species as a body involves considering the various activities of mankind as analogous to the functions of the different bodily organs. The care of the body is the model for conceptualizing collective effort. We saw in the previous section that for Narayanan it is not caste markers that constitute the true semiology of differentiation, it is the body that indicates difference. The body is not a bearer of signs, it is a sign in its own right. Without the distinctiveness of the human body, the identity of the human species is inconceivable. The unity of the social realm, founded as it is on the specificity of the human, refers us back to the human body.

Three concepts recur prominently in his discussions of the social realm. These are caste (*jati*), religion (*matam*), and community (*samudayam*). While pointing out that caste was a principle of false differentiation and needed to be rejected, Narayanan also argued that religion was purely a matter of inner beliefs and opinions. His

[78] Ibid.

argument on *jati* privileges, as we saw, the literal meaning of the word. In the case of religion too, he stresses the literal sense of *matam*, i.e. belief, opinion. In both these instances, current usage is criticized as an instance of historically generated misunderstanding. Appeal to a literal meaning leads to a redefinition of *jati* as natural kind and dissociates *matam* from birth and external institutions to establish its status as inner belief.

The third element, community (*samudayam*), signifies in Narayanan's writings a locus of concerted action and the sense of belonging that arises from this. Although earlier uses of *samudayam* referred to Brahmin collectives, and to committees engaged in the management of temples, by the late nineteenth century the word had come to indicate human collectivities in general, and religious and caste groupings in particular.[79] In Narayanan's texts the sense of *samudayam* appears to oscillate between the specific and the general, between collectives founded on a commonality of conditions of existence or of objectives of action on the one hand, and the human species as the most universal and pre-eminently valid form of community on the other. The second, general, meaning is evident in statements like 'Caste should go; there is no other way. All human beings belong to the same community.'[80] Narayanan uses the idea of a natural, universal human community as the original, literal standard against which other notions of the community must be measured or understood.

His own reform movement primarily addressed the Ezhavas, appealing to them to get rid of their caste markers and internally reform themselves into a *samudayam*. The word 'Ezhava' here ceases to function as a sign of differentiation according to convention and becomes the name of a community, i.e. the shared site of individual and

[79] Hermann Gundert's dictionary defines *samudayam* as 'an assembly; a council of Brahmans, committee for managing common property or the concerns of a temple.' Hermann Gundert, *Malayalam and English Dictionary*, 1039. Writings published in late-nineteenth-century newspapers and periodicals often use *samudayam* to signify human collectivities in general.

[80] Sanu, *Narayanaguruswamy*, 349.

collective practices. The construction of places of worship, the development of agriculture and trade, and the spread of education are actions which have specific communities as their locus. The deeper ambitions and assumptions of these reformist practices are universal—they are validated in terms of the concept of a virtuous life that pertains to the entire human species or human community (*manushya samudayam*). However, identification with the human species is actualized only when there is an eradication of false divisions like caste. This is implied in Narayanan's statement that the progress of the human soul towards spiritual happiness is facilitated by the extent of internal reform attained by the various communities (*oro samudayangal*).[81]

We saw earlier that Sree Narayanan considered the human being in its creatureliness as the locus of a special predicament, marked by *avidya*, which prevented it from recognizing its own kind or *jati* in its humanity, and commanded to perform ethical acts of compassion towards all creatures. *Samudayam* appears as the means by which the human being can learn to recognize human-ness, its species identity, as its natural kind. This apprenticeship works through an unlearning of false identifications of *jati*: the first step in that direction is to work through and destroy the caste character of Ezhava identity and reconstitute it as *samudayam*. The cleansing of the community, analogous to the cleansing of the body's caste markers, involved the removal of rituals like *talikettu* and *tirandukalyanam*, associated with the attainment of puberty by girls in the community. The concept of *samudayam* pointed in two directions: towards a caste identity, which it sought to annihilate, and towards a universalistic identification with the human species.

The twin-faced character of *samudayam* introduced in Sree Narayanan's initiatives made an appearance in discourses of social reform among other castes in Kerala too. The Nambutiri reform movement's motto, 'to turn the Nambutiri into a human being'

[81] Narayana Guru, 'Advaita Jeevitam', *Sreenarayanaguruvinte Sampurna Krtikal*, 1.

(*namboodiriye manushyanakkuka*) and its practices of internal reform invoked similar ideas.[82] An extension of this line of thinking can also be seen in a resolution passed in 1931 at a conference of the Nayars which declared that 'anybody who speaks Malayalam and observes Malayali customs can be admitted, regardless of their caste, as members into the Nair community.'[83] Membership of the *samudayam* is linked here to cultural, national identity. These grand assertions of universality, however, went along with a practical identification of the community with caste members.

Sree Narayanan's writings and organizational initiatives demonstrate similar ambivalences in his concept of *samudayam*. Without a universalist aspiration as its grounding, *samudayam* ran the risk of becoming an instrument of the caste struggle, a tool in the service of *jati* identity. Narayanan resisted this possibility and tried to ensure that the institutions he founded did not become exclusive domains for the Ezhavas; and that the untouchable castes of Pulayas and Parayas had free access to the schools, temples, and ashrams he founded.[84]

A *samudayam*, however, is unable to deny its moorings in the ascribed caste identity of its members. This was manifest in many of Sree Narayanan's organizational decisions, especially in the early years. Some pronouncements reported in *Vivekodayam* (the organ of the SNDP Yogam) in 1905 appear to work with a *jati* identity. When Sree Narayanan's attention was drawn to some Ezhava converts to Christianity who pretended in public that they were still Hindus, he is reported to have suggested that 'believers in other religions should not be allowed to attend the functions of the caste (*jati*), and

[82] Balakrishnan, ed., *Sree Narayana Guru*, 98–102.

[83] Ibid., 92.

[84] Sree Narayana Guru did not always succeed in realizing this objective. The Jagannatha temple in Tellicherry consecrated by him did not, contrary to his wishes, permit entry to lower untouchable castes like the Pulayas. See Sanu, *Narayanaguruswamy*, 194–5. Sree Narayanan also had serious disagreements with the SNDP Yogam in later years. See Bhaskaran, ed., *Sree Narayana Guru Vaikhari*, 264.

that if they renounce in writing their new religions then there is no objection to their participation.'[85] Similarly, in response to a question concerning a woman who had intimate contact (*samsargam*) with a man from another religion, Narayanan is reported to have ordered that 'the woman should be made an outcaste, depending on the seriousness of the evidence of the contact. On the basis of a penalty commensurate with her fault, she may also be pardoned and purified. The money paid as penalty should be kept as common property.'[86] Even in later years, Narayanan used rituals of inclusion, or the rehabilitation of people into the *samudayam*. In 1915 he took back into the community a number of Ezhavas whose families had converted to Christianity generations earlier. These families had offered worship in churches while retaining close contacts with the Ezhavas. In the light of the reform initiatives undertaken by the Narayana movement, they wished to sunder their connection with Christianity and return to Hinduism.[87] More interestingly, in 1919 Narayana Guru introduced some members of a caste group in Changanassery, known as Kanikkuruppanmar, into the Ezhava community.[88] A public meeting was held, after which Narayanan announced to the Kanikkuruppanmar that 'Your title "Kurup" is no longer valid from today. These people and you should dwell in future as *swajanangal*.'[89] The word *swajanam* (one's own people) is usually used to refer to kinship or caste affiliation.[90]

[85] *Vivekodayam*, vol. 1, no. 2 (1905), 41.

[86] Ibid., 41.

[87] See *Vivekodayam*, vol. XI, no. 9 (1915), cited in Sanu, *Narayanaguruswamy*, 293.

[88] Ibid., 339–42.

[89] Ibid., 342.

[90] Interestingly, Guru's admission of Kanikkuruppanmar into the Ezhava community was contested by some members of the community when one of the converts was recommended for appointment as a member to the Municipality. Sree Narayanan issued a certificate to endorse the Ezhava identity of the person in question. Moorkothu Kumaran, *Sreenarayanaguruswamikalude Jeevacharitram*, 178.

These examples may indicate how deeply the concept of *samudayam* was enmeshed in its caste moorings. However, Sree Narayanan also attempted gestures of inclusion and exclusion in order to redefine the *samudayam*. He once said that toddy tappers should be expelled from the *samudayam*; he saw this as analogous to amputating an organ infected by leprosy to prevent the affliction from spreading to other parts of the body. They can be rehabilitated, he said, after purification if they give up this 'dirty occupation'. When a devotee asserted that people took to toddy tapping because they had no other means of subsistence, Narayanan responded by saying that if one were to break a tapper's knife into four pieces, one might be able to make four shaving knives: it would be more respectable to work as barbers with these shaving knives than tap toddy and would bring in more income as well.[91]

Narayanan used a literalist definition for religion (*matam*) too, taking it to mean inner belief or opinion, a matter of autonomous choice by the individual. This view appears, at first sight, to be in tune with a modern privileging of religion as personal belief. 'It is wrong to subordinate matters of the community to religion or religious matters to the community. There should be no connection between community affairs and religion. Religion is a matter of the mind.'[92]

These views entailed no clear endorsement or opposition to conversion as a strategy in anti-caste struggles. In the early 1920s Ezhava leaders like C. Krishnan, C.V. Kunjuraman, and Sahodaran Ayyappan argued that Ezhavas should renounce Hinduism to free themselves from the caste system. C. Krishnan, who embraced Buddhism in 1926, was a propagandist for his religion in Malabar for several years,

[91] Ibid., 540. Dr Palpu held a different position on toddy tapping. He thought that the adverse effects of toddy could be removed with proper care and that it could be made into a lucrative industry, of great benefit to the community.

[92] Desabhimani, 15 July 1916, cited in Vaidyar, *Sree Narayana Guruvum Kumaran Asanum*, 5.

advocating that Ezhavas convert.[93] C.V. Kunjuraman and Sahodaran Ayyappan were largely sympathetic, the latter identifying himself as a Buddhist in a legal document around 1922.[94] Kunjuraman wrote an article entitled 'The Buddhist Faith is the Best for the Thiyyas' in 1926.[95] It is also said that he considered Christianity a possible alternative for Ezhavas.[96] Other leaders, like Kumaran Asan and T.K. Madhavan, were opposed to the idea of conversion, arguing for fighting the caste system from within Hinduism. Kumaran Asan's thinking, however, was strongly influenced by Buddhist philosophy.

Narayana Guru clarified his position on religious conversion in two conversations —with C.V. Kunjuraman and Sahodaran Ayyappan.[97] In his responses to them, Narayanan used the word *samudayam* in another sense. 'Religion (*matam*) has two sides: one internal and the other external,' he said, 'Which of these sides would you like to see changed?' He continued: 'If the desire is for change in the external aspect, it is not really religious conversion (*mataparivarthanam*), but change in community (*samudayaparivarthanam*). As for internal religion (*abhyantara matam*, also meaning inner belief, inner opinion), it is subject to constant and gradual change in all thoughtful people.'[98] Here he made a distinction between the inner and the outer dimensions of religion, equating the latter with *samudayam*. In this view, it was inner religion (*abhyantaramatam*) that really merited the appellation of *matam*. Nonetheless, Narayanan's views also resisted the elevation of religion as a source of stable identity. *Matam* is understood literally as inner opinion, subject to constant change in the intelligent person.

93 For a biography, see Achutan, *C. Krishnan*.

94 Ayyappan's conversation with Narayana Guru in 1922, in Shaji, *Narayanaguru*, 467–9.

95 See Kunjuraman, 'Tiyyarkku Nallatu Buddhamatam Tanneyanu'.

96 Sanu, *Narayanaguruswamy*, 347–8.

97 See Shaji, *Narayanaguru*, 459–66, and 467–9.

98 Ibid., 463.

Did Narayanan consider differences in *matam* inadequate grounds for differentiating communities? A *samudayam* may include followers of diverse practices for the attainment of *moksha*. This also meant that caste and its disabilities may not disappear by changes in *abhyantaramatam*—a different spiritual opinion and practice—at an individual level. This would require *samudayaparivarthanam*—the transformation of the community—according to principles and practices independent of and opposed to caste. Religious conversion as a response to the communitarian problem of caste did not, for Narayanan, resolve the relations between the external and internal dimensions of religion.

In his conversation with C.V. Kunjuraman, Narayanan said: 'What does India need today? Liberation from the struggles between castes and religions. Let everyone try to learn about all religions with equal attention and respect, and then mutually exchange that knowledge. One will then realize that the struggles are not on account of religion (*matam*) but because of one's arrogance (*madam*). The enthusiasm for religious conversion will also disappear then.'[99] He organized a conference of universal brotherhood in 1921 and an all-religions conference in 1924.

Narayanan introduced another element of complexity in his discussions on religion: in response to Kunjuraman's argument that those who oppose the conversion of Ezhavas have expressed their dissatisfaction with the Hindu religion (*Hindumatam*), as it exists in the present, he said:

> Then they are arguing for a conversion (*parivarthanam*) not only for the Hindus, but also for the Hindu religion. However, there is no religion called the Hindu religion. Foreigners used to refer to the inhabitants of Hindustan as Hindus. If the religion of the inhabitants of Hindustan is Hinduism, the religions of the Christians and Muslims who live in Hindustan now is also Hinduism. Nobody, however, says this. Now, Hindu religion is a common name for religions which have originated in Hindustan, excluding those like Christianity and Islam which came

[99] Ibid., 233.

> from outside. This is why some people consider Buddhism and Jainism as also a part of the Hindu religion. If it is not illogical to give the common name 'Hindu religion' to several religions such as Vedic religion, Pauranic religion, the Sankhya religion, Vaiseshika religion, Mimamsaka religion, Dvaita religion, Advaita religion, Visishtadvaita religion, Saiva religion, Sakteya religion and Vaishnava religion which are apparently different from one another, then what is illogical in referring by the word 'One religion' to all the religions formulated by various Acharyas for the liberation of the entire mankind (*manushyajati*) in accordance with their different times and places?[100]

Narayanan begins this passage by pluralizing the idea of religion and suggesting that the seeming unity of the Hindu religion conceals widely divergent *matams* or inner opinions. Then he goes on to project the same logic to religions in general. If the Hindu religion can presume to be one in spite of substantial differences, could one not overcome the seeming diversity and conflict among the religions of the world by bringing them under a common name, 'One religion' (*Ekamatam*)? This is an important sense in which the phrase 'one religion' in the Guru's motto—'One caste, one religion, one God for humankind'—may be understood.[101] Interestingly, the unity that Sree Narayanan stresses with this slogan is, in the light of the passage cited above, an argument for difference and plurality. It is the very diversity of religions that enables the use of the category 'One religion' as a principle of the subsumption of plurality.

The new rituals Sree Narayanan devised for the Ezhava community, however, were all within the horizon of Kerala's Hindu traditions. At the same time, Narayanan's argument for 'One religion' and his statements—such as 'It is enough if a man is good, whatever

[100] Ibid., 463–4.

[101] Several years before Guru's promulgation of the motto '*Oru jati, oru matam, oru daivam manushyanu*', 'Atmopadesatakam', v. 49, used the phrase '*immatam ekam*' (this is the only *matam*), in relation to all human endeavour being aimed at *atmasukham* (one's own happiness, or spiritual welfare). Narayana Guru, *Sreenarayanaguruvinte Sampurna Krtikal*, 379. I thank Guru Muni Narayana Prasad for bringing this to my notice.

his religion'—offered no grounds for arguing against advocates of conversion. In 1916 he issued a statement to the effect that he did not belong to any particular caste or religion.[102]

Gandhi's conversation with Sree Narayanan, during his visit to Travancore in 1925, reveals the complexity of Sree Narayanan's position. The Mahatma enquired if the Guru gave permission to those who wished to convert to other religions as a means for obtaining greater freedom. Sree Narayanan replied: 'It is often seen that those who convert to other religions are able to obtain freedom. Seeing this, it becomes difficult to criticize people for speaking in favour of religious conversion.'[103] Gandhi continued his enquiry: 'Do you consider the Hindu religion sufficient for the attainment of spiritual liberation (*adhyatmikamaya moksham*)?' The Guru replied: 'Other religions too possess paths for liberation (*mokshamargam*).'

> *Gandhi*: Let us leave aside other religions. Is it your view that the Hindu religion is adequate for the attainment of *moksha*?'
>
> *Narayana Guru*: 'For attaining spiritual liberation, the Hindu religion is amply adequate. However, it is worldly liberty (*laukikamaya swatantryam*) that people desire more.'

Gandhi then asked the Guru to set aside the unfreedom arising from untouchability and other similar practices, and state whether for spiritual liberation (*adhyatmikamaya moksham*) religious conversion was needed, to which the Guru responded in the negative.[104]

This conversation, in its twists and turns, highlights the differences between the approaches of the two thinkers to the political and religious domains. Sree Narayanan's reluctance to separate questions of worldly and spiritual freedom was in tune with the thoughts he articulated in 'Advaita Jeevitam'. Separating these two aspirations went against the grain of his thought on freedom. Then how do we understand his separation of the internal and external senses of *matam*

[102] Vaidyar, *Sree Narayana Guruvum Kumaran Asanum*, 6.
[103] Sanu, *Narayanaguruswamy*, 440.
[104] Ibid.

and his identification of the latter with *samudayam*? The distinction between the external and the internal, it seems, is not to be seen as identical to that between the worldly (*laukikam*) and the spiritual (*adhyatmikam*). It pertains, rather, to the levels of the collective and the individual. This would mean that the spiritual and the worldly are inseparably intertwined in Sree Narayanan's conception of *samudayam*. For him the spiritual dimension of *samudayam* was not to be sought in institutional religious forms; it was located in a primordial ethical orientation prior to the conception of the social domain and deriving from the creatureliness of the human species. A social collectivity grounded in a domain anterior to the social, *samudayam*, in Sree Narayanan's thought, maintained this paradox at its heart, as attested by the difficult negotiations of this idea in its worldly history.

One may say that *dharmam*—a concept central to Sree Narayanan's discourse—sums up this primordial ethical orientation of the human in its creatureliness and worldly destiny. The anteriority of this concept to the social domain is reflected in Narayanan's reluctance to endorse historical arguments clarifying the identity of *samudayam*. We noted his reluctance to explain 'Ezhava' through narratives of origin and arrival. This contrasted with the discourse of several important Ezhava intellectuals of the time who invoked history—especially a Buddhist past—as the principal ground for the community's ethical and political ideals.[105] Sree Narayanan's discursive innovations did not draw on the resources of historical narration; they worked, rather, through their deliberate avoidance, and through a carefully set up assemblage of the primordial and the contemporary. Historically momentous innovations introduced by Sree Narayanan had, as their discursive ground, not historicist narratives of a glorious past or a redeemable future, but the creaturely human subject in its worldly contemporaneity. In this one may find a conception of human history that is not narrativizable in the idioms of recovery or progress.

[105] Dr Palpu developed this argument in his letters, petitions and speeches, in an alternative, speculative historiography of caste in Kerala. See chapter 1.

3

Intensities and the Language of Limits

Marking Gender in the Poetry of Kumaran Asan

THE POETRY OF KUMARAN ASAN (1873–1924) signalled a crucial moment in the history of idioms of self-articulation in modern Malayalam writing. Asan was a disciple of Sree Narayana Guru and the first General Secretary of the SNDP Yogam. Drawing upon a meditative, ascetic strand in Sree Narayanan's thinking and, more generally, in Indian philosophical and literary traditions and the idioms of English romanticism, Asan forged a new, primarily monologic, language of intense passion and inner deliberation in his major poems. Here I look closely at this innovative poetic apparatus. Asan's protagonists are marked indelibly by their status as men or women. Gender is a matter of interiority in Asan's poetry, and this is articulated through trajectories of desire and agency pursued by his characters.

Kumaran Asan was born in Kayikkara near Trivandrum. After preliminary education in a village school, initial lessons in Sanskrit under a local scholar, and four or five years of training in a Malayalam school he worked for a few months as a teacher and for a couple of years as an accountant in a shop before deciding to study Sanskrit seriously. His meeting with Sree Narayana Guru in 1891 was a turning point in his life. He soon became the Guru's disciple, moved towards the path of bhakti, and read extensively in Vedanta, Yoga, Sanskrit, and Tamil. With Dr Palpu's help Sree Narayanan arranged for Asan's higher studies in Sanskrit at Bangalore and Calcutta, where he also gained close familiarity with English literature. He returned to Kerala in 1900 and stayed with Sree Narayanan at Aruvippuram as one of his favourite disciples, gaining popularity among the followers as *chinna swamy* (the little sage). He became secretary of the SNDP Yogam when it was founded in 1903 and held the office for sixteen years. To the surprise of many of Sree Narayanan's followers, Asan married in 1918 and entered *grhasthashrama* (a householder's life). He died prematurely in a boat accident in 1924. In his brief poetic career, from the publication of 'Veenapoovu' (The Fallen Flower) in 1907 to 'Karuna' (Compassion) in 1923, Asan wrote some of the important poems that shaped a modern poetic language in Malayalam.

To appreciate the significance of Asan's intervention, some familiarity with the dominant tendencies in Malayalam poetry at his time is necessary. The later decades of the nineteenth century saw poetry become an important part of the emerging print-public culture in Kerala. Kandathil Varghese Mappila, editor of the *Malayala Manorama*, was perhaps the first to start a regular column for poetic compositions in his newspaper.[1] Literary pages in magazines were initially dominated by competitions in versification such as *samasyapooranam*, where poets were invited to complete *slokas* for which only the last phrases were given. *Mangalaslokangal* (verses of felicitation) and compositions on predetermined themes were some of the other major genres of public versification.

It seems possible to identify two major trends in Malayalam poetry in the late nineteenth century. One of them, of which Keralavarma Valiyakoyil Thampuran was the most important proponent,

[1] Priyadarshan, 'Alpam Charitram', 16. See also Harisharma, *Kandathil Varghese Mappila*.

looked to the Sanskrit tradition for poetic norms. Poets of this bent showed a preference for Sanskrit words and metres. In contrast, a group of poets centred around Kodungallur—including Kunjikkuttan Thampuran and the Venmani poets—wrote in an idiom closer to ordinary Malayalam and often addressed themes from everyday life. Both these strands, and the poetic field of Malayalam in general, were dominated by the upper castes, especially Nambutiri Brahmins—linked to royal families and traditionally associated with Hindu temples. In spite of the active presence of several Christian poets and a large body of compositions in Arabi Malayalam by Muslim authors, the mainstream of Malayalam poetry was almost exclusively dominated by upper-caste Hindu writers.[2] The young Kumaran Asan—along with Muloor Padmanabha Paniker and C.V. Kunjuraman—was among the few Ezhava poets to be published by newspapers in the late nineteenth century.

Asan found his distinctive poetic idiom by moving decisively away from both these strands of writing. In language, versification, and choice of themes, his sensibilities were far removed from those of Kerala Varma; in fact, it was from A.R. Rajaraja Varma—Keralavarma's nephew and antagonist in some of the aesthetic debates—that Asan received substantial support and encouragement. Asan's poems also broke decisively with the work of the Kodungallur poets, especially Venmani Achhan Namboodiri and Mahan Namboodiri. He turned away, especially in his early writings, from any quotidianization of poetic themes. In his use of erotic sentiment and representation of women, Asan's work came to occupy a position diametrically opposed to the poetic universe of the Venmani poets and their successors.

[2] For a discussion of Arabi Malayalam writing, see Abu, *Arabimalayala Sahityacharitram*. An excellent discussion of the Christian contribution to Malayalam writing may be found in Thomas, *Malayalasahityavum Kristianikalum*, and in the annotations therein by Scaria Zacharia. See also Manavalan, *Kerala Samskaravum Kraistava Missionarimarum*; Kumar, 'Shaping a Literary Space'. For an interesting analogous discussion of the practitioners of Tamil poetry over the late colonial period, see Venkatachalapathy, *The Province of the Book*, chapter 1.

Asan and his contemporaries Vallathol Narayana Menon (1878–1958) and Ulloor S. Parameswara Aiyer (1877–1949) have been regarded as forming a triumvirate of great poets in modern Malayalam. Unlike Vallathol and Ulloor, Asan did not write in the genre of the *mahakavyam* or extended poetic narrative. His critical discussions of Vallathol's *Chitrayogam* (1914) and Ulloor's *Umakeralam* (1914), as well as his response to Vallathol's review of his elegiac poem 'Prarodanam', stressed the differences between his own poetic principles and those of his contemporaries.[3]

Asan's poetic innovation in relation to the erotic should be understood against the background of a long and rich tradition of erotically charged versification in Malayalam. Venmani Achhan Namboodiri (1817–91) and Venmani Mahan Namboodiri (1844–93) were the most prominent proponents of this strand in the nineteenth century. Some of the earliest poetic *manipravalam* compositions in Malayalam, such as *Unniyacchicharitam*, *Unnichiruthevicharitam*, and *Unniyadicharitam*—as well as the large number of *srngara slokangal* cited as examples in *Leelatilakam*, a medieval Sanskrit text on *manipravalam* poetry—attest to the longevity and popularity of this strand.[4] These poems revolved around courtesans from the non-Brahmin Hindu upper castes, with their physical beauty appearing as a principal focus of attention.[5] They displayed a consistent desire for voluptuous female bodies, marked by the frequent appearance of bare breasts, seductive glances, and expostulations of erotic fulfilment. Compositions in a genre known as Vaisikatantram (the art of the courtesan) used the format of advice offered by an elderly courtesan to a young woman about to enter the profession as a guise for outlining strategies of seduction. Venmani Mahan Namboodiri's 'Ambopadesam'

[3] See Asan, *Kumaranasante Gadyalekhanangal*, vol. 1, 75–8, 104–30, 133–42.

[4] Elamkulam P.N. Kunjan Pillai, *Lilatilakam*. See, for a discussion of this text, Freeman, 'Rubies and Coral'; and 'Genre and Society'. See also M.R. Raghava Variar, *Madhyakala Keralam*.

[5] For a discussion of these works, see Aiyer, *Kerala Sahityacharitram*, vol. 1, 442–58.

is a comic composition in this genre, in which a ninety-four-year-old woman lays out for her granddaughter the special techniques of her profession: the use of magic potions, cosmetics on one's body, skilful speech, and deft erotic attention. The *srngara slokangal* written by the Venmani poets sometimes adopt the same hard-hitting perspective on the economic underbelly of erotic transactions, cheerfully complaining about women who demand a price for letting men close to their enticing bodies. Poems that do not have a satiric intent are also often filled with an air of playful erotic festivity.

The feel of breasts and the taste of lips recur as tropes of fulfilment, the principal end to which the subject of these erotic poems constantly strives. The drama in this poetic theatre works with varied forms of apostrophe and appeal, with changes in tone ranging from sarcasm to a flirtatious feigning of indifference, to an avid declaration of obsessive desire. There is space only for two entities in Venmani's erotic theatre—an erotically charged male subject and a female addressee described largely in terms of her seductive body. One might even say that this theatre has only solo performances, since the female figure is often reduced to the status of a silent addressee by the male performer. This does not mean that the woman's presence is static or passive: her gestures and actions become objects of male erotic investment—a woman lifting her hand to place a ritual mark on her forehead, her sweet voice, and even her ability to appreciate the *sloka* that is addressed to her can be sources of sexual charm.[6] The woman's engagement is often a necessary moment in the scenario of enjoyment. She is imagined as being provocative with the male subject through feigned anger or mock challenge. Her postures are 'feigned' since the acts and counter-acts in this exchange function as props to generate the ultimately solitary pleasure of the male sensual subject.[7] The

[6] See, for instance, Venmani Mahan Namboodiripad, 'Srngara Slokangal', 464–7.

[7] The tropes of challenge and conquest are also invoked by Sree Narayanan and Asan in their '*vairagya*' poems. However, in them the challenge is no longer in the mode of play. It produces intense fear in the subject, as a symptom of the ultimate fear—of mortality.

anger, the fear, the challenge and the conquest—all these belong to the realm of 'play'. An unfolding of the encounter is thus made possible, permitting the emergence of a gaze that converts details of this dynamic into objects of enjoyment. The female partner is not allowed to be the subject of such a gaze, and this asymmetry restricts play to its proper, fictional locus.

The female body in these poems is the object of delight and enjoyment, no different from other such objects.[8] Yet this does not mean that it can be substituted with a combination of other objects of sensory enjoyment. There is something specific to sexual pleasure, as with other extraordinarily pleasurable sense experiences. In Venmani's poetic universe, the uniqueness of a female subject is conceived as the distinctiveness of enjoyment of each erotic encounter. Such encounters are particularized as experience, although the female partner's identity remains insufficiently individualized. Female figures in the writing of the Venmani poets appear as a series: each of them may be substituted for others by virtue of their function in the erotic encounter. Their bodies are not adequately differentiated; the features offered for erotic contemplation do not vary from poem to poem. These women are accorded a state of pseudo-subjectivity, a simulated space from which they can incite or respond to the initiatives of the male subject. The modes of subjectivity developed in Asan's poems appear in direct opposition to this.[9]

II

There is a story about Asan's first meeting with Sree Narayana Guru: in response to the Guru's demand, the young poet read out some of his poetic compositions. Narayanan was pleased with the young

[8] See, for example, the presentation of the female figures in Venmani Mahan Namboodiripad's 'Poora Prabandham'.

[9] The tendency to present female figures through enticing physical descriptions, strongly evident in the Venmani tradition, continued—despite the absence of explicitly erotic themes—in later Malayalam poetry. The best-known Malayalam poet among Asan's contemporaries, Vallathol Narayana Menon, arguably participated in this strand.

Kumaru's talent, but advised him not to write *srngara slokangal* or verses dominated by the erotic sentiment, at least for the moment.[10] Another, related story speaks of their offering prayers together at a temple soon after their first meeting: Sree Narayanan composed a verse apostrophizing the goddess and asked Kumaru to complete the *sloka*. Asan's instant composition was more sombre than the Guru's: it pleaded with the deity not to send him the merciless summons of death.[11] These stories have a special resonance in light of Asan's subsequent poetic career. A move away from the tradition of *srngara slokangal* and an intense preoccupation with mortality run through his work as constant, almost obsessive concerns. However, Asan's poetry shows a redefinition rather than abandonment of the erotic, and an incorporation of human finitude as an essential element in its phenomenology.

In his early work, Asan seems to have followed his guru's advice to the letter. Compositions from this period are devotional in nature, addressed to Siva, Subramanian, and Devi. Devotional compositions written a little later—such as 'Nijanandavilasam'— show a clear Advaitic orientation, adopting a *nirguna* conception of the divine in not addressing any particular deity. This parallels, as we saw, Narayana Guru's own literary itinerary. Compositions such as 'Vairagyapanchakam' in *Sivastotramala* and 'Kaminigarhanam' are good examples of Asan's early renunciatory poetics and his condemnation of the erotic. 'Vairagyapanchakam' appeals to God to protect the devotee from gazing at doe-eyed beauties who pierce his heart with their glances and throw him into the confounding welter of sensory attachment.[12] 'Kaminigarhanam' also warns against their killing glances.[13] As in Sree Narayanan's 'Mananateetam' and 'Siva Satakam', the speaking voice here views sensory attractions as the destructive path to his own mortality.

[10] Sanu, *Narayanaguruswamy*, 140–1.

[11] Ibid., 143.

[12] Asan, *Kumaran Asante Sampurna Padya Krtikal*, 756.

[13] Ibid., 786.

Mortality and the charms of the female body converge in Asan's early poems in another way as well. 'Vairagyapanchakam' highlights the transitoriness of sensory beauty by reflecting on the untimely death of beautiful women.

> Heavily tied hair and breasts
> Decked up in lovely attire
> Alas, she lies on the pyre now
> Not a dog will desire her.[14]

'Kaminigarhanam' invokes a similar image: the ornate body of a young woman returning to the five elements, becoming food for birds of prey.[15] We have already seen Sree Narayanan's invocation of corpses in his early poems: the woman in one's arms suddenly turns into a decaying cadaver, producing disgust and dread. In Asan's early writings the spectacle of the dead female body assumes another tonality: rather than inducing disgust and provoking the devotee's flight from the scene, it leads to a lingering gaze of mourning. The devotee is struck with the bewilderment of grief: how could this lovely young woman, all decked up in new clothes, suddenly become lifeless and unattractive? Mortality incites compassion and grief rather than disgust. The dead female body is not a frightening, nightmarish apparition, but the centre of a sombre theatre of bereavement. Acts of mourning in these poems offer a paradigm for imaging renunciation. The male devotee, his eyes sepulchral and downcast, recognizes the transience of phenomenal life; mournfully, he withdraws from the last scene of the body to contemplate a higher truth. These elements—dead women's bodies, funeral scenes, aspects of desolation, and the valedictory walk away from the venue—reappear with variations in Asan's later poetry. They are arguably among the most frequent, or at any rate the most strikingly visible, motifs in his work. They show us how Asan's early devotional writings and his later poems, in spite of their apparently contrasting approaches to erotic desire, are deeply connected.

[14] Ibid., 756.
[15] Ibid., 786.

'Veenapoovu' (The Fallen Flower), written in 1907 and generally considered Asan's first mature work, indicates the earliest links in this chain of continuity. Using the allegory of a wilted flower, the poet grieves over the passing nature of the sensory world. The last lines of the poem enact the retreating gestures of the mourner: the poet's voice appeals to its own gaze to withdraw from the scene, as the fallen, wilting flower will soon disappear into oblivion: this is our shared, tearful destiny; life on this earth is no more than a dream.[16] The 'killing glances' of female beauty in the devotional writings, inciting fear and anxiety, are no longer in evidence, and the mortal world of phenomenal beauty is approached with a mourner's sombre compassion. This involves more than the recognition of death's inexorable work: grieving for works by acts of remembrance, by devising a site where phenomenal life is retained as an image of beauty and finitude.

The story of the flower in the poem stands for an affective female life beginning with the innocent sportiveness of childhood and moving to a natural discovery of the joys of love. Death interrupts reciprocal affective longing and turns the lover into the first mourner. Death appears as an absolute limit in 'Veenapoovu', and reflections on the human body and on the inner sense take place within an irreducible locus of finitude. Notions prominent in Indian metaphysical thought, such as *vasana* (tendencies), *mukti* (liberation), *deham* (body), and *dehi* (soul), come up time and again in Asan's poems. The use of these notions does not ameliorate—on the contrary it intensifies—death's ubiquity in his work.[17] The shadow of cessation falls on the subject's gaze and thought. Poetry is not just epitaph; in its very vocation, it is thanatography or death-writing. 'Veenapoovu' mourns less the disappearance of animating life from the young limbs of the woman than the interruption of her vital, affective investment. Bereavement directed at the female protagonist extends to all phenomenal life and

[16] Ibid., 79.

[17] As we shall see below, in Asan's poetry, *vasana* also appears as a naturalizing element in the understanding of desire.

to the mourner-subject's relation to his own existence. A new cluster of concerns emerges around the dead body of the woman, linking memory, narrative, affective ties between men and women, and the ethical act of poetic reflection. Asan went on to explore this thematic terrain further in his later writings, in poems of female longing and the mourner-subject's acts of compassionate witnessing.

III

In the works that he wrote next—two long poems entitled 'Nalini' (1911) and 'Leela' (1914)—Asan firmly established his new poetic identity.[18] These poems, abandoning the metaphoric structure of 'Veenapoovu', directly engage with the figure of the woman in her live presence. The presentation of the female body continues to be fraught, though, and the heroines, Nalini and Leela, are hardly described in any physical detail. A reluctance to describe the woman's body persists in Asan's work almost till the end. Physical descriptions of characters such as Sita and Matangi have hardly any relation to sensory relish.[19] 'Karuna', his last work, is the only one to present its heroine, the courtesan Vasavadatta, with the language of sensory attraction.[20] This description, interestingly, has a paradoxical function: the heroine's beautiful body reappears in the second and third sections of the poem, bleeding and mutilated, staging finitude and corporeal fragmentation.[21]

'Nalini' and 'Leela' unravelled somewhat similar narratives at different levels of experience and intensity. 'Nalini' presents a heroine who goes into the forest in search of Divakaran, a young ascetic, whom she knew well in her childhood and whom she had steadfastly adored. She manages to catch up with him in a forest near the Himalayas, but

[18] Asan, 'Nalini', *Kumaran Asante Sampurna Padya Krtikal*, 99–139; 'Leela', in ibid., 149–226.

[19] Asan, 'Chintavishtayaya sita', *Kumaran Asante Sampurna Padya Krtikal*, 521–63, and 'Chandalabhikshuki', in ibid., 655–76.

[20] Asan, 'Karuna', *Kumaran Asante Sampurna Padya Krtikal*, 685–701.

[21] Ibid., 685 and 693.

Divakaran does not recognize her, and, even when he is reminded by her of their past association, is affectionate to her in a non-desiring, non-differentiating way. Nalini affirms her love for him and appeals to him to let her accompany him over his life. Divakaran turns her down, saying that it is the same emotion of love, in its intensity, that makes him abandon any desire for earthly union. He gives spiritual advice to Nalini and she attains enlightenment by receiving the *maha-vakya*. Paradoxically, this supreme moment of revelation turns into the moment of her death: she collapses, her face ecstatic with joy, and dies on Divakaran's chest.

Unlike in 'Veenapoovu', it is not the desiring male and the dying woman that form the axis of affective imagination in 'Nalini'. The poem is organized around a male yogi who has left behind the world of desire, and a woman protagonist single-mindedly devoted to her unreciprocated passion. In spite of apparent contrast, a deep thread of affective intensities connects them. The yogi's first appearance in 'Nalini' highlights a sense of calm harmony achieved through austerities; but there is an implied suggestion of covert, subterranean fire. The deep sigh that emanates from the yogi's tranquil body attests to elements unaccommodated by an ascetic understanding of perfection. However, from Divakaran's responses to Nalini's declaration of love, we understand that what is carried within, as if in a crypt, is neither a passion directed at an individual nor a series of personal memories. A link with the experiential universe—free from the details of a personal biography—survives under the yogi's calm demeanour. Divakaran understands by love the inexorable connectedness that emerges between creatures in their pursuit of diverse chains of action. In this sense, *sneham* (love) is a compulsion of the soul (*dehi*) in a state of embodiment.[22]

Nalini's love on the other hand is resolutely individuated. It is expressed in intense images of personal recollection:

[22] Asan, *Kumaran Asante Sampurna Padya Krtikal*, 129. See the end of this chapter for further discussion on this.

I remember, how the butterfly flew
Fluttering in the wind
And how we watched, and walked
Along the jungle, hands entwined.[23]

The flashback of personal memory is available to the yogi as well, but it is dim; even after he is reminded by Nalini's memory-images, his recollection does not gain affective intensity.

In Nalini's articulation of her love, a new configuration of bodily desire makes its appearance. Desire is not understood in her speech as directly corporeal; however, the physical dimension is not rejected. The body seems to mark a certain stage in the life of desire, which is eventually overcome. The true object of desire is not the body of the other, not even reciprocal bodily desire from the other, but a desire affirmed by the other's soul. Such feeling is possible in Asan's poetry only between a man and a woman: it depends on a differentiation of human beings into men and women, of which the body remains the primary sign. The law that ultimately governs gender differentiation and the operation of the passions belongs to the originary order of nature.

We have seen Sree Narayanan arguing against the false differentiation of the human species into castes by showing the natural sexual differentiation between the male and the female as an instance of true difference. Asan takes this line of thinking in a new direction. The treatment of love in 'Nalini' suggests that just as the body signifies the inexorable difference between the sexes, physical desire is the privileged sign of a passion that is ultimately grounded in the soul. The intensities the soul expresses, enjoys, and suffers remain inescapably connected to a discourse of bodily desire. Even the moment of spiritual revelation, where the soul's need finds its fulfilment in absolute separation from bodily experience, resonates with the ecstasy of bodily union: 'unable to bear the waves of ecstatic joy that inundated her inner states, her body gave way, like a reed on the river's bank. The yogi took her in

[23] Ibid., 120.

his arms, with care as if this wounded body were his own. As calm ripples merge, their hands entwined, and their bodies joined—sound to like sound, glow to like glow.'[24]

Paradoxically, the moment of bodily contact is also that of an ecstatic cessation of existence for Nalini. The yogi finds to his surprise that his body has now become the deathbed of this beautiful lovelorn woman. His response clearly marks the distance travelled by Asan's poetry from devotional verses in which the proximity of the female corpse evoked fear and disgust. Here it generates compassion and self-purifying mourning. The yogi recognizes in Nalini's love a form of asceticism akin to his own: at the end of the poem he recounts how the contemplation of her auspicious life has made his mind pure.[25] Elsewhere in the poem, Nalini is characterized as a *mahavrata* whose austerities are arguably as stringent as the yogi's ascesis.[26] Nalini's death signifies the ultimate sacrifice of the body and its universe of experience; yet this sacrifice is performed in honour of a love whose transcendental intensities maintain a relationship to corporeal existence.

'Leela', Asan's next major poem, is an occasion for unravelling these tensions further. This is evident from the Preface, where the poet says that the protagonists of his earlier poem 'Nalini' had almost fully relinquished *rajas* and had attained the *satvik* stage. 'However,' Asan continues, 'it is in stages prior to this that the sorrows of life and the secrets of the mind are contained in greater measure. Therefore, it was about lives situated at a stage lower than the protagonists of "Nalini" that I felt writing next.'[27] The complex transactions between the body and the soul in the experience of desire, indicated in 'Nalini' in a form all too abstract, could be explored further only if one moved closer to subjects who had not renounced worldly experience.

Asan also referred to another source of inspiration: 'Around this time, probably in the Central Hindu College Magazine, I came across

[24] Ibid., 133.
[25] Ibid., 137.
[26] Ibid., 107.
[27] Ibid., 143.

the picture of a Persian heroine published along with an essay by the famous Dr Coomaraswamy. That image stimulated my conception. I do not remember the essay containing anything in detail about the story.'[28] Asan's attempt to obtain a copy of the essay and the picture to aid him in composition was unsuccessful, and he had little to draw on except his imagination. Nonetheless, the passion Asan sketched in 'Leela' has resonances in narratives of love in the Persian tradition, as in Layla–Majnun: the links may not just be in onomastic resemblances between the protagonists.

Leela, the heroine of the poem, in spite of her deep love for Madanan, marries a merchant in accordance with the wishes of her father, and lives with him until his premature death. The lines in the poem on the consummation of Leela's marriage are ambiguous, although she is presented as persisting in her devotion to Madanan, and as distraught within her marriage. She returns to her parental village after her husband's demise, only to discover that death has stolen her parents as well, and that Madanan—still the enduring object of her desire—has left the village soon after her wedding and has subsequently been sighted wandering, like Majnun, in the forest like a madman. Here the similarities with the Layla–Majnun plot come to an end, and the poem picks up parallels from Asan's own earlier composition, 'Nalini': Leela too, like Asan's earlier protagonist, travels to the forest in search of Madanan. While Nalini expressed her desire in the form of a plea to be Divakaran's spiritual companion, Leela's affirmation takes a form more closely related to the body. She senses the proximity of her lover in the intoxicating fragrance of *chempakam* flowers in the forest and prepares to meet him by decorating herself with them.

The site of their meeting, even within the forest, is a garden abundant with the treasures of spring—wild colours, maddening fragrance, the sound of birds and bumblebees, and the gentle murmur of trees—indeed the topos of a sensual tryst between lovers.[29] Yet

[28] Ibid.

[29] Ibid., 208–10.

this space of sensual luxuriance is also a liminal site where bodily desire encounters its boundaries. When Leela finds Madanan and, holding him in her arms, reminds him of their past, Madanan remains unresponsive, his mind far away from the present. Slowly, he comes to remember her, responds to her gestures of love and, in a brief moment of intense passion, takes her in his arms and kisses her. This marks the limit of their tryst—he immediately walks away as if frightened and disappears into the torrential flow of the river to embrace his death. Leela follows him without hesitation and ends her life too in the river. Later, Madhavi, Leela's *sakhi* (friend), has a dream in which both Leela and Madanan reappear with new, unblemished bodies to tell her that no one disappears from this universe, and that there is no cessation for the love-entwined bond that unites the soul to the body.[30] Madhavi's acts of witnessing provide a conclusion to the narrative of 'Leela'. Spiritually transformed by this epiphanic moment, Madhavi becomes a *sanyasini.*

In the poetic universe of 'Leela' Madanan appears as another figure of the renunciant, carrying with him traces of the ascetic in 'Nalini'. However, Madanan is no *sanyasi*: his mind is focused solely on the image of Leela whose name he chants as he wanders through the forest.[31] Yet when Madhavi returns after her initial search for Madanan, she tells Leela that the creatures of the forest were all devoted to Madanan as no yogi had ever loved humans or the gods as Madanan had.[32] Forest-dwelling Malaya women compose songs to commemorate his supreme devotion to love.[33] The poem does not indicate that anything other than the memory of Leela ever preoccupies Madanan. Yet the purity and intensity of his love are perceived as comparable, if not superior, to the intensity of the love

[30] 'O, sakhi, no one disappears from this world; the bond that unites the soul to the body is entwined with love; it does not cease to be when the flesh is shed . . .' Ibid., 224.

[31] Ibid., 183.

[32] Ibid., 184.

[33] Ibid.

that a yogi feels for all humankind, for all creation, and for the divine. Here, as in 'Nalini', desire in its purity and constancy is a potent spiritual exercise—an intense *vrata*—which provokes the same response from nature as the yogi's ascetic steadfastness.

However, even while endorsing the ascetic intensity of pure desire, Madhavi tries to advocate prudence, discouraging Leela from following Madanan. Man was given two faculties for the enjoyment of the world, she says, desire and intelligence. Those who follow desire alone, giving it unrestrained play in the conduct of life, violate the rule of creation and thus insult the creator.[34] In countering this argument, Leela makes a distinction between two realms—the inner and the outer. Socially accepted norms of conduct belong to the realm of the outer and change constantly. True dharma, on the other hand, is located in the realm of the inner, which is the domain of love.[35] This is why incomplete lovers (*apoornaragikal*) obey the injunctions of social morality while full desire (*nirayum rati*) does not recognize these norms. In a familiar move, the inner/outer distinction is mapped on to that between the soul and the body. Leela goes on to say: 'The body is external, and so is the world which is dependent on that body. Pure love belongs to the inner soul (*antaratmikam*). How can human souls (*dehikal*) forget that?'[36] Therefore, those who do not value the mortal garment of the flesh (*mamsakanchukam*) do not fear the norms that prevail in society.[37]

Some critics have pointed out that Asan drew on the conceptual pair *jivatma* and *paramatma* in Advaitic thought for figuring the passion of Leela and Madanan.[38] The conception of love as a pure desire that orients the individual soul to the supreme would justify the attribution of a spiritual dimension to the sentiment of pure love. This understanding has been a major strand in Bhakti poetry, where

[34] Ibid., 192.
[35] Ibid., 193–4.
[36] Ibid., 194.
[37] Ibid., 195.
[38] Ibid., 148.

devotion often aims at fusion, and Asan's poetry does rework elements from this tradition. This has also been a prominent idiom in the Sufi poetic imagination. However, to read 'Leela' solely as an allegory of fusion between the individual and the supreme may be to miss the point. We need to remember Asan's Preface to 'Leela', in which he contrasts his new work with 'Nalini', wherein the protagonists had almost fully relinquished *rajas* and had attained the *satvik* stage. The *rajasik* stage involves a more concrete confrontation with the consuming intensities of earthly desire.

We saw that, in the forest, Leela and Madhavi came across a grove of *chempakam* flowers and that they inferred from this the proximity of Madanan who loved the intense fragrance of *chempakam* blossoms. The difference between the male protagonists of 'Nalini' and 'Leela' is obvious here. While Divakaran's ascetic life comprises a renunciation of the sensual, Madanan's *vrata* of desire involves an accentuation of the sensual and its incorporation as memory. The maddening fragrance of the *chempakam* becomes an object of supreme relish by virtue of the association of Madanan's memories with it, but these memories are not directly available to him for reflection. Waiting for Madanan's arrival, Leela asks Madhavi to decorate her as a floral bride. Bearing the signs of heady spring, she waits for her tryst, like a self-willed woman (*swairini*) in defiance of the social codes of propriety and restraint. The overcoding of Leela's body with signs of sensual intensity runs parallel to the undercoding visible in the skeletal frame of the male renunciant lover. When the protagonists meet, the moment of physical contact generates intensities that cannot be contained by the body, except in the ultimate experience in terms of which all intensities are understood in Asan's work—namely, death.

The laws of poetic necessity at work in 'Leela', however, require that the body reappear for the final conflagration of inner intensities. The ultimate earthly possibilities of desire can be expressed only through the body and the sensorium. Inner intensities retain something essentially corporeal about them, something erotic and sensual, which can only be expressed through a caress or a kiss. However, unlike in the tradition of erotic poetry that Asan rejected, the caress and the kiss do not seek their final destinies in bodily pleasure. They indicate, in an asymptotic way, higher intensities that rupture and exceed the body's powers of accommodation. The body in 'Leela' appears as the very limit of figuration. In seeking to fulfil its expressive function, it buckles: it is the moment of corporeal breakdown that comes to express unbearable, higher intensities.

IV

Asan's male and female protagonists occupy two distinct positions and postures in relation to the event of desire that erupts in his poems. There are similarities between 'Nalini', 'Leela', 'Chandalabhikshuki', and 'Karuna' in this respect. The female protagonists in these poems affirm and express desire while the males turn away—in detachment (Divakaran); or excessive, imploding attachment (Madanan); or in benign, non-reciprocal accommodation and sublimation (Anandan, Upaguptan). The woman is always the active subject in articulating desire. Her agency assumes forms ranging from invitation (Vasavadatta) and passionate declaration (Leela) to a readiness to follow the path of the beloved even if takes her away from the erotic to ascetic renunciation (Nalini, Matangi). Asan's women characters travel from their domestic and social locations to an uncharted realm of discovery and affirmation. This territory is imaged in Asan's poetic topography through liminal spaces: the forest in 'Nalini' and 'Leela', the funeral ground in 'Karuna', the monastery of the Buddha in 'Chandalabhikshuki'. In these final stations of women's journeys they meet men who remain 'elsewhere' in relation to their desire. The non-reciprocity of the male also takes several shapes: an ascetic non-recognition of the intensity of female affirmation ('Nalini'), intensities that shock and destroy the coherence of the male subject ('Leela'), an engrossment in the dharma of the social so that the dharma of individuated desire has to be abandoned ('Chintavishtayaya Sita'), and a compassionate ascetic plenitude which sublates desire in Asan's later work with its various figurations of the Buddha ('Chandalabhikshuki', 'Karuna').

In none of these instances is there a male equivalence of the woman's desire, and this renders all symmetry and reciprocity impossible. Men and women are differently placed: the woman embodies the realm of transformation while the man stays beyond the pale of change. He may inhabit a position of fullness where change is anticipated and contained, as in the Buddha figures, or he may be incapable of conscious agency, as in Madanan. The woman, on the other hand, deliberately performs acts of reflection and resolution, even when she eventually submits to the law embodied in the male. These two dimensions—of deliberate action and submission—are sketched vividly in the figure of Sita in 'Chintavishtayaya Sita'. Her actions in Asan's poem conform to the events narrated in the Ramayana, but her inner intentions are vastly different. Asan's Sita is animated by a spirit of independence and a profound relationship to herself. Sita's sense of autonomy and resoluteness is shared, less explicitly, by Asan's other female protagonists as well.

Asan's male characters, by contrast, are either silent or located in a non-reciprocal 'elsewhere'. A crucial moment in 'Leela'—when Madanan kisses Leela, breaks away from the kiss, and flees in fear—reveals this well. His fear is anticipated in an earlier verse in the poem, when he attempts to touch Leela's body and reciprocate her caresses:

> Together with her, he tried,
> mutual bodily caresses
> but fumbled, confused,
> A child close at a mirror
> faced with its own face.[39]

The male subject who flees from an uncanny specular vision stands in clear contrast to the deliberative self-relation of the heroine in 'Leela'. The self-destroying mirror stage reveals a mechanism by which

[39] Ibid., 217.

male identities are constituted in Asan's work. The male protagonists of 'Nalini' and 'Leela', in turning away from women's desire, redeem themselves from the intense passions of the phenomenal world. The male subject attains his identity as a renunciant only through a disavowal of desire. This renunciatory passage permits the male subject to be compassionate to the woman and places him in a superior position of understanding. In the Buddha figures—Anandan, Upaguptan or the Buddha himself—disavowal is not directly thematized; an achieved spiritual stature is assumed. In the case of Divakaran, the protagonist of a more personalized drama, disavowal takes the form of forgetting: even after listening to Nalini's detailed recollection of events from their childhood, he is unable to insert himself into an autobiographical narrative of experiences and affects. However, disidentification with his past enables Divakaran to offer redeeming spiritual advice. Even though he is momentarily shaken by Nalini's death—by her use of his body as her pyre—he is able to proceed on his spiritual path with greater sanctity. For Madanan, the *rajasik* male subject, the disavowal of desire is traumatic. The sensual female body, bedecked with *chempakam* blossoms, becomes the mirror image of male desire. His flight from the female body appears to be a traumatic disavowal of his own desire and life.

In other words, gender identities are assumed in Asan's poetry through the staging of a non-reciprocal drama. While desire finds discursive expression in the woman, the male subject disowns it in order to exit the pale of attachment. In this new position, he turns into the mourner-witness of the woman's passion and extinction. Facing the dead female body, the male subject mourns an identity that he has refused for himself. Asan's major poetical works stage the construction of a masculine identity which, paradoxically, is carried out through the elaboration of the female subject's desiring interiority.

In Asan's writings, gender is marked not only by the relationship assumed by the subject towards desire; it also has a bearing on one's discursivity: one's relationship to language and articulation. While the discourse of male subjects displays fulness or nullity, wisdom or inarticulateness, female discourse is tremulous with remembrance, deliberation, and longing. The differentiation of these two languages and the way subjects implicate themselves in them was perhaps Asan's most significant contribution to the craft of Malayalam poetry. It is to these gendered territories of language that we turn next.

V

In his major poems—'Nalini', 'Leela', 'Chintavishtayaya Sita', 'Duravastha', and 'Karuna'—Asan developed a new discursive machinery. The primary source of discourse in these poems is neither the meditative imagination of the poet reflecting on objects or situations, as in 'Veenapoovu' and 'Oru Simhaprasavam', nor the unravelling of a narrative, as in 'Balaramayanam' and 'Sreebuddhacharitam'. It is to be found, rather, in acts of inner deliberation and autobiographical enunciation performed by a female character-subject. 'Chintavishtayaya Sita' provides a prime example of this: in it the protagonist, 'unable to contain her turbulent mind, emitted inner utterances in the language of thought.'[40] Sita's monologue presents thoughts that are possible only in a first-person account consisting of I-statements; her language, in its form and texture, is constitutively linked to inner self-reflective acts. This connection is anticipated to some extent in 'Nalini' and 'Leela', while Asan's later works, 'Duravastha' and 'Karuna', conform to this logic in oblique ways. In these four poems the protagonist produces a first-person account, a discourse of the 'I', in the context of a conversation. In 'Leela' and 'Karuna' the interlocutor to whom the statements are addressed is a *sakhi*, while in 'Duravastha' Savitri's long monologue is addressed to a parakeet—which responds by mimicking and echoing human speech. The interlocutor offers a context for voicing inner thoughts but does not determine the course of what is said dialogically. This is true even in 'Nalini', where the heroine's self-revealing statements are addressed

[40] Ibid., 523.

to Divakaran in a context of non-reciprocity. These conversations need to be understood not as instances of dialogue or dialectic but as self-analysing monologues.

Asan's portrayal of Sita provides a typical illustration of the monologic moment: away from male presence, the female subject immerses herself in inner speech: 'Not knowing how to calm her agitated mind, using the language of thoughts, with grief she spoke within.'[41] Inner turbulence is constitutive of Sita's monologue and her first thoughts are about the unsteady state of her own mind. They then move to her past through an invocation of memory images, the slowly unfolding elements of a narrative which returns her eventually to the present. It is a transformed subject that returns, having overcome inner conflicts through a resolute taking hold of one's own destiny. Parts of Sita's inner speech are addressed to others, and some of the best-known passages of the poem are directed at Rama. However, he is an absent addressee and there is no expectation of a response. It is in fact the absence of the addressee—the addressee's virtual character and non-reciprocity—that makes Sita's interior monologue possible. Her inner speech does not aim at convincing or persuading this absent addressee and at resolving an external conflict, but at 'calming one's inner turbulence', at reaching a moment of inner resolution. This preoccupation with oneself in one's autonomy—in its lack of dialogicality—shapes the autobiographical monologues in Asan's poems. The monologue indirectly draws on the structure of the testimony.

Testimonies make their truth claims on the basis of a first-person, experiential relationship to the content of their statements. All autobiographical acts involve the modality of the testimony and found their truth claims on I-statements, i.e. statements made by a first-person subject on its own experiences. Sita's arguments on justice are grounded in a direct, reflexive access not only to her own purity and innocence, but also to her pain and anger. Her monologue makes its claims in a language of authenticity: even when

[41] Ibid., 523.

unruly emotions make her thoughts defy norms of propriety, these transgressions also bear testimony to the genuineness of self-revelation. Asan's monologic form allows an incorporation of such excesses into an economy of inner deliberation. Memories, feelings of pain and indignation, a narrative consolidation of one's own self—these elements in this economy finally lead to a moment of decision. Sita's gesture of leave-taking from the world appears in Asan's poem as a form of renunciation, withdrawal from life, and perhaps even suicide, taking to its logical conclusion the convergence between self-authentication and agency, autobiographical narration and self-transforming decision.

These patterns are evident in the structure of the dramatic monologue used in 'Chintavishtayaya Sita'. In 'Nalini', 'Leela', 'Duravastha', and 'Karuna' they are less directly displayed since these poems are not monologic in their outer form. However, each of them shows the female protagonist narrativizing her life through a process of inner deliberation and a moment of irreversible decision. In 'Nalini', as we saw, the heroine reminds Divakaran of their shared past and tells him the story of her subsequent life. In 'Leela' autobiographical testimony is presented in a third-person account, but deliberation and agency centre on Leela's conversation with Madhavi. This conversation, like Savitri's utterances to the parakeet in 'Duravastha', is monologic in its basic impulse. Self-narration in these texts does not display all the features found in Sita's monologue. Not much is revealed about Vasavadatta's past history—her autobiographical utterances articulate a present condition of desire.

Unlike these women characters with their autobiographical narratives, Asan's male protagonists adopt forms of speech located outside the borders of personal recollection and analysis. Divakaran's utterances work with impersonal resources of discourse, such as maxims (*aptavakyam*), cited repeatedly in tradition as a source of authority and guidance. His conversation with Nalini closes with spiritual teaching and the (possibly silent) instruction of the *mahavakya* (the great proposition).[42] Nalini, in contrast, begins by noting the inadequacy of language to reveal her inner domain: what she has to say has not been said before; she needs to forge a new language and risk errors and misprision.[43] The speech of the male protagonists is often not directed at any particular individual, as in the case of Divakaran, Upaguptan, Anandan, or the Buddha; or they are silent (Madanan), or not fully articulate (Chathan). Male discourse arises either from a position of sublimation and transcendence of desire or dissipates into a silence that marks an inability to identify oneself as the subject of desire. The temporal orientation of the discursive subject, a central feature of female autobiographical articulation in Asan, is missing from male speech. Asan's men do not think of themselves in terms of a history. The spiritually accomplished among them consider their past as having already been renounced: it no longer exists. For Asan's inarticulate male subject—Madanan—there is no past; it has been incorporated as the timeless present of an obsessive melancholia.

However, it may be a mistake to read into Asan's female characters a discourse of history. Their monologues show an ambivalent relationship to alterity. The desiring subject in Asan is structurally placed in a situation of non-reciprocity. Even as Asan's women affirm worldly life as desire, they are enveloped in a profound solitude which isolates them from family and society. Desire, Leela says, is about the realm of the inner, while the body is regulated by the rules of the outer and the social.[44] This makes the articulation of love free from restrictions made on the basis of social distinctions like caste and class, a point Asan stressed in some of his later poems. The

[42] Ibid., 132. The stanza says: as Nalini contemplated Divakaran's face, luminous with the divine glow, he told her the meaning of the Mahavakya, impossible to communicate in words. Sanu's commentary identifies the Mahavakya as '*tat tvam asi*' (thou art that), the well-known non-dualist proposition.

[43] Ibid., 118.

[44] Ibid., 194.

discursive space marked as inner is the space of female autonomy and transgression rather than patriarchal control. The pursuit of desire in these poems takes women away from the social world towards a moment of solitary resoluteness. There is a non-narrativizable core (of decision or resolution or realization) which escapes and determines autobiographization in Asan's female monologues. They all conclude in moments of exit from the world. It is as if there is no space in the world for the resolute female subject, and the autobiographical monologue is the only keepsake she leaves for the living.

One might point to 'Duravastha' as an exception. In terms of its narrative, 'Duravastha' does not follow the features of Asan's earlier works. The poet referred to it as a *vilakshanakrti* (uncharacteristic or non-normative work).[45] Written against the background of the Mappila revolt of 1922, the poem presents the story of Savitri, a young Nambutiri woman, and Chathan, an untouchable Pulaya youth. Savitri flees her home when it is attacked by rebellious Muslims who rape, kill, and abduct her family members. She takes refuge in the hut of Chathan, who protects and looks after her with keen devotion. Even after the revolt is suppressed, Savitri resolves to stay with Chathan and lead the life of a Pulaya woman. The poem ends with Savitri inviting Chathan to share her bed and be her husband. While Left criticism has found in 'Duravastha' a laudable precursor of Marxist 'progressive literature', the poem was criticized by many contemporaries and later critics on aesthetic (its propagandist element), moral (its fostering resentment against the elite), and political (its allegedly anti-Muslim verses) grounds.

Although Savitri and Chathan are united in happy conjugality at the end of 'Duravastha', asymmetry and inequality are central to the configuration of their relationship. Chathan's personal qualities are objects of praise by Savitri, but they are not part of the latter's self-consciousness; they have no way of figuring in his own discourse. An inheritor of centuries of slavery, Chathan's place is at the edge of

[45] Asan's 'Preface' to 'Duravastha', ibid., 591.

articulate language; he occupies a space of 'infancy'. Savitri too, in spite of her elite lineage, is an outcaste. Her inner thoughts sketch a future in which she will work in the fields alongside other Pulayas and remedy Chathan's infancy through education. One might say that this apprenticeship begins already in the poem's present, when Savitri explains the meaning of her name to Chathan by narrating the Puranic story about chastity. Asan's Preface stressed the need to restructure Hindu society, ravaged by centuries of caste oppression and existing in the present in dramatic mutilation after the Mappila revolt. Is the poem then a programme of Hindu reform and reconsolidation, and is Savitri's desire a means to effect it?

In his Preface, Asan characterized the union of his protagonists as configured in a state of intractable crisis, a fall without recourse (*gathyantharmillatha pathanathil*), stressing the link between desire and destitution in the poem.[46] It is as if desire in 'Duravastha', as in Asan's other poems, cannot inhabit the social domain: Chathan's hut is a topos of destitution, similar to other liminal spaces in the poems mentioned earlier. Chathan's inarticulateness is marked by an absence of social habitability; Savitri's transgressive desire emerges from a moment of denudation of the world rather than from a discourse of social equality. An exception to Chathan's infancy is offered in the poem when, on his way back from the fields, he is moved by the beauty of lotus blossoms in a pond, one of which he plucks and presents to Savitri as an offering.[47] This moment works through a contrast with Savitri's Puranic education. The affect visibilized in Chathan's act occupies a plane prior to the acquisition of culture through education. He represents a dimension of affective life that in Asan's thought is more primordial than history and society; it comes not only before culture but also before what culture identifies as nature and before figures of bodily or sexual desire.

'Duravastha' places the union of its protagonists alongside the beautiful confluences of the universe—as in earth reaching out to

[46] Ibid., 592.
[47] Ibid., 635–6.

the skies through its mountain ranges, clouds coming down to kiss treetops, and rivers merging with the ocean—which cannot be prevented by human will.[48] The law that governs these urges for union is not that of instincts, which exist at a level of embodiment. Desire's location is prior to this, in the earliest links between the soul and the body; it is desire that makes life and embodiment possible. Destitution and infancy—the free fall without recourse—is where such desire can be delineated. The universality of love reveals itself in the outcaste woman and the inarticulate slave, as they occupy the degree zero prior to the charting of the social and historical domains.

VI

Asan used several words to refer to the interior realm of the individual subject, including *antarangam*, *manataru*, and *antakaranam*. The last of these, *antakaranam* (inner sense), merits special attention, as Asan used it in his non-poetic discourses as well to refer to the interiority of agent.[49] In modern Malayalam, *antakaranam* refers to the domain of inner thoughts and feelings, and the word was already used in this sense in ordinary language in Asan's time.[50] Chandu Menon's

[48] Ibid., 646.

[49] Asan used the word *antakaranam* in his Presidential Address at the twentieth annual conference of the SNDP held in Quilon in May 1923, where he argued against mass Ezhava conversion to Buddhism or Christianity on the grounds that conversion goes against the logic of one's inner sense. Asan, *Kumaran Asante Gadyalekhanangal*, vol. 2, 54. See also his 'Mataparivartana Rasavadam'. For a criticism of Asan's use of *antakaranam* in this argument, see Kunjuraman, 'Adhakrtarkku Buddhamatamanu Nallathu', 4.

[50] In the mid-eighteenth century, Benjamin Bailey defined *antakaranam* as 'the heart, the mind, understanding.' Hermann Gundert's dictionary, published in 1872, has 'the inner organ, heart, mind' in its entry on the word. Bailey, *Dictionary of High and Colloquial Malayalam and English*, 25; Gundert, *A Malayalam and English Dictionary*, 31. Several articles published in periodicals in Malayalam in the early twentieth century discussed the concept of *antakaranam*. See, for example, K.M., 'Antakarana Samskaram'; Embrantiri, 'Antakaranam'.

Indulekha, for instance, mentions the protagonists of the novel at the beginning of the story as having already performed *antakaranavivaham* (a marriage of minds).[51] The word *antakaranam* has its conceptual origins in classical Indian philosophy and refers to the inner perceptual apparatus. Like the external sense organs, *antakaranam* engages with the phenomenal world, and this differentiates it from *atman* and *sakshi*, which occupy a non-phenomenal final level in the subject's perception of reality. It is conceived as physical (*bhautikam*), consisting of the five elements and dominated by *tejas*, which accounts for the inner sense's instability and constant transformations into various forms known as *vrtti*.

Our concern here is less with classical Indian doctrines of knowledge than with the semantic associations of this word in Malayalam at the time Asan was writing. We find the use of the notion of *antakaranam* in the compositions of both Sree Narayana Guru and Chattampi Swamikal. In 'Atmopadesasatakam', Sree Narayanan mentions it along with the sense organs, the body, and the perceptual world as the sacred body of the supreme being, i.e. knowledge. Furthermore, he compares *vrtti*—the forms assumed by the inner sense in the process of knowledge—as the wick in the lamp where the *atman* burns, accompanied by its corporeal shadow.[52] Chattampi Swamikal's 'Advaitachintapaddhati' offers a doctrinal discussion of *antakaranam*. He defines it as 'that organ which has been composed of the *sattvika* aspect of the five elements and which has knowledge as its object.'[53] *Vrtti*, the evolute of the *antakaranam*, has four forms, namely *manas*, *buddhi*, *chitham*, and *ahankaram*. Since these function within, as distinct from the external sense organs, they were called *antakaranam*.[54] *Ahankaram*, or the sense of the 'I', which is a part of the inner sense, when united with the *sthula sariram*, begins

[51] O. Chandu Menon, *Indulekha*, 27.

[52] Narayana Guru, *Sreenarayanaguruvinte Sampurna Krtikal*, 352.

[53] Chattampi Swamikal, *Chattampi Swamikal: Jivitavum Krtikalum*, 623.

[54] Ibid., 624.

to identify itself with the body and to think of itself as 'dark or red, tall or short.'[55] For Chattampi Swamikal, as for Advaitin thinkers in general, this sense of the 'I', as well as the *antakaranam* on which it depends, is, in the final instance, the result of a deluded perception, similar to that which sees a serpent in a rope.[56]

Kumaran Asan translated *Maitreyi*, a short novel written in English by a Bengali scholar named Pandit Sitanath Tatvabhushan. It was first published serially in *Vivekodayam*, the organ of the SNDP Yogam, when Asan was its editor, and then published as a book in 1913. Asan gave it a subtitle: 'A story which depicts the religion and community practices among Hindus in Vedic times'. Asan's interest in this narrative was twofold: firstly, he wished to suggest that the varna system in the Vedic period was based on one's actual qualities (*guna*) and occupational engagements (*karma*) rather than on birth. Secondly, the narrative contained two long discussions on Advaita thought between Yajnavalkya, Katyayani, and Maitreyi. In the course of one of these discussions, Yajnavalkya responds to Katyayani's objections to believing in the permanence of the *atman*: 'Your problem has arisen from confusing the *atman* with the inner sense (*antakaranam*) or with the psyche (*manas*). *Manas* is in a sense inseparable from the *atman*. Yet, in another sense, they are different from each other. The impermanence and instability you referred to are those of *manas* and not of the *atman*.'[57]

In Asan's poetry *antakaranam* is used as part of a field of words denoting personal interiority. These words are deployed in a variety of senses, ranging from the flux of thought and the turbulence of emotions to the locus of inner reflection. While most of these are in tune with the philosophical conception of *antakaranam* in the tradition we indicated above, as the site of the 'secrets of the mind', the word acquires in Asan's hands a clearly individualized sense; it became central to the use of this word in modern Malayalam. One of the principal functions of the monologic method in Asan is to make

55 Ibid.

56 Ibid., 625.

57 Asan, tr. *Maitreyi*, 42.

it possible for the subject to reflect on the activities of *antakaranam*. At the same time, the monologue is also a manifestation of one's inner state.

Asan's reflections on inner thoughts and the role they play in shaping our experience of the universe also show the influence of Buddhist thought: 'As one is, so is one's world. Each state in the universe is firmly rooted in our inner experience of that state. It is not important to look at the external state. This is because all that [external state] is a reflected image of the state of our inner sense (*antakaranam*).'[58] This is even more pronounced in his reflections of the soul (*atmavu*): 'Each human life experiences events, helpful or difficult, depending on the quality and the strength of its inner life of thoughts. The body is a mixture (*samavayam*) of the experiences and thoughts condensed in the soul, as well as the temporary vehicle for articulating them. Therefore, our real soul (*yatharthamaya atmavu*) is none other than our thoughts.'[59] This reading introduces a dimension of individuation to the Buddhist conception of the subject, a strand in his thinking also seen in some of his other works. Asan translated James Allen's *As the Man Thinketh* into Malayalam under the title *Manassakti*, emphasizing its arguments regarding the determining role played by our thoughts in creating the world that we inhabit. Inner sense, as individualized personal interiority, with its relations to the bodily and the worldly, was for Asan the site for unveiling the 'truth' about the subject.

Two features are striking in Asan's portrayal of women subjects: firstly, they embody a self-conscious and reflective notion of inner agency, which identifies them as unique individuals; secondly, the instability of female *antakaranam* is contrasted with the stability of the enlightened male subject. The woman's turbulent inner self is, as we saw, often framed in Asan's work by the man's immutable spirituality. A temporal unfolding of human agency is not found in his male figures; one needs to turn to Leela or Savitri for this. Asan's valorization of female agency is ambivalent: it is oriented in

[58] Asan, *Kumaran Asante Gadyalekhanangal*, vol. 2, 137.

[59] Ibid., 138.

the last instance towards spiritual fulfilment; the woman though is an apprentice-subject, finding the destination of her spiritual journey in guru-like male figures who are outside the ambit of self-transformation. Her lack of perfection allows the woman to be the locus of individuation. The woman, for Asan, is the agent of autonomous initiatives and the transgression of social norms; at the same time, she is an object of instruction by male figures who have transcended the world of desire.

Kuttikrishna Marar read into the narrator's silence in 'Leela', on the cause of death of Leela's husband, an implied suggestion that he was murdered by the heroine. In the same vein, Sita's final disappearance may be seen as the veiled manifestation of a transgressive, suicidal agency. We noted the parallels between Nalini's emotions in front of Divakaran and female erotic experience. Leela and Vasavadatta express their desire through their physical seductiveness. Even in Matangi and Savitri, religious conversion and the move against caste are motivated by a movement of erotic desire. All these initiatives and transgressions are, however, framed within a narrative of female, spiritual apprenticeship. The erotic is sublated into the spiritual by the male subject. Matangi's desire in 'Chandalabhikshuki' is the ground from which her spiritual initiation arises: 'The blessed One understanding her sentiments towards Ananda made use of them to open her eyes to the truth, and took her among his disciples.' These lines from Lakshmi Narasu's *The Essence of Buddhism* form part of the summary narrative cited by Asan at the beginning of 'Chandalabhikshuki'.[60] The woman is the desiring subject, but she is also the object par excellence of instruction.

This conception of female agency seems to draw upon two distinct strands. It reworks the paradigm we saw in the *vairagya* compositions, which express a strong fear of woman's desire. At the

[60] Asan, *Kumaran Asante Sampurna Padya Krtikal*, 652; Narasu, *The Essence of Buddhism*. Asan is also likely to have consulted Paul Carus' *The Gospel of Buddha*, which he cites as a source for 'Karuna'. Carus' recounting of the Matangi story stresses her feelings for Anandan. Carus, *The Gospel of Buddha*, 196–7.

same time, this conception joins the efforts in Asan's time to address the woman as an object of reform and instruction. In addition to the novel, a large number of prescriptive texts—some authored by women and several by men—appeared around this time in Malayalam, elaborating on the notion of *streedharmam*. Asan reviewed some of them with approbation.[61] Often using verse, these texts drew on ideas, tropes, and idioms from Hindu prescriptive writing to outline the duties of women within the household and in relation to their body and conduct. Such reiteration of familiar propositions was made necessary by the changes in the role and status of women and in the relationships between men and women. The normative tenor of the genre helped in conferring a sense of authority on their responses to contemporary challenges.

The newness of these concerns was acknowledged more openly in the larger body of prose writing on these themes. Much of the content of early women's periodicals—such as *Sarada*, *Mahila*, and *Lakshmibai*—were of this genre.[62] Articles published in *Sarada*, for instance, often addressed topics such as *bhartrsusrusha* (care of one's husband), *veettuvela* (house work), and *vyayamam* (physical exercise).[63] *Lakshmibai*, a magazine that began publication from Trissur in 1905, announced that it would make available to native women writings in Sanskrit and English on subjects such as *garbharaksha* (pregnancy care), *sisuparipalanam* (childcare), *arogyarakshamargam* (health care), *pachakavidhi* (recipes for cooking), *grhabharanam* (governing the household), *bhartrsusrusha* (caring for one's husband),

[61] Reviewing one of them, entitled *Bharyadharmam*, Asan commented with approbation that the men who happen to read this book would indeed buy copies as gifts for their wives. *Kumaran Asante Gadyalekhanangal*, vol. 1, 46. Asan also reviewed M.V. Parvathy Amma's *Sthreedharmam* (ibid., 29), Muloor Padmanabha Panikkar's book of the same title (ibid., 20–1), and P.M. Govindan Vaidyan' *Sootikamrtam* (ibid, 23.).

[62] For a discussion of the social and discursive processes of gendering in Kerala during this period, see Devika, *Engendering Individuals*.

[63] See, for example, P. Bhageerathi Amma, 'Vyayamam'; 'Veettuvela'; K. Padmavati Amma, 'Bhartrsusrusha'.

pativratamhatmyam (the glory of chastity), and *manyamaraya oro streekalude jeevacharitram* (the biographies of reputed women).[64] *Streedharmam* too appeared as a theme in many essays. T.B. Kalyani Amma, one of the editors of *Sarada*, argued that 'women's duties in the world are twofold. The first and the more important one is to be performed in their homes; the second is as a member of their community. Indian women in our times are performing only the first of these; the second needs to be demanded of them.'[65] Some discussions of *streedharmam* cautioned women against the passion for modern ways (*parishkarabhramam*), which was seen as a reckless imitation of Western practices.[66] Women's education was frequently discussed in these magazines, and it was often extolled on account of its possible benefits for the family, especially for the sound upbringing and education of children and for the intelligent, prudent running of the household.[67] The education of women was also seen as the best means of forestalling unwanted attractions and changing the everyday preoccupations of women, such as gossip and popular entertainment. The nature of the education appropriate for women, and the language and contents of the curriculum, were matters of debate.

The construction of the woman as an object of reform and education in nineteenth-century India has been extensively discussed in the scholarly literature. The relationship of this configuration to the emergence of nationalism, to novel forms of patriarchy and domesticity, and to new senses of the community and tradition has been noted for colonial Bengal and North India, as well as other regions.[68] Advice manuals and literary works written especially for

[64] *Lakshmibai*, 1:1 (1905), 5–6.

[65] T.B. Kalyani Amma, 'Streedharmam', 1.

[66] Ammini Amma, 'Streedharmam'.

[67] See, for example, T. Ammukkutti Amma, , 'Streevidyabhyasam'; 'Malayalikalum Streevidyabhyasavum'; M.K.; 'Streevidyabhyasam'.

[68] See, for instance, Tanika Sarkar, *Hindu Wife, Hindu Nation*; idem, '*Streesiksha* and Its Terrors'; Geraldine Forbes, 'Education for Women'; Charu Gupta, *Sexuality, Obscenity, Community*; Partha Chatterjee, 'The Nationalist Resolution'; Judith E. Walsh, *Domesticity in Colonial India*.

women, magazines, and periodicals addressed to and sometimes run by women, and sessions for women in conferences held by community organizations—all these were spaces crucial to the elaboration of a new discourse on women.

In Kerala, although a substantial part of this literature was written by men, sometimes under assumed female names, women also became important participants in producing and altering the terms of this discourse. Many of the writings by women stressed the virtues and necessity of women's education and of women's freedom, although the latter was initially presented within the frame of male protection. Essays by women brought into the public domain of writing the texture of domestic life, everyday activities in the lives of couples and families, and a new tone of worldly experience, alongside aspirations for participation in professional and public arenas which had been the preserve of men. New notions of female agency, which sought autonomy in thought and expression, developed in the pages of women's journals.[69]

Asan's poetry primarily envisaged the apprenticeship of the woman as spiritual rather than worldly. The woman's capacity for transformation was in her autobiographical constitution, which opened her interiority—fraught with negotiations between the corporeal and the spiritual and traversed by intense desire—for insistent discursive articulation. In contrast to the disciplines of modern gender recommended for women in contemporary texts of *streedharmam*, which Asan applauded, the women characters in his poetry were sketched in the incandescence of a desire which transgressed the social coordinates of womanhood: family, marriage, and the body. In the female subject's ambivalent links to the corporeal—connected through primordial ties of desire and made uninhabitable through the body's embeddedness in the social world—Asan's poetry found a fleeting promise of freedom and a new grammar for the subject's presencing in language.

[69] For an excellent discussion of women's essays in periodicals, see Devika, 'Introduction', in Devika, ed. and tr., *Her-Self*, xix–xxxi.

4

Unsteady Luminosity

Reading the World in Early Novels

PREMAMRTAM (1913), C.V. RAMAN PILLAI'S satiric 'social novel' set in the late nineteenth century, has within it a curious moment when Ayyappan Thampi—a young graduate gainfully employed by the Travancore government and therefore an eminently eligible bachelor—looks at the photograph of a prospective bride brought to him by Panki Paniker, an interested go-between. As he gazes at the image, he finds himself extraordinarily transported:

> His fleshly vision clouded over. For the first time, the eyes of love that his inner body possessed became capable of sight . . . These eyes saw not a form created by the arrangement of light and shade, but the purity of a slender virgin leaning on a chair immersed in intense thought. . . Thampi felt that the heavenly beauty of divine virginity had appeared before his eyes draped in innocent piety and assuming a pure, sublime state of femininity.[1]

As he emerges from the spell—captured with all its intense vicissitudes—Thampi is convinced that the referent of the image could not be of this world; it could only be the replica of an ideal. But ideals are beyond the realm of photographs; could the photo then be of

[1] C.V. Raman Pillai, *Premamrtam*, 110. (Also hereafter 'C.V.')

a painting which had conferred fleshly lineaments upon an ideal? Was this not in fact the photograph of a painting by Raja Ravi Varma? Who but that unsurpassed master could conjure up such an image of ideal beauty?

Thampi is invited the following day to meet the ineffable original of which the photograph, for all its superlative charm, is but a copy. He is taken to a decorated chamber festooned with images of ideal beauty. Heavenly women in attitudes of erotic charm confront him from paintings on three walls: on the eastern wall is Menaka in seductively loosened clothes, lit up in an amatory glow; a thinly veiled Rambha bathed in moonlight is on the northern wall, sternly forbidding the approach of those without a taste for the amorous; on the south, Urvashi recounts her passion for Arjuna and is ready to curse those blind to beauty's charms. In the room's centre, surrounded by these ethereally sensuous images, stands a round table upon which is placed another photograph of the girl he has come to meet. This portrait shocks Thampi: it scarcely resembles the one he has so ecstatically contemplated the previous day.

> if the second photograph is accurate, it is a certain elegant seductiveness (*chetitvam*) that is dominant in the woman whom he has come to visit. . . As it was a full-length portrait one could see the rare exuberance of her hair. If a girl who has such copious hair is ready to comb and hold it up before a photographer, thus displaying the taste of a seductress, her heart was untouched by the venerable trait of modesty, and she did not possess sufficient majesty to become spouse to the heir of Chambrangottu *taravad*. . . He put the photograph down on the table. Paniker's hopes dimmed. He said: 'Same girl in both pictures. You can see the very original if you wish.'[2]

Soon enough the girl enters the room, heralded by the intoxicating scent of rose flowers and attired in white in the North Indian style. Her physical presence, instead of resolving the conflict between the two images, serves only to multiply appearances and compound the

[2] Ibid., 116.

confusion: 'Amidst the dark abundance of her hair, which indicated the profusion of natural riches, her face shone with the glory of the golden image of a goddess . . . and Thampi felt that this face was not familiar to him through either of the photographs he had seen. Radiant like the full moon, on that face played childlike purity as well as traces of frivolity . . .'[3] The visual enchantment is intensified by the extreme beauty of her voice as she begins to play the veena and sing a *srngara padam* (a verse of erotic love), with a slight smile at the aptness of the words: 'What wrong have I done thee, my love . . .' The singer's aesthetic self-abandon, surprisingly, leads to the spell's abrupt undoing.

> Thampi's taste identified in the bluish glow of the singer's eyes the flicker of an animal emotion. On her red lips tender like buds, glowed a fire that could rage and burn down the sacred abode of matrimony—thus he analysed her natural propensities. A strong awareness shone inside him that the beautiful fingers which were now playing the veena as if they were dancing on the hood of the serpent Kaliya, those same fingers could turn into snakes with multiple tongues for the man embraced by them.[4]

The extraordinary predominance of visual images and their apprehension in these passages could serve as a point of departure for our engagement here with early novels in Malayalam. C.V.'s obsessive preoccupation with visuality, even if exceptional in its intensity, is not unique. Many novels of the period appear to be concerned with presenting a visible world within which characters live and move, and which they frequently attempt to make sense of. Readers are interpellated into a new imaginative practice in which the configuration of vision and language, seeing and saying, becomes difficult to disentangle. Through their perceptual and discursive economies, these early novels found ways of inserting subjects into new, complex domains of worldliness and speech.

The account of obsessive visual scrutiny in *Premamrtam* makes no distinction between a photograph and a painting, or between

[3] Ibid., 117–18.
[4] Ibid., 120.

images and reality: the body in its immediate presence also works as an image, eliciting an equally intense visual investigation. Even the animated body, which resists static contemplation, is regarded as a moving picture: the viewer's compulsive gaze becomes even more alert to track momentary corporeal transitions and register the slightest signs that flicker across a face.

C.V. Raman Pillai, unlike his French contemporary Marcel Proust, was not concerned with a hermeneutic configuration where personal jealousy produces and, in the same movement, impedes the affective work of love.[5] Neither the unique personal history nor the inner intentions of the woman directly command Ayyappan Thampi's anxieties. His concern is rather with her natural proclivities, her *swabhavam* or *swabhavadharmam*.[6] Close observation and relentless speculation about bodily testimony mark this pursuit. We also see another relationship at work. This is not defined by sceptical distance: the spectator is affected by the image, being carried away to a realm that lies not only beyond the viewer's encounter with the photograph but also the moment captured and presented in the image. While looking at the first image, Thampi does not notice the luxuriant length of the woman's hair or the style of its arrangement; his gaze does not register details of the represented body. He sees only emotions and abstract virtues, which, we realize later, have their provenance in his English education, in his exposure to Western literatures and ideas. The narrator does not translate details of the image into linguistic description, but documents the imagined drama produced by the photograph. 'In the figure standing in profile, decorated with the hair falling on the cheek, the eye half-closed in inner agony seemed to be in prayer beseeching the helping hand of a virtuous ally. The soft cheek appeared to quiver as an outward manifestation of uncontainable suffering.'[7]

[5] For a discussion of the semiology and hermeneutics of jealousy in Proust, see Deleuze, *Proust and Signs*.

[6] Raman Pillai, *Premamrtam*, 120.

[7] Ibid., 110.

It is difficult to disentangle visual information and abstract ideas, and the passage appears to be pulled simultaneously in two directions: an allegorical vision where pure ideas are made visible, and an extreme verisimilitude where the image begins to come alive and acquire a corporeal immediacy. The living image makes demands on the viewer, in the form of a prayer or a quivering cheek, and his responses find their expression in a language of essences: virtue, innocence, divine beauty. The spectator—and the narrator—are not reading the image according to a well-formulated iconography: the code that links essences to appearances seems rather to be an offshoot of the viewer's transformation in the presence of the image. The image exerts an uncanny power over Thampi and draws dramatic freezes from his acquired imaginary.

The second photograph, by contrast, breaks the spell of this virtual production. The viewer's gaze abandons the search for transcendental essences and focuses on the prosaic conditions of picture-making. The photograph appears to represent nothing more than a model who has combed up her hair before a stranger, the photographer. The viewer is located outside the auratic world produced by the image; the gaze is obsessed in its eagerness to reconstruct the scene in the studio and make inferences. The photograph possesses no virtual dimension and offers no transcendence from the conditions of the studio. Enchantment, however, reclaims its dominance when the heroine enters the room: her physical presence offers a third, more complex image next to which the two earlier photographs pale in comparison. Idioms of transcendence to imaginary scenes and the reduction of the image to its conditions of production recede into the background, and a new, intimate engagement with the face begins. A tense competition between enchantment and interpretation, a passive submission to the power of the female figure, and an active hermeneutic dominance become discernible. Musical performance accelerates and complicates this tussle when Thampi listens to the singing voice in rapt attention even as he scans the singer's face for signs. The fleeting appearance of a bluish glow of animal desire, apprehended by the viewer's agile powers of discrimination, provokes no turbulence: Thampi feels neither attraction nor revulsion but reaches a composed judgement with which he detaches himself from the image, having now become immune to its powers.

Later in the novel another suitor, Karta, entranced by a fleeting encounter in the street with the same woman, goes through the same steps. However, the chamber looks different now: on the walls we find images of deities instead of heavenly nymphs in erotically charged postures; books are displayed on the tables; the decorated bed in the corner is hidden away by a screen. The new suitor too is captivated by the first photograph that had bewitched Thampi's imagination, but he quickly dismisses the second as the handiwork of an inept photographer. And the appearance of the woman leads not to a musical performance but to the mutual avowal of love through a combination of Westernized rituals of romantic love and native gestures of propriety. The mastery of the second, successful suitor over the unstable world of visual appearances, however, does not last forever. Later in the novel he becomes prey to a far stronger misrecognition of the woman's fidelity on account of an inadequate and misleading visual encounter.[8]

Visual experience plays a vital role in shaping the narrative in these passages, but it is marked by deep instability. In contrast to the novel's celebrated claim to describe things as they are, these passages chart the difficulty and insufficiency of vision: instead of revealing an indisputably existent world available through the senses, visual experience is put into crisis by dimensions that conflict with the empirical. No pre-existing codes of decipherment appear to guarantee the significance of objects of vision and the stability of the viewing subject. Yet this perceptual and discursive instability—the lack of surefootedness in sensory apprehension and in the choice of the

[8] The central moment of crisis in *Premamrtam* arises when the protagonist wrongly doubts his wife's chastity. The darkness of the night and unsteady illumination lead here to a crucial misidentification of bodies. Ibid., 201–2. See also Kumar, 'Seeing and Reading', 180.

code that will unlock its significance—does not appear to hinder the novel's work: rather it appears as a vital source of the form's energy, as the kernel of the aesthetic experience offered by fiction's new imaginary.

The proliferation of visual images in *Premamrtam* is in tune with the transformations in scopic regimes and technologies of image-making at the time the novel was written. Raja Ravi Varma did indeed produce oleographs of Rambha and Urvashi, akin to the ones described as decorating the imaginary walls of the bridal chamber in C.V.'s novel. It is possible that the attire 'in the northern style' in which the heroine appears before Thampi was borrowed from Ravi Varma's paintings, which drew on eclectic sources to produce ideal costumes for female characters from Indian mythology. But it is not the portrait but the photograph that occupies the centre of the drama whose unfolding we traced in *Premamrtam*. Sujith Kumar Parayil has noted the arrival of photography in Travancore and the establishment of the early studios in Trivandrum during C.V. Raman Pillai's lifetime.[9] Could there be a relationship between these new visual technologies of photography and the scopic environments of the early novel?

In her study of the relationship between fiction and photography in nineteenth-century England, Nancy Armstrong argued that literary realism converted 'a particular kind of visual information—infinitely reproducible and capable of rapid and wide dissemination—into what was both a way of seeing and a picture of the world that a mass readership could share.'[10] Her contention is that realism involved a pictorial turn, a supplanting of the word by the image: visual information became the basis for the intelligibility of verbal narrative. This led to a conjunction between the interests of literary realism and photography: 'in order to be realistic, literary realism referenced a world of objects that either had been or could be photographed', and 'photography in turn offered up portions of this world to be

[9] Parayil, 'Photography(s) in Twentieth-Century Kerala', especially chapter 3.

[10] Armstrong, *Fiction in the Age of Photography*, 7.

seen by the same group of people whom novelists imagined as their readership.'[11] Based on this shared ground between realist fiction and photography, Armstrong makes larger claims about the 'image' and its epistemological centrality in modern social life: 'in establishing a relationship between fiction and photography, I will insist that the kind of visual description we associate with literary realism refers not to things, but to visual representations of things, representations that fiction helped to establish as identical to real things and people before readers actually began to look that way to one another and live within such stereotypes. It is the referent common to both Victorian fiction and photography that I mean by the term "image".'[12]

For Armstrong the new fictional regime—of literary realism and photography—did not refer to a world of things and people; its referent was the image, which occupied a field of images and gained its value from differential relationships within the field.

In *Premamrtam*, however, the stress is not on the capacity of images to bear reliable visual information; it is rather the power exerted by the image on the viewer and the difficulty of hermeneutic decipherment which come to the foreground. The light that makes images visible also obscures them: the shifting luminosities of the photograph, and the barely perceptible glow of emotion on the singing face are moments in an uncertain struggle; it is within this tussle that the spectator-subject of C.V.'s novel is formed. Do differences in perceptual regimes between Victorian England and early-twentieth-century Travancore account for the distance that separates this from Armstrong's account?

Thampi's praise of Ravi Varma highlights the painter's ability to give visible form to an ideal beauty for which there is no analogue in the living world. The image is not a stereotype under whose regime human beings will relate to and read each other; it marks a limit where the world is surpassed and astonishment overpowers the viewer. This

[11] Ibid., 7–8.
[12] Ibid., 3.

is not pivoted on a stable distinction between the empirical and the ideal; it is the power of the image, regardless of its origins in experience or imagination, that matters. Even the photograph, with all its claims to mimetic accuracy and indexical relationship to the world of objects, is well within this regime of power and affect. Historians of early photography in India, like Judith Mara Gutman and Christopher Pinney, have shown how this emergent visual technology inserted itself into the dominant scopic regimes in an India where visuality and other embodied practices played a vital role in public culture, and produced effects and relations at variance with their histories in the West.[13] The use of painted photographs, photolithographs which present composite images taken from different sources, and the simultaneous representation of all elements in the picture field—as if it were happening in an 'idealized and timeless space'—were all distinctive features of the popular practice of photography in India.[14] The power of the image and the transformative effects it could have on the viewer imply, according to Pinney, a corposthetic rather than aesthetic approach. The modality of the Darshan—described by Diana Eck in the context of religion and invoked subsequently in the study of popular print culture and cinema—'mobilizes vision as part of a unified human sensorium, and visual interaction as physically transformative.'[15] Vision and language in early novels in Malayalam, and the new modes of imagining subjectivities they offered, worked within the ambit of a corposthetic dimension of images and the transformative power of seeing and saying.

Discussions of the early novel in India have recognized the many ways in which the representational strategies of this genre deviated from its Western predecessor. Even as early novelists claimed novelty for their compositions on grounds of representational realism, what

[13] See Gutman, *Through Indian Eyes*; Pinney, *Camera Indica*.

[14] See Chatterjee, 'Critique of Popular Culture', 172.

[15] Pinney, *Photos of the Gods*, 9. See also Eck, *Darsan*; Rajadhyaksha, 'The Phalke Era'; Prasad, *Ideology of the Hindi Film*.

they offered was manifestly different in expectations of verisimilitude, representational conventions, plausibility of plots, and other aspects of narrative organization. Critics have tried to understand this difference in terms of the novel's allegiance to earlier literary forms and techniques. Meenakshi Mukherjee pointed out that the physical appearance of characters is described often according to conventions of head-to-toe description (*nakha-sikha* or *apadachooda varnana*) inherited from the Sanskrit poetic genres (*kavyas*).[16] The novel's self-proclaimed distinction from the traditional *kavya* seems to be belied by its reliance on the latter's representational norms. Are these novels to be seen as continuous with the *kavyas*, or did they fashion a new literary technology that put to innovative use earlier representational strategies? The vocabulary of hybridity may not, on its own, help us describe with precision the ways in which the novels worked as discursive assemblages. And large categorical distinctions between the pre-modern and the modern or the Indian and Western may not take us close to a positive description of the nature of the perceptual world offered by the early novel, with its objects, characters, and events.

II

A set of tropes recurs in accounts of the origins of the new form offered by early Malayalam novelists. Prominent is a desire to tell new stories and widen the scope of entertainment for readers who had only puranic tales at their disposal; a shift away from supernatural extravagance to showing things as they appeared in real life; an intervention in the contemporary world with a social or moral purpose, or to document in detail the customs of one's community; and a deep entanglement with translation—failed, abandoned, or partially carried out—where derivativeness and originality do not function in strict opposition to each other. These go alongside occasional comments on language: how does one make one's language assume

[16] Mukherjee, *Realism and Reality*, 10.

a new literary voice and a new mode of address and make it capable of showing and saying things in a way it has not done before?

Literary historians are known to quibble about the 'first' novel of a language, marking the commencement of a genre; while doing this they often posit an immediate prehistory revealing a number of 'not-yet' novels which anticipate the emergence of the genre without belonging to it. However, these texts, judged as having failed to reach the normative benchmark for the genre, anchor an alternative history, enabling us to see an unstable terrain of discourse before its subsequent settlement and regulation. This is less a matter of generic or textual properties and features than of literary habits, imaginaries, and publicly affirmed aesthetic pleasures. In Malayalam, several early attempts at long fictional narratives in prose came from Protestant missionaries and native Christian writers. These efforts, often translations of Christian literature, did not usually consider themselves as aiming at the reader's aesthetic attention. Hana Catherine Mullens' *Phulmoni Ennum Koruna Ennum Peraya Randu Streekalude Katha* (The Story of Two Women Named Phulmoni and Koruna), a schematic narrative about Indian converts to Christianity, originally published in Bengali in 1852, was translated by Joseph Peet into Malayalam six years later. Mrs Collins' novel *Slayer Slain*, set in Kerala, was translated by her husband, Rev. Richard Collins, as *Ghatakavadham* and published in 1877. Archdeacon Koshy, who translated John Bunyan's *Pilgrim's Progress* in 1847 (another translation by Joseph Peet was published by Basel Mission in the same year), authored a text called *Jatibhedam* (Caste Difference) in the 1860s in the form of a fictitious debate. This was republished in 1887 with the title *Pullelikkunju*. Apart from these stories with a direct Christian religious intent, Kalloor Oommen Philippose wrote *Almarattam* (Impersonation) in 1866 as a loose, non-dramatic translation of Shakespeare's *Comedy of Errors*. *Kundalata*, written by Appu Nedungadi, was published in 1887 and soon found recognition as a novel, although its principal role in subsequent literary histories has been to serve as a precursor to O. Chandu Menon's *Indulekha*, published two years later and hailed as the first properly modern novel in Malayalam.

Nedungadi's Preface to *Kundalata* shows an awareness of the newness of his project:

> In English there are several books by the name of 'novel'—meaning stories of a new kind—in which readers find much distraction. Since there are no books of this sort in Malayalam, the majority of Malayalis who lack proficiency in English are unable to feel the pleasures of narration and dexterity of language in these books. As a result, they pass their time in a pitiable state, reading again and again without enjoyment some Puranic stories found in a few books like Ramayanam, Mahabharatam and Nalacharitam, which in all probability their parents had already narrated to them in their childhood. It is also a matter of surprise that the few capable Malayalis who possess knowledge of the English language have not been trying to change this situation.[17]

It is clear that Nedungadi conceived his readership as essentially Hindu, as having been shaped by Hindu mythological narratives and the literary tradition that derives from Sanskrit. Interestingly, *Kundalata*'s story is closer to Shakespeare's *Cymbeline* than to English novels. However, the texture of the novel has much in common with the Sanskrit literary tradition and its afterlife in Malayalam poetry and drama. This is evident from an inaugural compositional move: although Nedungadi stresses the newness and invented nature of his work as well as its similarities to the English novel, he takes care not to place it in a world familiar to the Malayalis from experience: 'Names of kingdoms like Kalingam and Kuntalam and personal names like Kundalata and Taranathan have been used in this novel mainly to remind the readers that the story is said to have taken place in an alien land far away from Kerala: in case [readers] find in this mores and practices out of tune with the customs in Kerala, these may be in accordance with the ways of those countries. However, readers should not think that the story took place in countries famed by these names in the Puranas and which are now called differently.'[18]

While the names of places and persons would appeal to the reader's familiarity with native literature, the narration seems to bring

[17] Nedungadi, Foreword to the first edition, *Kundalata*, v.
[18] Ibid.

it closer to the reader's own temporal frame. In spite of their royal status, characters are described in their ordinariness: even the mystery surrounding Kapilanathan is eventually resolved in favour of motives that are not extraordinary or elevated.

The descriptions that punctuate the early chapters of the novel rehearse this combination of strangeness and ordinariness. The first chapter, which presents a mysterious hermit, who is later revealed to be a renowned former minister in disguise, is succeeded by descriptions of a hunt, assembling details and actions that have no consequence for the turn of events or the reader's understanding and affective response to the principal characters. The exteriority of the description—its role as an element in assembling a picture of the strange kingdom, far away from Kerala—seems to be its own justification. The same tendency is evident in a detailed description of the house of Aghoranathan. The garden, each of the rooms, and the principal objects that decorate them are profusely described without aiming for a totality of effect. Each object is a curiosity in its own right. The detailing reveals no rationale other than the operation of an implied, imaginary gaze which registers things and notices their strange and special qualities without trying to integrate them into an overall image.

This tendency is pursued in a number of early Malayalam novels. In Ammaman Raja's *Indumatiswayamvaram*, the heroine Indumati sends a message to her lover Sukumaran asking him to meet her in secret in a bungalow to discuss some matters of the utmost urgency. Indumati and the reader are both aware that the king has turned against Sukumaran, and that he is going to be expelled from the palace. At this vital moment, the narrator cheerfully interrupts the progress of the story:

> Now, for the delight of the readers, I shall briefly describe the excellences of this bungalow. It was set in the middle of an exceedingly beautiful garden in Srinagar, the capital city of Kashmir, renowned all through the country. On both sides of the paths that take you beyond the steps, on the beautiful iron fencing that enchants the minds of viewers and in the bowers specially built for the enjoyment of the breeze in the middle

> of gardens dense with plants and bushes, spread fragrant, flowering creepers in abundance. Even the heavenly garden Nandana will be put to shame at this sight. On the outer edge of these bowers, four or five ponds—a yard or two in depth and some sixty or seventy yards in length and breadth, and filled with limpid unsullied water—have been lavishly constructed with special moonstones and illuminated by lamps placed on short pillars cast in copper and coated in gold. At their centre, above the water stand female forms sculpted in marble; from the artificial lotus flowers held in their hands water fountains emerge and spread out fanlike and fall. Different kinds of fish nurtured there flit around and play all the time. Who can help being delighted by the beauty of this garden adorned by all this?[19]

This description uses techniques from the *kavya* tradition, especially in the triumphant comparison with Nandanodyana, but it would be a mistake to see this as an instance of the survival of a pre-modern poetic device. The detailing of the features and forms of the garden, the mention of measurements, the precision in the description of the fountain all follow the same principle we found in *Kundalata*, that of detailing without consolidating or totalizing. This tendency is taken further in Cheruvalathu Chathu Nair's novel *Meenakshi* (1890), where the entire village is mapped in a similar way before locating the heroine's house and describing it in detail. Even though the raison d'être of the description is the production of a total subjective, aesthetic experience of delight and marvel, the narrative appears to be guided by a desire to master the object inch by inch, detail by detail.

Chandu Menon's *Indulekha* (1889) is remarkable for adopting a somewhat different and far more diverse set of descriptive procedures. Interestingly, in the author's Preface it is vision and language that serve as the ground for defining the uniqueness and novelty of his venture. *Indulekha*, Menon says, had its origins in a failed attempt at translating Disraeli's novel *Henrietta Temple*.[20] A direct translation, he

[19] Ammaman Raja, *Indumatiswayamvaram*, 45–6.
[20] Chandu Menon, Preface to the first edition, *Indulekha*, 7.

realized, posed two major problems: firstly, it was far more difficult to reproduce the flavour of the original in an accurate written translation than in oral retelling, where a wider range of expressive and explanatory resources were available to familiarize the listener with the world and culture in the English novel; secondly, a straight translation into Malayalam of passages in the English novel 'where *srngaram* dominated as rasa' would not be aesthetically pleasing.[21] The choice of the word *srngaram* to refer to scenes of romantic love in the English novel is in itself an act of translation, predicated as it is on an apprehension of the English novel by Indian literary habits. Chandu Menon's oral retellings were also of this kind, drawing on native imaginaries to grasp alien literary gestures. His aim was to find a substitute, in the domain of writing, for the flexible inventiveness of his oral translations. This is what led him to write a 'novel book in Malayalam more or less in the manner of English novel books.'[22] A paradoxical notion of creativity: the new composition's originality derives precisely from its status as an imitation. *Indulekha* was addressed to an audience mostly unfamiliar with the English novel, and this made it impossible for Menon to anticipate their possible response to his work. This raises questions regarding the literary habitus presupposed by the new form, and the grounds on which it appealed to its readership.

Menon did not directly address these questions; but his clarification of the nature of his project does give us some leads. It was to visual representations and ways of speaking that he turned for analogues of the novelty of *Indulekha*. In response to the scepticism about his choice of ordinary affairs of contemporary life and his avoidance of marvellous incidents, the novelist had this to say:

> Before the European style of oil-painting began to be known and appreciated in this country, we had painted, in defiance of all possible existence, pictures of Vishnu as half man and half lion, pictures of the

[21] Ibid., 8.
[22] Ibid.

> deity of the chase, pictures of brute-headed monsters, pictures of the god Krishna, with his legs twisted and twined into postures in which no biped could stand and blowing a cowherd's horn, pictures of Ananthan wearing a thousand cobra-hoods, pictures of gigantic demons, and all these executed with a touch and colouring so coarse as to banish all idea of chiaroscuro, perspective and proportion.[23]

Against this older indigenous mode of visual representation, Menon placed an emergent form of new visuality:

> A taste has set in for pictures, whether in oil or water colours, in which shall be delineated men, beasts, and things according to their true appearance, and the closer that a picture is to nature the greater the honour paid to the artist. Just in the same way, if stories composed of incidents true to ordinary life, and attractively and gracefully written, are once introduced, then by degrees the old order of books, filled with impossible things, will change, yielding place to the new.[24]

Are we to see in this a simple opposition between traditional indigenous practices of stylization and modern, Western norms of realistic representation? The former is shown here not by classical traditions of stylization but by popular prints whose draughtsmanship and colouring are criticized as tasteless and crude. Does this analogy hold in the domain of literature too?

W. Dumergue, then Acting Collector of Malabar District and former Malayalam translator to the Madras Government, was the first to render *Indulekha* into English. His praise for Menon's novel was more than equalled by his outright denigration of literary practices in Malayalam: 'The popular literature, with its unnatural and supernatural paraphernalia, belongs to an age when the human mind was still in a go-cart, its language is as obsolete as the language of *Piers the Plowman*, and as it is without exception founded on the venerable Sanskrit, there is a total absence of originality.'[25] Menon's

[23] Ibid., 10. Translation by W. Dumergue, in Chandu Menon, *Indulekha: A Novel from Malabar*, xiii–xiv, slightly amended.

[24] Ibid., xiv.

[25] Dumergue, 'Translator's Preface', in Chandu Menon, *Indulekha*, vii.

relationship to the poetic culture in Malayalam was very different from Dumergue's. His avid enthusiasm for Kathakali was well known; he shared a close literary friendship with Keralavarma Valiyakoyil Thampuran, a great proponent of the classical strand in Malayalam poetry in his time.[26] Menon, as an enthusiastic reader, inhabited the very poetic tradition that Dumergue rejected as worthless. These differences are obliquely reflected in Dumergue's translation of Menon's Preface: the word 'supernatural' appears twice in the English, once without any warrant from the original and once as the equivalent for *ascharyam* (marvel, wonderment); the word *sadharanam* (common, general, ordinary) in Menon's Malayalam is rendered as 'natural'. Dumergue insistently foregrounds an opposition between the natural and the supernatural (and unnatural) which has religious and colonial-historicist overtones, while Menon's Preface appears more interested in distinguishing the ordinary from the exceptional and differentiating the modes of representation associated with them. The contrast set up between coarsely coloured prints in which figures appear in improbably stylized attitudes and recent watercolours and oil paintings that tastefully depict things as they appear to us—was Raja Ravi Varma in Menon's mind?—ought to be seen against this broad background. The word *swabhavam* (translated by Dumergue as nature) captures the complexities and ambivalences of Menon's aesthetic formulations, pointing variably towards verisimilitude, probability, and innate tendencies, with an eclectic mix of intellectual resources and histories of usage as their background.

Menon's second point in the Preface is about the language of his novel. The word *sadharanam* makes an appearance again. The novel, Menon says, is written in a Malayalam that is ordinarily spoken in Kerala's households. This move challenges the rules of literary language in Malayalam, which were largely derived from Sanskrit. The word *vyutpathi*, of Sanskrit origin, he says, is usually pronounced *vyutpathi*

[26] For accounts of Chandu Menon's life and work, see Moorkothu Kumaran, *Oyyarathu Chandu Menon*; Balakrishnan, *Chandu Menon*; Sankara Menon, *Makers of Indian Literature*; Arunima, 'Glimpses from a Writer's World'.

by Malayalam speakers, and that is how the word will appear in his novel.[27] This deviation from 'correct' pronunciation will appear as a mimetic device in the speech of characters; it will be a part of the novel's linguistic normativity, which conflicts with the protocols of correctness and felicity in literary language. Ordinary, common usage—the *sadharana* form of language—is not merely the object of this new idea of literature; it is literature's very stuff, what it is made of: one might even say that it is the *swabhavam* of the novel. While defining the ordinary language spoken at home, Menon had educated upper-caste Hindus in Malabar in mind. But does the ordinary, even in this restricted sense, displace literary language and fully assume its place in his novel?

The opening chapter of *Indulekha* does keep the promise of a simple, ordinary style of narration. However, at the beginning of the second chapter, when the heroine is about to make her first appearance, the narrator begins to forget the principles announced in the Preface by the author and suddenly adopts an elevated style:

> I confess that it is impossible to describe the joy and the happiness and the fervour and the excitement and the intense desire and the grief that arises in the minds of men when they see Indulekha's complexion which resembles the colour of gold, her teeth which resemble gems, her lips red like coral, her eyes which make dark flowers feel like slaves, her face which has the glow of red lotuses, her dark hair, her heavy breasts, and her slender waist.[28]

The passage sounds like the paraphrase of a verse from a Sanskrit *kavya*—its syntax is modelled on the long and complex sentences of *anvaya-artham* that appeared in print after each stanza of Sanskrit verse in Malayalam prose translations. Its vocabulary and rhetorical tropes also follow Sanskrit poetic conventions, frequently used in Malayalam poetry of the time, which describe female beauty through a series of schematized similes and metaphors. The change in register is aimed at producing an experience of the exceptional,

[27] Chandu Menon, Preface to the first edition, *Indulekha*, 10–11.
[28] Ibid., 25.

and a corresponding sense of wonder and awe. Menon, we saw, had alerted his readers about the impropriety of direct translations from English novels when *srngara rasam* was dominant; the exceptional beauty of the heroine—intimately linked to the production of *srngara rasam* in readers—seems to demand stylization in description. Her body cannot appear in the natural light of everyday perception, or be written of in the ordinary language spoken at home without resulting in a loss of literary decorum; there is a need to place a screen of cultivated language before the gaze of ordinary readers. English novels do not supply the material for this screen; it is the language of poetic formulae, the oft repeated, the schematic, that helps Menon to veil—and make visible—the heroine's body. In fact, this allows him to describe his heroine's body with an explicitness which, without this inflection of the poetic, may have appeared vulgar and indecorous: 'One may say that at this time her breasts had begun to become hard and heavy. Which youth will bear the sight of those pots of gold growing incessantly in their roundness?'[29]

Ammaman Raja, in his novel *Indumatiswayamvaram*, used formulaic descriptions from the *kavya* tradition in their straightforward conventionality:

> Indumati's dark, long and curly hair, exceedingly beautiful forehead, her eyes that give agony to dark water lilies, lips that put ripe red fruit to shame, her lotus face that diminishes the beauty of the full moon, round breasts that stun even the globes of elephants, her slender waist that seems about to break under the weight of her breasts, and her limbs that defeat *sirisha* flowers in softness and *chembakam* flowers in colour—it is impossible to describe the fluctuating emotions that arise in the hearts of young men as they see all this.[30]

The passage draws on the convention of describing the body from head to foot, known as *kesadipadavarnana* or *apadachooda varnana* in the *kavya* tradition. In Komattil Padu Menon's *Lakshmikesavam* (1892), this form of description is found not only in the narrator's

[29] Ibid.
[30] Ammaman Raja, *Indumatiswayamvaram*, 21–2.

initial presentation of the heroine but even in the protagonist Kesavan Unni Nair's inner imaginings.[31] The narrator's presentation of Lakshmi's beauty concludes with a volley of figures of speech like *upama* and *utpreksha*, to despair at the inadequacy of all rhetoric to present her ethereal beauty. Formulaic similes from Sanskrit poetry are paraded to suggest that the leaves of the banyan tree keep trembling because they are excited by the voluptuous beauty of the heroine's hips.[32] Early novelists did not always borrow such images directly from Sanskrit originals; they were available in abundance in Malayalam poems of the times. These formulaic descriptions were attacked by a new generation of English-educated critics such as C. Anthappayi and Thatha Kanaran. 'Malayalam poets think nothing of appropriating, or rather misappropriating the ideas and sentiments of others', wrote Kanaran, 'and the same figures and expressions are repeated over and over again by each successive writer without the slightest acknowledgement or the least compunction.' Kanaran's examples are precisely of the kind that we encountered in the early novels:

> For instance, columns of dust and smoke commenced carrying their complaints to Indra so far back that one might reasonably expect that even the slowest of tribunals had settled their case long ago, but at any rate it is high time indeed they are allowed to rest in peace. The abdominal contour of some beautiful damsel centuries ago had struck terror into the peepul leaves so effectually that they have not yet ceased trembling, though the recent innovations in the female habiliments of the natives of the country obviate all necessity for further anxiety on that score.[33]

Kanaran's criticisms were based on aesthetic norms derived from Western literatures, especially English; interestingly, the early novels in Malayalam, which also looked up to Western literature for their aesthetic models, provided a happy habitat for the formulaic similes and metaphors condemned by him.

[31] Padu Menon, *Lakshmikesavam*, 151.
[32] Ibid., 143.
[33] Kanaran, *A Comparative Study*, 146–7.

The accommodation of poetic cultures in early novels complicates not only Menon's linguistic characterization of the novel, but also his visual analogies. Formulaic poetic descriptions are more in tune with a visual culture of stylization than with a representation of things as they appear. There is a partial justification for their use in the narrator's initial discussion of female beauty and the difficulties of describing it. The narrator accepts as correct the features of female beauty upheld in classical Sanskrit texts; they are appropriate for Indian women, while Western ideals of beauty—upholding a totally different set of features—are right for European women. There is an attempt at formulating a universalistic principle for beauty: it is based on lustre (*sobha*) as well as on the pleasing quality of all features individually and in their togetherness.[34] Indulekha is introduced as foremost among the beautiful women in whom these conditions are fulfilled. While discussing the relativity of beautiful features, the narrator says dark skin, although generally not considered attractive, might appear beautiful in felicitous combination with other features, but quickly interrupts himself to warn readers against thinking even for a moment that Indulekha is of dark complexion. The description of the heroine, in fact, begins with her skin: 'since her skin was of the same colour (*savarnam*) as the golden brocade, no one could tell with certainty where the brocade ended and her body began.'[35] The word *savarnam*, which also means Hindu upper caste, appears like a symptom of the caste underpinnings of the narrator's alacrity. The colour of Indulekha's lips finds its equals only in the lips of European women, the narrator tells us, thus violating his earlier pronouncements on the local embeddedness of ideals of beauty. The description of Indulekha's eyes and breasts shifts focus from the objects to their effect on the viewer: the scorching heat of her glances, the insufferable beauty of her breasts. It is as if the viewer's turbulence makes static contemplation and clear description impossible. In the concluding sentence, attempts to describe the heroine's beauty

[34] Chandu Menon, *Indulekha*, 23–4.

[35] Ibid., 24.

through the subjective experience of the spectator are also given up: it is as if citationality, with its formulaic panegyric centred on features, provides the final screen through which the reader may look at the heroine's beauty without bringing it into the promiscuous proximity of naturalist description. The stimulation and interruption of the reader's voyeurism deftly negotiate a new public visibility of the heroine's body while simultaneously protecting caste propriety and female dignity. Stylized ways of saying—phrases that Thatha Kanaran had condemned for being unimaginative and insincere—come alive as both spur to and brake on the desire for visual pleasures set in motion by the novel's direct prosaic presentation.

Such direct representation in these early novels appears to require, when the object warrants it, a non-naturalist, stylized enhancement which works by interrupting and replacing earlier descriptions even while retaining and drawing on them for its effects. There may be parallels between this and the use of paint in the history of early photography in India. Pinney notes that while European photographers had used paint 'to retouch the negatives and to enhance colour on the final print', many of the Indian instances from the 1860s 'deploy paint as much more than a supplement to the photographic image; rather the overlay of paint completely replaces the photographic image in such a way that all or most of it is obscured.'[36] Paint, in India, thus acquired a new valence and offered a new sort of pleasure on the photographic image, obscuring and transforming it. Similarly, in the early novel, formulaic representations from the *kavya* tradition found a new function: that of interrupting and supplanting naturalistic descriptions and thus spurring a new experience of desire.

III

Stylized, schematic descriptions of female bodies in early novels were not always about formulaic praise. Sometimes they were there to supply cues for reading characters and their inner propensities. The

[36] Pinney, *Camera Indica*, 77–9.

body in such instances turned into a semiological space: it suggested character traits according to a taxonomy of personality types or of emotional states. In Padu Menon's *Lakshmikesavam*, the emotional transformations in the heroine were represented through bodily changes: 'Meenakshi thought, "Her body is fatigued like a tender leaf under the scorching sun. Her breasts do not appear to have any firmness at all. Face resembles the full moon caught in a thin cover of clouds. Even when I fan her, she speaks of feeling warm. Medicines do not have any effect on her."'[37] The withering creeper and weak breasts have their origin in the Sanskrit *kavya* tradition; the passage may have directly derived from a verse in Kalidasa's *Abhijnana Shakuntalam*.[38] Cheruvalathu Chathu Nair's novel *Meenakshi* (1890) incorporated inferences based on *samudrikasastram*, a traditional method for reading bodily signs, into a description of the heroine's physical beauty: 'From the width and the rise of her forehead, anyone familiar with *samudrikasastram* will conclude without a doubt that she is highly intelligent and fortunate.'[39]

Descriptions of this sort create a sense of exteriority in the presentation of characters. Inner propensities are worn on one's body: they take the form of physiognomic characteristics, changes in the body, and recurring expressions on the face. The last necessitates a closer gaze at the individual's face and a description of expressions, and this helps produce a sense of individuation and interiority. Comparing *samudrikvidya* in vernacular print in nineteenth-century India with colonial phrenology, Shruti Kapila suggests that

> [f]undamentally, the point of application for *samudrik* practices of decoding and giving meaning to markers of physical distinction was at the level of the self. In other words, the operative logic was diametrically opposite to that of race and phrenology. In the latter, (individual) skull and other physical materials were representative of a type. For *samudrik*,

[37] Padu Menon, *Lakshmikesavam*, p. 153.

[38] Kalidasa, *Abhijnana Shakuntalam*, scene 3: *Kshamakshamakapolam*, 62. This *sloka* is also cited in *Indulekha*.

[39] Chathu Nair, *Meenakshi*, 74.

> on the other hand, the self or the individual carried unique signifiers and marks of physical distinction that needed to be rendered meaningful. Further, it was the random nature of the presence of signs on the entirety of the body and in relation to the head and face that needed a coherent strategy of interpretations. It was quite unlike the case of phrenology for which the key signifier of distinction, the head or the skull was a fixed one.[40]

We found an attempt at determining the individual through a close reading of the face in *Premamrtam*, although there was no settled taxonomy or code which guaranteed accurate decipherment. In his first novel, *Martandavarma*, C.V.'s descriptions are more closely determined by a schematic orientation. Consider the presentation of the heroine:

> I cannot find a simile for her face, which is slightly elongated and not entirely round. But her eyes display a steadfastness that seems to keep her suitors at a distance. Some may feel that our heroine's beauty is not pure and aesthetic, as the emotions that appear to play on her lips and eyebrows are not seductive. Those who have seen emotions arise on her face in different situations, however, have compared her to holy women like Sita and Draupadi.[41]

C.V. invites the reader to adopt a gaze trained in the significance of bodily features and expressions, but unlike in Padu Menon's novel the description works through differentiation, with some inferences rejected and new types invoked from literary and mythological traditions. Are Sita and Draupadi to be regarded as sources of visual schemata? Is C.V. drawing on visual imaginaries of his own time in the description of the heroine of his historical novel, situated almost two centuries earlier? In any case, his description focuses less on features than on facial expressions, linking them closely to ideas of 'character', for which he sought a typology by referring to mythological heroines. The word *swabhavam*, primarily meaning 'natural disposition', also

[40] Kapila, 'Race Matters', 503.
[41] Raman Pillai, *Martandavarma*, 71.

possesses in Malayalam the sense of 'individual character'. In addition, the dramaturgic idea of character, as a principle of coherence for diverse propensities, actions, and expressions, underlies C.V.'s search for a schematism of characterization. I shall discuss this in greater detail in the next chapter.

Kavyas and puranas were not the only resources used in early novels for a taxonomy of characters. Technologies such as photography, as we have seen, gave rise to the emergence of new schematisms, especially an aesthetic of 'sameness' produced, as Walter Benjamin noted, by the assault of technological reproducibility on a culture of uniqueness.[42] While the photograph documented fleeting moments and testified to the unique identity of individuals (as would become normative for major identification documents), it also nurtured investigations into recurrence and sameness: the use of photography in establishing racial and criminal types in the nineteenth century has been well documented. Photography became an important component of the colonial ethnography of castes and tribes in India, as the images in Edgar Thurston's seven-volume *Castes and Tribes of Southern India* demonstrate.[43]

Potheri Kunjambu's novel *Saraswativijayam* shows an interesting use of the photograph as an indisputable document of identity and source of typification. Towards the end of the novel, Marathan, a Pulaya supposedly murdered by a Namboodiri landlord's Nayar manager, is revealed—years later, at the conclusion of the murder trial—not only to have survived but also to be present in the very courtroom as the presiding judge. His identity is established through a photograph taken by a German missionary, who testifies to its authenticity and explains the circumstances in which it was taken.

> I took that photograph when I was informed that some scholars in England needed to study the physiognomy (*dehaprakrti*) of members of various castes in Kerala. In particular, the man you see in this image had

[42] Benjamin, *The Work of Art*.
[43] Thurston, *Castes and Tribes of Southern India*.

> come to join the Christian faith. If his physiognomy were to undergo some change later, it was necessary to know how much that change would be. These pictures would be very useful in later years for scholars who inquire into the physiognomy and the state of civilization of people from various countries from all over the world. This picture, therefore, was taken and preserved before he was admitted into the Christian faith.[44]

An intriguing passage, not only on account of the way a document of ethnographic intent is turned into the decisive piece of evidence for establishing a singular individual identity; more importantly, the photographer's explanation confuses the discourses of ethnicity, civilization, and religious belonging. The image is made to serve diverse expectations: represent the physiognomy of a caste group in racial terms, to establish relations between stages of civilization and physiognomy, and to help measure the physical changes that might take place over the years after conversion to Christianity! The burden placed on the body and on photographic evidence testifies to the inseparability of questions of religious conversion and caste mobility for the novel's imaginary. The borderlines between bodily features and attire begin to blur in the concept of visual stereotypes for communities. Photography is seen here as a recording device not merely of the empirical but also of the typical, and is endowed with a magical capacity to track transformations in the subject through religious conversion.

Schematic representations of the body were not always directed at the subject in question. In Chandu Menon's description of his heroine, we saw a movement from bodily features to their effect on the viewer: the description of Indulekha's eyes turned into a paean on the erotic power of her glances and their grievous effects on the onlooker. It is not necessary for the woman to intentionally address such potent glances to her victim. The eroticism of the glance is intransitive in its orientation. Chathu Nair's novel *Meenakshi* has a description of its heroine's glances: 'Her eyes were the seats of several gestures of the erotic emotion (*srngaracheshtakal*) which flickered inside her. They

[44] Kunjambu, *Saraswativijayam*, 119.

appeared like containers of some secret medicine for attracting and captivating the minds of valiant men.'[45]

Gestures that produce erotic emotion are neither voluntarily produced nor directed at anyone in particular. Meenakshi's glances are signs of an inner erotic attractiveness; they refer not to an intending consciousness but to taxonomic determinations of female beauty. We saw in the previous chapter that this separation of the individual's singularity from her outer expressions was a prominent feature of traditions of sensual poetry in Malayalam. In the compositions of the Venmani poets the female subject was primarily the source of an overwhelming seductiveness. In *Indulekha*, Madhavan's initial romantic expostulations to Indulekha are couched in the same idiom; the poetry he recites to her during their courtship is very much in the style of *srngara slokangal*.[46] Interestingly, neither of them, in spite of their avid reading of English literature, cites anything from English love poetry.

If the intransitivity of expressions pushes descriptions away from inner intentions, another element adds to their complexity. Since expressions rely on schematic readings for their intelligibility, it is also possible to perform them as pure artifice; they were always shadowed by the possibility of deceptive imitation. If the signs of love and valour could be determined by convention, they could then also be imitated and reproduced at will. The anxiety of the viewing subject of photographs in *Premamrtam* has at its root the fear of the iterability of signs and the possibilities it opens for deception. It is not an accident that disguise comes up repeatedly in many of the early novels. This trope draws on Sanskrit plays, indigenous performance traditions, and Western literature—notably the plays of Shakespeare. In many novels, disguises acquire the same degree of coherence and concreteness as full-fledged characters. This is not surprising, given the reliance of character descriptions on exteriority and the link between

[45] Chathu Nair, *Meenakshi*, 74.

[46] Chandu Menon, *Indulekha*, 37–40.

disguise and performance. The singularity of the individual is at times fleetingly produced in the gaps between the different roles adopted by characters, which are all described in exterior terms. Schematic descriptions, performance routines, and disguises play a vital role in C.V. Raman Pillai's novelistic imaginary. They will return to our attention when we discuss his historical novels in the next chapter.

IV

The regime of bodily descriptions discussed above had important consequences for the articulation of love and erotic desire in the early novel. The connections between these, especially in the upper-caste novels of Malabar, merit consideration against the background of debates around the marital practices of matrilineal castes in the late nineteenth century. *Sambandham* arrangements were regarded by colonial administrators as a form of concubinage and condemned by Nayar reformers as the sexual exploitation of Nayar women by Nambutiri Brahmins. Conceptions of 'primitive' and 'civilized' stages in the history of conjugal institutions, issues of justice in the inheritance of property, and ideas of the 'natural' strength of filial relations dominated these criticisms.[47] The lack of constraints on annulling conjugal arrangements and on substituting one partner with another were seen by both colonial and reformist critiques as the morally inadmissible core of *sambandham* relations. Chandu Menon, as a member of the Malabar Marriage Commission, formally disagreed with the recommendations for change that eventually led to the Malabar Marriage Act of 1896, arguing that the *sambandham* practices prevalent among the Nayars in Malabar were actually forms of marriage, and their invalidation by the state through a marriage act would be offensive to the customs of the community and destructive of its sense of 'nationality'.[48] *Indulekha*, written just two years before

[47] See Arunima, *There Comes Papa*; Kodoth, 'Courting Legitimacy'.

[48] See 'Appendix IV: Chandu Menon's Memorandum to the Malabar Marriage Commission', in Chandu Menon, *Indulekha*, 248–62.

his memorandum to the commission, makes a powerful attempt to interpret native custom as being in tune with modern Western conceptions of matrimony and monogamy. The heroine of the novel makes a strong argument for the autonomy customarily enjoyed by Nayar women, and claims that her community's matrilineal practices actually resulted in an enhancement and not a weakening of the respect for chastity among Nayar women.

Suri Namboodiripad, the profligate Brahmin of innumerable loveless *sambandhams* in *Indulekha*, represents the economy of decadent desire against which the novel pitches the values of monogamous romantic love. The object of Suri's sexual desire keeps changing: he begins by desiring Indulekha, shifts his attentions to Indulekha's mother Lakshmikkutty, and then to her maid Ammu, before finally fixing them on Indulekha's poor cousin Kalyanikkutty. There is an important conversation on the nature of erotic desire between Suri and his friend Cherussery, an erudite Nambutiri Brahmin who is favourably contrasted with Suri in several respects. In response to Suri's contention that the end justifies all means adopted for the realization of sexual desire, Cherussery proposes a distinction between *agraham* (wish, desire) and *bhramam* (madness, passion), the word which Suri uses to denote sexual desire. Cherussery says: 'I do not understand well what you mean by *bhramam*. If you mean *agraham* by this, when a man realizes that the woman [he desires] does not reciprocally feel such *agraham* towards him, he ought to conquer his desire by his will and relinquish his wish for sensual enjoyment with that woman.'[49] Suri, innocently lascivious, is perplexed by this ethical burden: 'Why should one relinquish one's desire? Shouldn't I try and see if the woman can be obtained?' Cherussery corrects him. 'What one needs to try and find out', he says, 'is not if a woman can be obtained [for sexual gratification], but whether love can arise in her.'[50]

Cherussery's distinction between *agraham* and *bhramam* is based on the principle of reciprocity: the legitimate space for *agraham* is

[49] Ibid., 167.
[50] Ibid.

reciprocal desire. If the object of your desire does not desire you in return, your *agraham* becomes illegitimate and its realization impossible. Suri is bewildered by this argument—why should one abandon one's desires merely for lack of reciprocation? Cherussery's answer elevates reciprocity as the essential marker of a distinctively human experience of desire:

> For a man to say that he has had the enjoyment of a woman (*streesukham*), he would have to have pleased (*sukhippichittu*) her erotically (*ramippichu*). It is from giving erotic pleasure (*ramippikkunnatil*) to a woman and from knowing that she is having erotic pleasure (*ramichu sukhikkunnu*) that a man should derive his own experience of pleasure (*sukhanubhavam*). Similarly, a woman can say that she has enjoyed (*sukhichu*) herself with a man only if she gives him erotic pleasure (*ramippichu sukhippichal*). For this experience of enjoyment to be fully and reciprocally possible, an intense mutual sentiment of love (*anuragam*) needs to be present. Those who seek the [sexual] enjoyment of a woman (*streesukham*) in any other way are like animals—even if they obtained their aim, they would have only performed some antics with each other.[51]

Sexual desire in its human vocation is for Cherussery predicated on a mutual mirroring of recognition and gratification. *Agraham* essentially seeks another *agraham*. As in Kojève's Hegel, the true object of desire is always and only another desire.[52]

Agraham, in this model, obliges the subject to withdraw from situations where it does not find reciprocity: its economy is marked by a will that discriminates and controls itself. This approach to desire chimes with an earlier moment in the novel where, in a conversation with Madhavan, Indulekha denies the very possibility of unattainable desire: her mind, she says, possesses a natural ability not to set its desires (*agraham*) on unattainable objects. She claims this to be an innate attribute of her mind rather than a result of external control or conscious self-disciplining. Indulekha offers the example of romantic desire: 'I am a young woman. I see a handsome young man. Before

[51] Ibid., 167–8.

[52] Kojève, *An Introduction to the Reading of Hegel*, 5.

my mind determines whether he is fit to be my husband it does not invest itself in that man. Here it is not as if my mind gets invested first and then I free it with my will [*dhairyam*, literally "courage"]. My mind does not invest itself in him to begin with.'[53]

Indulekha goes a step ahead of Cherussery by placing discrimination and restraint at the very origin of desire: it is as if *agraham* is by its very nature self-reflective. Restraint from the start rather than a suppression of already existing desires; the inception of desire presupposes a prior, instinctive discrimination and orientation. In *Indulekha*'s erotic ethics, the opposite of *agraham* is *bhramam*, the very word used by Suri Namboodiripad for erotic desire. *Bhramam* in Malayalam, derived from Sanskrit *bhram*, signifies a turbulent, uncontrolled state of mind. It is often used in situations where a character subject has 'lost his/her head' and entered a state of intense attachment or infatuation, be it with an object, an activity, or a person. In this it displays its generic affinities with madness or *chitthabhramam*. The word *bhramam* appears with striking regularity in essays and stories in Malayalam in the late nineteenth century. 'Kesari' Vengayil Kunjuraman Nayanar, with characteristic humour, identified *vasana*, *bhramam*, and *bhrantu* as three gradations of the same affliction of the mind: while *vasana* is a positive aptitude for and interest in a certain object or activity, *bhramam* is a contagious obsession which spreads through imitation. It can take any form, ranging from *kathakalibhramam* (passion for Kathakali) and *streebhramam* (for women) to *udyogabhramam* (for government employment) and *parishkarabhramam* (for new fashions).[54] Much of the discussion of *bhramam* in late-nineteenth-century Kerala stresses its link to colonial modernity, and is critical of the unreflective imitation of English ways. In *Indulekha*, however, *bhramam* is associated with decadent tradition; it is what the new subject eschews.

[53] Chandu Menon, *Indulekha*, 32. The word that has been translated as 'invest' is *praveshikkuka*, which literally means 'enter'.

[54] Nayanar, 'Bhramam', 54–6.

In Indulekha's ideal of a natural discrimination working at the very origin of desire, we can find the diametrical opposite of *bhramam*'s anarchy. Even after recognizing her desire for Madhavan, Indulekha is shown as denying any expression to those feelings until his examination results come in and marriage becomes a clear possibility between them. This is no cold calculation; her feelings are presented as even more intense than Madhavan's, since she contains them within herself, denying them all expression.[55] The stress on self-restraint does not mean an ascetic denial of the sensual; desire, in the appropriate circumstances, does not shy away from sensual gratification. The physical attraction and erotic enjoyment of young lovers are indicated in many early novels, resulting at times in some tension between the language of self-restraint and the display of erotic acts. When Indulekha finally acknowledges her desire, her words combine unrestrained gestures of physical intimacy with a declaration of conjugal commitment:

> Indulekha, suddenly overwhelmed by an irrepressible rush of intense grief and love, went to the couch, joined Madhavan's handsome face to her own moon-like countenance, and with a long sigh, gave a kiss on his lips.
>
> 'My husband, the lord of my life! Why do you grieve like this? It is two years now since in my mind I accepted you as my husband. My body and my mind are all yours to rule. . . My mind has never desired anyone but you; nor will it ever!' Saying this, she lay on Madhavan's chest for a minute. Wiped his tears with her hand. Then got up.[56]

We must recall Chandu Menon's reluctance to translate English novels directly into Malayalam, especially those moments where *srngara rasam* dominates. His attempt here is to sketch a declaration of love in which the daring representation of the woman's kiss is balanced by the formal, marital—even if impassioned—register of the declaration. The kiss acquires a new symbolic value as the signal performative

[55] Chandu Menon, *Indulekha*, 37, 39.
[56] Ibid., 51.

of conjugal acceptance. C.V. Raman Pillai's *Premamrtam* satirically identifies the kiss as the gesture of love par excellence in the 'English tradition', indicating its derivation from English novels: 'She moved as if she wanted to wriggle out of his embrace, muttering something. He thought that she was saying something about the ignoble background of her family. "O, you don't obey?" he said, "All right, let me make you mine, register you as mine, and put brakes on your freedom." Saying this Kartha gave her a kiss, that seal or sign of love allowed in the English tradition.'[57]

The use of the legal metaphor of registration is not an accident; *Indulekha* and *Premamrtam* were written at a time when the legal registration of Nayar marriages was actively debated in Malabar and Travancore. Romantic desire in the early novels, mostly written by Nayar novelists, finds its most intense, definitive expressions in a marital, institutional vocabulary. Heroines, at the ecstatic moment of a declaration of love, apostrophize their beloved as 'husband'. In *Lakshmikesavam,* when the heroine wakes from a dream about her lover, she cries, '*Ayyo,* the lord of my life (*prananatha*), where have you gone? My dear husband (*bhartavu*)!'[58] In *Meenakshi* the heroine refers to her beloved as her husband much before their marriage is fixed.[59] The new discourse of romantic love in the early novel suggests not only that marriages need to be founded on autonomous desire but also that desire ought to be institutionally oriented: it should find marriage as its proper locus, as both its horizon of possibility and its *telos.*

Satires on the new routines of romance in the early novel treat them as derived from English: 'He uttered the English word for *priye,*'[60] the narrator of *Premamrtam* tells us once. One of the characters says: 'The situation that English authors eloquently speak of as "love" has enveloped me.'[61] Kizhakkeppatt Raman Kutty Menon's

[57] Raman Pillai, *Premamrtam*, 151.

[58] Padu Menon, *Lakshmikesavam*, 150.

[59] Chathu Nair, *Meenakshi*, 271.

[60] Ibid., 149.

[61] Ibid., 118.

Parangodi Parinayam, a scathing parody of early novels in Malayalam, shows its heroine grooming herself according to the conventions of English romantic novels, preferring courtship to actual marriage.[62] The example of a *bhramam* for emulating modern, Western routines!

These satiric exaggerations nonetheless touch upon an important aspect of early Nayar novels: the bodily gestures and speech of the new, educated woman were meant to exceed conventional semiologies of female body types and emotional states derived from *kavya* literature and suggest a new, schematic order of acts and utterances. *Indulekha* linked its idealized heroine with an education that brought together all that was good in both English and Sanskrit traditions; they inculcated in her both autonomy and deference to customary propriety:

> When she was about three years old, her uncle [. . .] Kochukrishna Menon, who was well-versed in various skills such as Sanskrit, English and music and who was employed as a Diwan Peshkar at a salary of eight hundred rupees, took Indulekha with him to where he worked and educated her till the age of sixteen. English was taught very well. Sanskrit was taught till the [advanced] level of drama and poetics (*natakalankarangal*). In music, she was trained to sing [in the Indian classical style] up to *pallavi* and *ragavistaram* as well as to play the piano, fiddle and veena with felicity. Further, the uncle also arranged for his extremely beautiful niece to be familiarized with embroidery and drawing in which European women are trained. One may say that Kochukrishna Menon realized to a great extent his desire to provide Indulekha, by the time she was sixteen, with the skills, knowledge and conduct that a girl in England would be educated in.[63]

While Madhavan wears Western clothes and goes hunting, he also keeps a long tuft of hair and ties it in the manner of his caste; even as Indulekha plays the piano and reads English novels, she has not abandoned the ways of being of a 'Malayali woman': 'she is totally unaffected by atheism or hatred for Hindu religion or that contempt towards one and all which unfortunately is often found among

[62] Raman Kutty Menon, *Parangodi Parinayam*, 218–69.
[63] Chandu Menon, *Indulekha*, 25–6.

educated youth.'[64] Interestingly, as we saw, English novels and English poetry do not figure as a discursive resource in the love talk between protagonists. Indulekha and Madhavan never discuss novels or poems in English but do read parts of *Shakuntalam* to each other and use it as a code for romantic banter. [65] In the famous eighteenth chapter, Madhavan summarizes, for the benefit of his father, arguments by English writers, especially on religion, but these readings do not make an appearance in his conversations with Indulekha.

In an important sense, English education in these novels is not really about the English language. When Kesavan listens to Lakshmi singing in the Indian style, he is 'overcome by so many different emotions', and, as the song comes to an end, the first question he addresses to her father is whether she has had an English education. When the father replies in the affirmative, Lakshmi and Kesavan exchange glances and smile furtively at each other, as if they know each other's minds.[66] Both Suri and Panchu Menon regard Indulekha's English education with some trepidation: they see it as making it difficult for them to infer her intentions from what she says, and to control her. Panchu Menon feels she is speaking in English even when she is responding to some of his questions in plain Malayalam. What he identifies as English is not words or sentences, but the arguments, and, more importantly, the way in which Indulekha inserts herself into language as a subject. What is at issue is an education in modernity; or rather modernity as education.

Education crops up as the dominant metaphor for reform and self-making in most of these early novels. However, seeing English education as a new styling of the self which enables a new relationship to tradition—making possible a new way of owning and inhabiting it—seems to be a feature of the upper-caste—especially

[64] Ibid., 26.

[65] There are hardly any references to the English novel in *Indulekha*, although Indulekha's novel reading is alluded to in Panchu Menon's bizarre summary of a 'false story' she narrated to him and to Govinda Menon's recommendation of a novel to her. Ibid., 71.

[66] Padu Menon, *Lakshmikesavam*, 149.

the Nayar—novels we considered above. We can see another strand among the early novels which focused on lower-caste life, primarily in the context of conversion to Christianity. Some of them, like Joseph Mooliyil's *Sukumari*, were written by lower-caste converts, while others, such as Potheri Kunjambu's *Saraswativijayam*, highlighted caste oppression via a plot in which conversion to Christianity offered possibilities of survival and redemption.[67] In *Sukumari*, education is essentially a matter of instruction in religion: the new self is formed by religion, and part of this education is considered primarily as the acquisition of skills—the ability to read and write, to understand new forms of knowledge, and proficiency in arithmetic. In fact, *Sukumari* voices a critique of state-supported English education as a substitute for religious instruction: without teaching religious virtue, English education will merely prompt an imitation of English manners and a consumption of English goods.[68] Unlike in the Nayar novels, English education does not lead here to a new corporeal and discursive styling of the erotic subject, especially the woman.

The new styles that Nayar novels proposed for their heroines had two important consequences. Firstly, they produced an effect of the possession of autonomy among female protagonists, manifest in the reorientation of their desires through a restraining interior agency. Secondly, this very sense of autonomy caused anxiety among male suitors, who perceived the inner self of the desired woman as obscure and inaccessible. Romantic gestures and declarations of love, and even their institutionalization in conjugal contracts, do not fully eliminate anxieties over the very autonomy of the woman which made her the object of male desire in the early novel. In *Indulekha*, when Madhavan receives false intelligence of Indulekha's wedding to Suri, he oscillates between belief and disbelief. The two conflicting inclinations prove, on a closer look, to be linked to the two ways of understanding desire in the conversation between Suri and Cherussery, discussed earlier: '"Perhaps that is what the female

[67] See Kunjambu, *Saraswativijayam*; Mooliyil, *Sukumari*.
[68] Mooliyil, *Sukumari*, 330.

mind is . . . Perhaps Suri is cleverer and more interesting than I am. Perhaps Indulekha was infatuated (*bhramicchirikkam*) . . .", he would think and then immediately he would [correct himself] . . . "Will my Madhavi ever desire (*kamkshikkumo*) another man? What a fool am I? . . ."'[69]

Such novels bore conflicting marks of a transition in thinking about the body and individuated desire. The difficulty that Chandu Menon faced in translating the language of love from the English novel is accompanied by an attempt on the part of the novelists discussed to elaborate a new, more appropriate language of love where the presentation of the body does not fully abandon schematic description. At the same time, these novels try to subordinate this description of the body to notions of an internal will and individual desire, both of which find their natural and true vocation in being oriented institutionally towards monogamous marriage. The complex exchange between two impulses remained unresolved in the early novels discussed above. However, these economies pertain primarily to the Nayar reform novels: ambiguities and tensions about bodily desire are not central to Ezhava anti-caste novels such as *Saraswativijayam*, and to novels of Christian conversion such as *Sukumari*. Bodily desire is peripheral to the projects of self-fashioning in them. While *Saraswativijayam* concludes with the heroine wedded to the Pulaya judge, the novel does not even sketch the growth of their romantic involvement or affective intimacy. Autonomous marital choice is important in *Sukumari*, but its idioms—of life partner and helpmeet—are resolutely kept away from the intensities of erotic longing.

V

Early novels in Malayalam drew on tensions between various ways of showing and seeing—of describing and interpreting—not solely in the portrayal of female subjects and erotic relations; they used them, more

[69] Chandu Menon, *Indulekha*, 189.

importantly, to differentiate between subjects on the basis of their perceptual relations to the world they inhabited. In *Indulekha* we find Kesavan Nambutiri, an underconfident and somewhat unremarkable Brahmin, fascinated by the modern world and describing a new kind of object:

> Siva, Siva, Narayana, Narayana! What can I say! The cleverness of these white men is truly astounding. Lakshmi, you will be amazed if you see it. What a marvel! The spinning mill that we hear so much about is actually an iron wheel. This wheel makes all the yarn. And what turns this wheel? Smoke, pure smoke! But this smoke does not hurt our eyes like in our kitchens. The factory has a long tail raised upwards, like the flagpole in a temple. They say it is for the smoke to pass, but I have my doubts. There must be some trick inside it. That these clever white men will not reveal.[70]

The factory is for him a new, illegible object, a locus of obscurity and concealment. This tricky thing can be tamed only through a process of reading, which translates it into familiar, legible signs and produces a world of stable objects and meanings: 'Smoke is a very potent substance. Does the smoke of ritual offering (*homam*) not have power? I have another doubt. I suspect this is also a *homam* for some deity. Perhaps some idols or *chakras* are kept inside the flagpole. Who knows? Perhaps the deity likes this *homam* very much and the factory turns because of its blessing. God alone knows!'[71] In *Indulekha*, as in many other early novels, the inaccuracy or inappropriateness of such translations becomes a source of humour. The reader is invited to laugh not merely at the characters' ignorance of facts, but also at the farcical floundering by men and women used to older ways of living when they encounter incongruous new objects and incompatible modern spaces.[72]

[70] Chandu Menon, *Indulekha*, 79.

[71] Ibid., 80.

[72] Kizhakkeppatt Raman Kutty Menon's *Parangodi Parinayam* (1892), which parodies the emerging formulae of the new genre of the novel, represents this incongruous object in the figure of a white man riding a

The satiric representation of Suri Namboodiripad in *Indulekha* is pivoted on his misdirected translation of an unfamiliar world: he reads the polite gestures of a modern, Western sociability as sure signs of an extreme, delectable promiscuity. Suri has two white acquaintances whom he calls, in hilarious approximation of their original names, 'Meghadantan' and 'Makshaman'.[73] When 'Makshaman' introduces his wife to Suri, she extends her arm to shake hands with him: 'Madamma sayippu held my hand—goose pimples rose all over my body . . . I held her hand for a very long time. I found her figure very enjoyable. Makshaman, that fool, stood close by, observing all this with a smile.'[74] The distance between the Englishwoman's gestures and Suri's reading of them stands for the distance between two modes of seeing and reading—of visibility and legibility. The same objects, bodies, and gestures may appear to two different kinds of subjects as occupying two widely divergent but equally coherent and meaningful worlds. For new objects or gestures (the factory; the white woman's handshake) to become legible, for them to possess value or meaning, they need to be made part of a world of coherent relations that can be imagined or assumed as existing. This is indeed what Suri and Kesavan Nambutiri are trying to do. They are placed at the receiving end of these jokes, but one never knows who has the last laugh: Kesavan Nambutiri has astutely bought shares of the spinning mill, and his capitalist entrepreneurship throws a different light on his seeming ignorance of the way machines work. Suri gifts the Madamma a ring and incorporates her into his imaginary erotic-affective circuits of patronage; he has met with no success in similar moves with Indulekha and her mother. Objects and practices, in changing times, are enmeshed in contradictory circuits of exchange: of material and symbolic value. Ambivalence and contamination in

---

horse, which is mistaken to be a fiendish, centaur-like figure. See Raman Kutty Menon, *Parangodi Parinayam*, 229.

[73] Chandu Menon, *Indulekha*, 93–4, 104.

[74] Ibid., 93–4.

these systems constitute the novel's conditions of possibility; at the same time, they threaten the coherence of circuits of value in the novel, inducing attempts at control and resolution.

Collections of objects, organized by personal taste as in private collections of individuals or by disciplinary knowledge as in modern museums, directly thematize issues of coherence and value. *Indulekha* presents two kinds of collections. The first is Suri's personal collection of valuable objects, all gold and silver, which he prepares to carry with him on his visit to Indulekha's house: 'On a table was spread out about fifteen golden shawls, about twenty special *mundu*, several rings, a box made of solid silver with a gold handle on the lid, betel-leaf rolls made of gold, a silver jug, silver lamps, silver jars, a gold watch which can be worn as a necklace with a gold chain . . .'[75] By contrast, the novel also speaks of 'English sorts of objects, beautifully collected' in Indulekha's rooms.[76] They form part of the discursive elaboration of a new space of a modern cultivation and style in the early novel, especially in the description of the rooms of educated Nayar men in Malabar or in Madras. Round tables, reclining chairs, painted mirrors, embroidered covers, glass lamps, carpets, and, as mentioned already, in the centre glass cupboards of books in English and in Sanskrit, beautifully bound and embossed with golden lettering—all these objects conjure a new world of coherence, a universe of new civility and new values.[77] The distinction between these worlds is made not merely in terms of discrete objects and their mutual connections, but in terms of the owner's and viewer's relationship to them. Both collections, Suri's gold and the educated Nayar's ornamental objects and books, are marks of distinction in Bourdieu's sense of the term.[78] For Suri, his golden objects are valuable possessions, available only to rich people; the educated Nayar's urban objects are signs of taste as

[75] Ibid., 102.

[76] Ibid., p. 26.

[77] Chathu Nair, *Meenakshi*, 41. See also Padu Menon, *Lakshmikesavam*, 131–2.

[78] Bourdieu, *Distinction*.

well as expendable wealth, obtainable only through cultivation and worldly success.

The treatment of attire in *Indulekha* is a point of entry here. Suri's clothes are chosen according to a sign system where gold is the original and paradigmatic emblem of all value:

> As soon as the palanquin reached the front courtyard, Kesavan Nambutiri opened its door. Immediately, a golden form jumped out. Yes, it was truly an idol in gold, a golden statue. Head covered in a gold cap, body covered in a gold shirt and gold-coloured dhoti, gold-gilded slippers on the feet, gold rings on all ten fingers, on top of all a golden shawl thrown over the shirt and a gold-cased mirror in the hand to look at oneself. Gold, gold, all gold. What can I say about the glow when [Suri] Namboodiri stepped out from the palanquin into the mid-day sun. Around him in a one-metre circle the glare of the sun turned yellow, acquiring a golden glow.[79]

Indulekha's clothes, predictably, provide a contrast by expressing a taste that turns away from ostentatious display to signify simple elegance:

> Indulekha was not very fond of jewellery. Her mother, grandmother, or uncle had to plead hard to make her wear some ornament as an exception on festive days . . . However, although not overtly fond of jewellery, Indulekha took particular interest in her clothes. *Onnara* and *melmundu* with special weave and gold border had to be kept ready, white and clean, every morning and evening when she bathed. She was always seen with a white *melmundu* with gold border covering her breasts.[80]

Against the dominance of gold in Suri's attire is placed the gold border on Indulekha's elegantly clean white clothes (a gold border indistinguishable from her skin in colour). They suggest wealth and aesthetic discrimination, respectively. It is not that Suri does not have any aesthetic claims: he likes to recite Sanskrit *sloka*s and displays an obsessive enthusiasm for Kathakali. However, the novel

[79] Chandu Menon, *Indulekha*, 108.

[80] Ibid., 26–7.

discredits these claims: Suri can neither remember the Sanskrit verses accurately nor understand their meaning. His passion for Kathakali or ***kathakalibhranthu*** (literally, Kathakali madness), although admitted to an extent by the narrator, is mocked by Indulekha as mere ***bhranthu*** (madness), a semantic kin of ***bhramam***. The arbitration of aesthetic taste, even in traditional art forms, is ultimately vested in modern subjects. When Panchu Menon finds his grand-niece Indulekha reclining on a couch and reading Kalidasa's *Shakuntalam*, the conversation serves primarily to provoke laughter at the old man's ignorance of the basics of printing technology.[81]

The presentation of objects in early novels is largely about their status as props for self-fashioning. Familiarity with new objects—the ability to use them rather than merely look at them in wonder—and the conversion of possessions into expressions of their owner's interior qualities are marks of distinction that identify the new subjects being endorsed. Yet these novels do not entirely give up the use of idioms of the marvellous in relation to new objects. In fact, the narrator often invites the reader to marvel at this new world of people and objects. We have encountered the painted mirrors and chairs and clocks that crowd the living rooms of educated Nayars who live in the regional metropolis of Madras. Madhavan's travels to Bombay and Calcutta become occasions for the release of the marvellous. The description of the Bombay port occasions a narrative abandon that can only be compared to the description of Indulekha's body when she makes her first appearance in the novel.[82] Such passages offer an indulgence in visual excess, a feast for the senses rather than a discerning reading of the objects presented. This reaches its culmination in the description of Babu Govinda Sen's bungalow, appropriately called Amaravati, in Calcutta, which produces the longest and most exuberant of descriptions. It concludes with an admission of inadequacy by the narrator, recalling the earlier confession of inadequacy in the des-

[81] Ibid., 76.
[82] Ibid., 199–201.

cription of Indulekha's beauty: 'As I do not have the eloquence to convey the nature of all the objects seen thus by Madhavan in Amaravati Bungalow, I shall now be brief. I can only say that Madhavan, on seeing the balconies, ponds, pearled couches, libraries and gardens depicted above, experienced immense joy. He felt as if he had been transported from this earth to the heaven or some such place full of comforts that he had never experienced before.'[83] The narrator also provides a scale to help Malayali readers imagine the inconceivable wealth possessed by Babu Govinda Sen, and thus overcome the limits of their provincial experience:

> In this book I have referred to Panchu Menon and [Suri] Namboodiripad as 'hugely wealthy' and have called Namboodiripad 'Kubera' in one or two places. I have also spoken of Babu Govinda Sen as hugely wealthy and as a Kubera. But my readers should not think that they are all at the same level in the wealth they possess. There is a huge difference between a Kubera in Bengal and a Kubera in the Madras state. This difference can be understood by gauging their wealth. A person who has possessions worth five lakhs of rupees would be considered a very wealthy person in Madras. In Bengal, such five-lakh people would be regarded as the fourth-class among the rich. There people with five crores would be very wealthy. To refer to someone unhesitantly as 'hugely rich' or as a Kubera, he would need to have wealth amounting to more than fifteen crores. Govinda Sen and his younger brother Chitra Prasad Sen were at the top of the rich who possessed more than fifteen crores.[84]

In this comparative chart of wealth as worth, one may see signs of another pedagogy, to train the subject to move from the native provincial backwardness of Malabar to the urban headquarters in Madras, and then to Calcutta, the capital of colonial India. The apprenticeship of the subject, however, is less a matter of economics than that of affect, a training in what to marvel at and how much. Suri Nambutiri's fascination with gold for its monetary value is

[83] Ibid., 207.
[84] Ibid., 209–10.

discredited; but money in modern circulations of exchange possesses not only economic but also symbolic value. The large numbers invoked here function less as accurate estimates of wealth than as harbingers of wonder. The modern world is not characterized solely by disenchantment and a secular, sceptical mode of perception. It is also a source of enchantment. It is not through a single idiom, but through divergent and at times conflicting frames, that the world is made available for perception in the novel.

An instance in *Indulekha* illustrates this well. Madhavan's sense of shock when he hears the rumour that Indulekha has married Suri Namboodiri, is described not once, but twice, in the novel. The two accounts use strikingly divergent tropes that derive from distinct worlds of discourse: 'As he listened to this, Madhavan immediately understood the matter. Not only in his mind but all over his body, he felt a sense of shock or an intense pain, as if he had touched the electric box called the battery when that machine is turned on.'[85] This is soon followed by the following exchange:

> Madhavan: Is what I heard just now about Madhavi right?
> Sankara Sastrikal: Yes.
>
> The word 'yes' was like a thunderbolt; it was the very fire of lightning. Madhavan's face and his body turned ashen, burnt-out. Like the deformation of Nala when the serpent Karkodaka bit him, one might say.[86]

The relations between the two descriptions cannot be easily understood as complementarity or contrast: one description does not complete the other to form a whole, nor does one negate the other to propose a more adequate account. The descriptions present two discontinuous discursive worlds: their coherence is produced only through the novel's act of juxtaposition. The space inhabited by these divergent representations defines the emergent genre of the novel. These early novels produced a new field of perception and enunciation

[85] Ibid., 189.
[86] Ibid., 190.

precisely through unresolved diversities. They reveal no simple concatenation of the indigenous and the colonial, or the traditional and the modern; they produce a new discursive space where ideas and tropes from varied resources—from Sanskrit *kavyas* to English political treatises—acquire vernacular contemporaneity.

We began this chapter by looking at the configuration of visibility. Conditions of perception and orientation in relation to the world in the works discussed serve as a major trope for exploring a new placement for the subject. The complex and uncertain nature of these conditions offered the novel one of its most fertile resources. The unsteady luminosity within which characters negotiate their apprehension of the world is not a deficiency, a failure to achieve an ideal transparency; it is a productive device from which the fictional world of early novels, with its fragile integrity and imprecise boundaries, emerges. This also gives us an insight into the internally inconsistent language of these novels: their value does not come from a status of anticipatoriness and backwardness in relation to the full-fledged languages of representation found in later novels. They reveal to us a discursive economy in its own right, where language, in its inner diversity and dissonance, offers a new site for depicting and describing people, objects, and emotions. Technologies of seeing and saying devised in them show a space being created within public literary language for articulating the subject's reflective relationship to worldly experience and inhabitation.

5

Sovereignty and Mourning

C.V. Raman Pillai and Fiction's Performance of the Past

THE NOVELS DISCUSSED IN THE previous chapter highlighted the newness of their time. Through hybrid and unstable arrangements of sight and language, they brought for literary enjoyment new experiences, objects, emotions, and people. Newness is paradigmatic for the sense of contemporaneity in these novels: their imaginaries often overtook the everyday worlds shared by their readers and authors. When Chandu Menon published *Indulekha*, there was a widespread feeling that no Nayar woman with Indulekha's accomplishments existed in the society of the time.[1] In these novels,

[1] However, Chandu Menon argued that many Nayar women did possess Indulekha's diverse qualities. He wrote to Dumergue: 'The only thing which my readers might reasonably take exception to is Indulekha's knowledge of English; but as one of my objects in writing this book is to illustrate how a young Malayalee woman, possessing, in addition to her natural personal charms and intellectual culture, a knowledge of the English language would conduct herself in matters of supreme interest to her, such as the choosing of a partner in life, I have thought it necessary that my Indulekha should be conversant with the richest language of the world.' Chandu Menon's letter to W. Dumergue, 19 December 1889, published in Chandu Menon, *Indulekha*,19–25.

contemporaneity is experienced as a sort of untimeliness; it gestures towards a dimension of the present that has surpassed chronology.

In this chapter we turn to a different figure of untimeliness, invoked now under the sign of the past. C.V. Raman Pillai's three major novels introduced new and complex ways of staging the past, placing an affective, talismanic invocation of history at the core of processes through which political subjectivities were fashioned and endorsed during his age. This, we shall see, introduced a distinct dimension to idioms of self-articulation in Malayalam writing. Speaking about oneself began to involve acts of possessing, owning up, and thematizing a dimension of the past which was integral to the sense of location and selfhood. As in the previous chapter, techniques of fictional narration were vital to the forging of a language in which one could express one's inhabitation of historical time. C.V. Raman Pillai's novels, with their complex layering of the past and intricate use of performative and narrative forms, allow us to address this important chapter in our story.

C.V. Raman Pillai, popularly referred to as C.V., was born in Trivandrum in 1858 and had a traditional early education which included Sanskrit and Ayurveda. He went on to the Maharaja's College, Trivandrum, for his Bachelor's degree, where he came under the influence of his teachers, especially the Scotsman John Ross. C.V. became thoroughly conversant with English letters in addition to gaining mastery over the literature, folklore, and traditional performing arts of Travancore. He left home for travel, stayed in Hyderabad during a period of emotional turbulence, and is said to have developed close friendships with a number of Muslim families there. After his return to Trivandrum he worked as a superintendent at the Government Press. His first novel, *Martandavarma*, was published in 1891, though it has been claimed that an earlier draft version was completed years before. He did not write another novel for the next two decades but was active, often behind the scenes, in contemporary campaigns around Malayali and Nayar identities. The distinction between these two political signs was not very sharp over the period because the Nayars saw themselves as historically the leaders of native communities.[2] C.V. played a major role in drafting the Malayali Memorial petition submitted to the Maharaja of Travancore in 1891. He wrote political essays, mostly under pseudonyms, in newspapers in English and Malayalam during this time. He wrote two sequels to *Martandavarma*—*Dharmaraja* was published in 1913, and *Ramaraja Bahadur* in 1918–19. He also wrote the satirical social novel *Premamrtam* (1914), and several farces (*prahasanam*), some of which were staged in Trivandrum. He died in 1922.[3]

C.V.'s three major novels—*Martandavarma, Dharmaraja*, and *Ramaraja Bahadur*—are read as a trilogy on major political events from the eighteenth century, a crucial period in the history of Travancore marked by the reign of two powerful kings, Anizham Tirunal Martandavarma (*r.* 1729–58) and Karthika Tirunal Ramavarma (*r.* 1758–98). The novels were named after these kings: Ramavarma Raja was referred to as 'Dharmaraja' to highlight his moral uprightness, and 'Ramaraja Bahadur' was one of his honorific titles. It may be short-sighted, however, to regard these three novels as segments of a dynastic saga. It was probably in the long gap between *Martandavarma* and the two later novels that C.V.'s fictional project took final shape. He regarded *Dharmaraja* and *Ramaraja Bahadur* as the first two volumes of a trilogy whose actual theme—in spite of the prominence of the maharajas in the title—was the life of Raja Kesavadas, the renowned Dewan of Travancore during the reign of Ramavarma Raja. C.V. did not live to complete the final novel of

[2] Some scholars have made a distinction between the political thinking of C.V. and C. Krishna Pillai, the other major leader of the Nayar campaigns. They argue that while C.V.'s conception of the Malayali was more inclusive, with the Nayars occupying the position of leader-protectors of all native communities within this frame, C. Krishna Pillai stressed a Nayar rather than Malayali identity, anticipating the competitive consolidation of caste communities in later years. See Balakrishnan Nair, *Sakshal C.V.* Also Vinod Chandran, 'The Counter Narratives of Power and Identity'.

[3] For a biography of C.V. Raman Pillai, see Parameswaran Nair, *C.V. Raman Pillai*.

the trilogy which, it is believed, was to deal with Raja Kesavadas' last days and tragic end.[4]

The author's preface in *Martandavarma* began by stating that the book was 'made with the intention of producing in Malayalam a model of the narrative form in English called "historical romance".'[5] The influence of Walter Scott, especially *Ivanhoe*, and Bankim Chandra Chatterjee's *Durgeshanandini* has been noted. Generic antecedents aside, C.V.'s vital sources were all from closer home. Published and unpublished histories of Travancore, literary works such as Ramapurattu Variar's celebrated poem *Kuchelavrttam Vanchippattu*, Devarajakavi's Sanskrit play *Balamartandavijayam*, a poem of unknown authorship *Martandamahatmyam*, and the folksong traditions of southern Travancore—including 'Matilakatukatha', 'Neelikatha', 'Iravikkuttypillaiporu', 'Ponniratalkatha', 'Mavaratam', and 'Valiatambi Kunjutambi Kataipadal'—the repertoire of indigenous expressive forms that C.V. drew on was vast and variegated.[6]

There may be difficulties in reading into C.V.'s historical novels the distinctive imaginaries of modern nationalism which have attracted recent scholarship. His political concerns revolved around the princely state of Travancore and the claims of native subjects, especially the Nayars. His historical fiction had at its centre what he saw as the sacred, magical bonds of protection and loyalty between the maharaja and his *praja*, and the intense ties of blood and affect that united people. These tropes rubbed at times uneasily against normative idioms of historical progress and the forms of political life in C.V.'s own time. In fiction's incantatory universe the production of

[4] Raja Kesavadas (1745–99) fell out of favour after King Rama Varma's death in 1798. He was kept under house arrest and was probably poisoned to death by a rival group that had gained ascendancy in the Travancore court.

[5] Raman Pillai, 'Peethika', *Martandavarma*, 52.

[6] See Venugopalan, '"Martandavarma": Srshtiyum Swarupavum', in Raman Pillai, *Martandavarma*, 11–50, esp. 33–8. He notes that P. Govinda Pillai's *attakkatha*, *Veeramartandacharitam*, dealing with the same theme, seems to have been written around the time C.V. wrote his novel.

subjects of historical inheritance was less a matter of knowledge than of affect; it was not primarily in cognitive terms that the past asserted its presence and made its claims there. C.V.'s fiction performed an aesthetic work of memory-making, fashioning a perceptual and enunciatory economy in relation to the past: it is this work that we follow here.

A preoccupation with history-writing had emerged in Travancore in the second half of the nineteenth century. Vaikkathu Pachu Moothathu published the first history of Travancore in 1867, and a decade later there appeared P. Shungoonny Menon's first official history in English.[7] Pachu Moothathu began with a seemingly simple definition of history as 'the true account of great people, focusing on their nature, the beneficiary deeds they did in life, their land and other forms of wealth, and other qualities.'[8] Shungoonny Menon's *History of Travancore* offered an avowedly royalist account in which the lineages of rulers and their achievements served as the main principle of narrative organization. Menon claimed an exceptional status for Travancore: it was one of the rare kingdoms 'whose dynasty continued to exist in an unbroken line of succession, from the time of its foundation to the present day', and 'one of the very few living specimens of a pure Hindu government, the institutions of which have never been affected by the Muhammadan conquest.'[9] However, his history had a strangely asymmetric structure, which P. Sundaram Pillai was quick to notice. 'Mr. Shungoonny Menon begins,' he noted, 'his history with *Brahma* the Creator, but he fills up his first chapter which brings down the account to His Highness Martanda Varma, who began his rule just 164 years ago, i.e., within the memory in all probability of the historian's own grandfather, with . . . questionable materials.'[10] In several dynastic narratives 'the earliest links in the

[7] Moothathu, *Tiruvitamkoor Charitram*; Shungoonny Menon, *A History of Travancore*.

[8] Moothathu, *Tiruvitamkoor Charitram*, 14.

[9] Shungoonny Menon, *A History of Travancore*, vii.

[10] Sundaram Pillai, *Some Early Sovereigns of Travancore*, 4.

genealogical chain are not meant to be taken as facts in the way that the latest links clearly are, with their dates, regnal years, and highly specific locations.'[11] However, Menon's condensation of several centuries and expatiation on the recent fifteen decades is interesting. Sir T. Madhava Rao, Dewan of Travancore from 1857 to 1872, attempted a history in English but he too completed only sections dealing with the years of Martandavarma and Ramavarma.[12]

The reigns of these two eighteenth-century kings dominated the nineteenth-century historiography of Travancore; the dramatic compression of the historical past appears to have conferred on their times the grandeur and weight of distant origins. The importance of Martandavarma and Ramavarma was no doubt linked to their role in the formation of a modern state in Travancore. Susan Bayly has argued that it was in the eighteenth—not in the nineteenth—century that 'a wholly new political system was built up in the region, and with the rise of the new Keralan states came rapid and dramatic change in many of the most fundamental institutions of the society.' The reign of Martandavarma and Ramavarma was a period of 'thorough-going changes in military organization, in the machinery of state, in caste leadership and in the structures of court culture and religious life.'[13] Not surprisingly, Martandavarma is often referred to as the maker of modern Travancore.

S. Raju has shown that words such as Raja (King) and Rajyam (Kingdom) make an appearance in the official records of Travancore only around the eighteenth century.[14] He argues that notions of *swaroopam*, *muppu*, and *vazhcha* were the operative concepts earlier, and that they indicated a different conception of self-location, seniority, and form of existence, all intimately linked to the *sabha* (council)

[11] This argument is made about *karanam* writers by Narayana Rao, Shulman, and Subrahmanyam, *Textures of Time*, 100.

[12] This text was translated into Malayalam and published in 1873. See Madhava Rao, *The History of Travancore*.

[13] Bayly, 'Hindu Kingship and the Origin of Community', 177–8.

[14] Raju, 'Politics and Culture in Kerala'.

which governed the affairs of the Padmanabha Swamy temple in Trivandrum. The decisive shift that took place in political configuration and discourse in the eighteenth century, Raju contends, is suppressed or elided in the historiography of Travancore from the nineteenth century on, which projects more recent ideas of sovereignty and territoriality—those of the Raja and the Rajyam—to earlier times. The eighteenth century, paradoxically, came to signify not a historical rupture and the emergence of the modern, but a paradigmatic formation that shaped Travancore's sense of identity and memory.

The eighteenth-century rulers of Travancore and Cochin, Bayly points out, 'were *parvenus*, sat-sudra warriors who had built up domains possessing no precedents in Keralan history and no clear standing in the Hindu moral and religious orders.'[15] This, she says, explains Martandavarma's use of new rites of sacralization to improve his symbolic, caste status. The rituals of Hiranyagarbham and Tulapurushadanam reconstituted the king's body as sacred, as twice-born. Bayly understands the import into Kerala of Brahmins in this light: a large number of *uttupurakal* or feeding houses funded by the state came up as a means to reward thousands of non-Malayali Brahmins who were brought to Kerala during Martandavarma's time.[16]

For C.V., Martandavarma's and Ramavarma's reigns did not represent the origins of the present; they stood for an almost mythical past whose glory his own time was unable to recapture. What did this grandeur consist of? '*Anungalillatha kora, valiya kora*' (The lack of men, a huge lack), C.V.'s friends remember him saying this in conversations often, as a comment on his own time. The past was a time of men and manliness.[17] Masculinity in C.V.'s world is a form of political existence. '*Anayippirannal oru ottapperunkaiyenkilum nokkanam. Allandu piraviyentinu, uyirentinu?*' (If you are born a man,

[15] Bayly, 'Hindu Kingship and the Origin of Community', 190.

[16] Ibid., 191.

[17] For a description of the importance of *paurusham* (manliness) in C.V.'s moral and political thought, see Balakrishnan Nair, *Sakshal C.V.*

you should play a big hand at least once; or else, what is the use of birth, of life?), says one of his characters.[18] It is in the display of an irrepressible impulse to grand deeds that manliness as political value emerges, inspiring awe and emulation.

The relationship between history and emulation, even without the foregrounding of masculine valour, was a familiar theme in historical writing. Pachu Moothathu saw it as the principal use of recounting the past. 'Exposure to the stories of meritorious people will lead to a gradual enhancement of worth among young boys. Therefore some great men, to facilitate access to such knowledge for people at large, have described in various books the stories of venerable personages who have lived in different times and places.'[19] This made political history rely on forms of biographical recall, making individual persons and their deeds determine the form in which the past could be narrated. This prevailed in other domains as well. P. Govinda Pillai, who wrote the first literary history in Malayalam, saw as one of his aims 'paying homage to a lineage of poets who had countered several obstacles (*pratyuhavyuhangal*) in the path of the language's development in years past.'[20]

C.V.'s novels too conjured up the past through a biographical mode; they did so by sketching images of extraordinary figures in a quasi-mythological register. It was possible for him to elevate events from the eighteenth century to the status of myth because the modern Travancore consolidated by Martandavarma had gone through vital, irreversible changes in the intervening period. Nowhere was this more pronounced than in Travancore's subservience to British colonial power and in the reduced autonomy of later rulers. The moment captured in C.V.'s three novels belongs to the last phase of pre-colonial sovereign rule in Travancore. Martandavarma's reign witnessed belligerent contests between foreign trading powers and early de-

[18] Raman Pillai, *Dharmaraja*, 97.

[19] Moothathu, *Tiruvitamkoor Charitram*, 13.

[20] Govinda Pillai, Introduction to the first edition, *Malayalabhashacharitram*, xvii.

cisive steps in Travancore's alliance with the East India Company; Ramavarma's time saw a strengthening of this dependence, and the signing of a formal treaty which involved substantial obligations on Travancore's part for English military support. It is important to see the quasi-mythic biographical register in C.V.'s account of the past against the backdrop of his concern with sovereignty.

The nineteenth century was a period not only of the ascent of colonial control over Travancore; the period also saw major transformations in governance and administration, especially during Ayilyam Tirunal's reign (1860–80) and Sir T. Madhava Rao's period as Dewan (1857–72).[21] These changes, it has been pointed out, were introduced at the advice of the imperial government through residents and sometimes under the veiled threat of annexation.[22] C.V. saw the new arrangements as altering the links between the sovereign and his subjects. He published a series of critical essays on the dewans of Travancore under the title *Videshiyamedhavitvam* (Foreign Rule). It was during Dewan Madhava Rao's tenure, C.V. argued, that the easy access of subjects to their sovereign was interrupted. In contrast with earlier times, when the king regularly consulted leading householders in order to understand the desires and grievances of his people, Madhava Rao introduced Western modes of governance, making the palace 'an inaccessible fortress' dominated by the dewan. Instead of subjects directly approaching their sovereign as their protector (*rakshitavu*), a new practice of petitions and offices came into existence. The highest office for the submission of petitions, C.V. remarked, became the headquarters of the police, or the secretariat of the government (*hajoor kaccheri*).[23]

The main target of C.V.'s political criticism was the office of the dewan and other higher positions in Travancore's administration,

[21] For an account of the refashioning of state architecture in Trivandrum during this period, see Heston, 'Mixed Messages in a New "Public" Travancore'.

[22] See Desai, 'Indirect British Rule'.

[23] Raman Pillai, *Videshiyamedhavitvam*, 1.

largely occupied by non-Malayali Brahmins. The Malayali Memorial of 1892 had made a strong case against the employment of high officials from outside Kerala. What C.V. regarded as 'foreign' in *Videshiyamedhavitvam* was not the dramatically increasing colonial influence in the administration: 'By the word "foreign" we do not mean the imperial power which functions in alliance with the king. At present, we include under this category only those who, with the help of some groups of important individuals in Madras, come as beggars to Travancore and steal its wealth through the exercise of their power, reduce its prosperity, and then leave this country.'[24] The political essays in *Videshiyamedhavitvam* deflected the dramatic decline in the king's sovereignty under colonial rule by foregrounding the problems of governance by non-Malayali dewans. Political campaigns led by the Nayars in C.V.'s time made a distinction between the sovereign and the dewan, holding the latter responsible for the objectionable policies pursued by the government. The dewan's appointment required consent from the imperial government and therefore was not of the king's choosing. The dewans of Travancore at the turn of the nineteenth century played a highly prominent role in policy-making and administration. During a period of attenuated kingship, before the introduction of popular representative bodies, they shaped most of the important policies and decisions under the direction of the British resident.

C.V.'s historical romances conjured up an alternative model of the relations between the king and his subjects. At the centre of these relations was the image of the native Nayar dewan, committed to his people and loyal to the king. Raja Kesavadas epitomized these qualities. And as a counterpoint to the contemporary decline in the king's sovereignty, the novels offered valorized images of Martandavarma and Ramavarma, in whom the two favoured attributes of the sovereign—the sacredness of his person and his indissoluble bonds with his subjects—came together. The figure of the king guaranteed

[24] Ibid., 16.

through his protective persona the autonomy of native communities. C.V. injected these ties with anachronistic political blood, producing a notion of the 'people' drawn from popular memory, sentiments, and desires available in his own period. The eighteenth-century universe is attributed the sacredness of an authentic tradition through a suppression of its new, emergent character.

This imaginative reworking of history posed a problem. The consolidation of the state of Travancore in the eighteenth century had been accomplished through brutal violence. According to Shungoonny Menon's history, Pappu Thampi and Raman Thampi, the former king's sons, challenged the custom of matrilineal royal descent and staked their claim to the throne. They were killed in a planned encounter: one of them died fighting Martandavarma's guards and the other was stabbed to death by the king himself.[25] Martandavarma's victory also involved the destruction of traditional Nayar power. The strong Nayar chiefs who challenged him—the Ettuveettil Pillamar—were executed, their houses demolished, and their property confiscated; their women were given away to fisherfolk to prevent the resurgence of family lines. The celebration of eighteenth-century kingship as an idealized locus of relations between protecting sovereigns and loyal subjects was belied by the violent destruction of Nayar power that lay at its very foundation. We see C.V.'s novels as being engaged in a complex aesthetic negotiation of this ambivalent historical inheritance.

An early sign of this is found in the silences in *Martandavarma*: the novel does not recount the execution of the Pillamar and the destruction of their families: instead, the victorious king is shown as granting pardon to enemies in an attempt to repair his bond with prominent subjects. The last chapter, which offers a summary of events over the final three years, directs the reader to the annals of Travancore's history for the subsequent story of the Thampimar and Ettuveettil Pillamar. Critics have pointed out from the very beginning that the novel's toning down of the king's ruthlessness in favour of

[25] See Shungoonny Menon, 123–4.

gentler qualities was not only historically inaccurate but had also diluted his valour (*veerarasam*).[26] This move was in tune with C.V.'s fictional reworking of questions of sovereignty. The second and third novels in the trilogy, written after twenty years, presume the destruction of the Pillamar by the king and offer indirect homage to their valour. But at their centre is an alternative conception of the Nayar subject presented in the figure of the dewan, Raja Kesavadas. C.V.'s configuration of historical memory draws on the complex affects produced by these conflicting images of Nayar heritage.

In the novelist's formulation, the stability of the kingdom was pivoted on the vital relationship between the king and his Nayar minister. Just as the *sat-sudra* king underwent a ritual process of sacralization, the traditional figure of the Nayar was invested with a new aura of dignity and valour. Dewan Kesava Pillai, renowned as Raja Kesavadas, served for him as a prototype of the dignity of the new Nayar subject, in striking contrast to the self-seeking non-Malayali officials of later regimes criticized in C.V.'s political writings. However, apart from Raja Kesavadas, eighteenth-century Travancore did not supply C.V. with enough resonant prototypes for shaping a new figure. The energies of plot and action in *Martandavarma* of course revolved around Anantapadmanabhan, the charismatic Nayar protagonist of the novel. The scholarship on C.V. has considered this character an entirely fictitious creation.[27]

[26] See C.P. Achyuta Menon's review of *Martandavarma* in *Vidyavinodini* (1891), reprinted in *C.P. Achyuta Menonte Sahitya Vimarsanam*, 66–70.

[27] However, the Nadars of erstwhile southern Travancore have claimed that the character of Anantapadmanabhan was modelled on a Nadar of the same name who shared a close friendship with the king and offered him protection and support. These, they claim, have been recognized in subsequent gifts from the king recorded in copper plates. If this is true, the production of Anantapadmanabhan as a Nayar subject seems to have been the work of C.V.'s fictional imagination. I thank B. Rajeevan for alerting me about the possible Nadar origins of C.V.'s Nayar hero. Examples of these claims can be found in Nation Master, Encyclopaedia, Internet. http://www.nationmaster.com/encyclopedia/Pandiya-Kula-Kshatriya-Mara-Nadar; http://nadarsangam.com/whoswho.html

C.V. followed royalist histories in regarding the conflict between Prince Martandavarma and his cousins—the two Thampis—as a confrontation between the custom of matrilineal inheritance prevalent in Travancore and an unorthodox, patrilineal claim. A contrary strand of commemoration is seen in 'Valiya Thampi Kunju Tampi Pattu' (The Song of the Brothers), a folksong from southern Travancore, performed by lower-caste bow-song singers, which places the sons of the former king on the side of custom. The Thampis are sons of Abhirami, a beautiful woman from Ayodhya whom Raja Ramavarma, Martandavarma's maternal uncle, met in Suchindram, fell in love with, and married. The conflict in the song revolves around the king's wish, rejected by the Thampis, to wed their younger sister Ummini Thanka. The song associates Martandavarma with sexual desire, deceit, and violence, and the Thampis with virtue and valour. C.V., given his close familiarity with the folk traditions of Nanchinadu, must have been aware of this alternative tradition of commemoration.[28] His novel reversed the ethical equation and attributed deceit and sexual predatoriness to the Thampis. The alliance between the pretender brothers and the Nayar chiefs represents, in the novel, a corrupt counterpart to the valorized relationship of devotion between Martandavarma and his loyal Nayar supporters. The novel pivots not on the contrast between custom and innovation, but between two models of sovereignty and subjection: one of them virtuous and gentle, the other wicked and violent. In the later novels C.V. rethought the stark terms of this opposition, re-estimating the legacy of Ettuveettil Pillamar and the form of power they embodied.

Why was C.V. obsessed with the question of sovereignty? The history of Travancore in the nineteenth century, subsequent to the period dealt with in his three historical novels, was crucial in shaping his ideas. The war against Tipu Sultan and his defeat by the British

[28] See, for a discussion of 'Valiyathampi Kunjuthampi Kathai Padal' (The Story of the Elder Thampi and the Younger Thampi], Venugopalan, '"Martandavarma": Srshtiyum Swarupavum', 37–8. For a translation and discussion of a performance of this song, see Blackburn, 'The Death of the Little Brothers'.

in 1792 led to a reconfiguration of sovereign power in Travancore. In 1795 the princely state was forced to enter into a treaty with the British, with an agreement to pay for the protection they received from the East India Company's army. Colonel Colin Macaulay was appointed British Resident to Travancore in 1800 and major decisions by the king, including the appointment of the dewan, required the Company's approval. Growing interference in administration and onerous financial demands by the British met with stout opposition from Veluthampi, the Dalawa of Travancore. Joining forces with his counterpart in Cochin, he revolted against the Company in 1807 and killed several Englishmen, but the rebels were eventually defeated by an army dispatched from Madras. Veluthampi mobilized an insurrection via a powerful anti-British proclamation from Kundara but the uprising ended in his defeat and suicide, leading to the firm establishment of British supremacy in Travancore and Cochin. Veluthampi's dead body was captured and publicly displayed on a gibbet to underscore the brutal and total suppression of native rebellion against the Company. This was followed by disarming the people and disbanding all militia.[29]

C.V. Raman Pillai, like many of the Nayar intellectuals of his generation, looked at these events almost a century later as an intensely poignant, tragic phase in the history of his people. The last novel he began writing and left incomplete, it is said, was to have as its theme Veluthampi's inspiring life and heroic death. As we saw, C.V. had considered *Dharmaraja* and *Ramaraja Bahadur* as parts of a trilogy on Raja Kesavadas' life: this largely unwritten last novel would have narrated the political machinations against the dewan which led to his death, supposedly by poisoning. Interestingly, the two works promised but not completed were to commemorate the heroic defeat and death of the two most venerated Nayar ministers in the history of Travancore. The novels C.V. published offered homage to erstwhile images of sovereignty and subjecthood through praise and worship,

[29] For a discussion of Veluthampi's period as Dalawa and the rebellion, see T.K. Velu Pillai, *The Travancore State Manual, Vol. II: History*, 448–97.

while the unwritten works were to be elegiac lamentations. Could the affective tenor of these unwritten works be of consequence to what was written and published? Could it be that C.V.'s narratives of praise derive their acuteness and power from the suffusion of a displaced tone of tragic mourning?

II

The registers of historical expression in C.V.'s work are several. Palace records, royal edicts, and ministerial orders went into the shaping of his idioms of narration. The novels also drew heavily on commemorative forms, such as folksongs of adventure and mourning, popular parodies, and performative storytelling. The speech genres deployed in his novels track the ritual work of power in a range of domains: the monarch and the state, communities and castes, family histories, and the ordinary spaces of everyday life. The biographical mode works in these texts alongside a discursive frame of ritual commemoration and veneration. Even as the king appears as a character whose qualities of kindness or resolution are revealed in action, he also appears as a valorized image successfully calling for acclaim and worship. More than emulation, a devotional attitude defines the relationship between the narratorial voice and the presence of the sovereign. At the same time, the king is not the actual locus of narrative elaboration; as we saw, in the later two novels it is the minister—the dewan—Raja Kesavadas, who is the centre of the action and invites admiration and emulation. Circuits of affect in these novels gather further complexity when figures and lineages opposed to the king are drawn into the ambit of veneration.

C.V.'s novels did not seek to narrate historical events: that was not, at least, their principal aim. Narration works more like a prop in a commemorative ritual to draw participants into a magic circle of incantation and enactment. A fictional language which broke with habits of literary narration was fashioned to serve as the vehicle for this mythical conjuring up of the past. Unlike Chandu Menon, who preferred the simple Malayalam of the Nayar home for his novels,

C.V. deliberately wrote in a stylized language unsuited to ordinary use. It was made up of multiple elements: a high-sounding Sanskritized diction in narration and a range of registers, dialects, and languages in the speech of characters, marking regional and caste differences. However, it would be wrong to regard his sonorous narrative style as a sign of classical purism. Several usages in *Martandavarma* were judged erroneous by the renowned Sanskritist of the time, Keralavarma Valiyakoyil Thampuran. Though C.V. did eventually accept some of the suggested corrections in the second edition of the novel published two decades later, his initial reaction was one of defiance. He scribbled on the margins of Keralavarma's letter, commenting on the excisions he had recommended: '[B]ut I thought let them stand. Nothing like boldness to write . . . Worship of blind authority . . . Fellows like myself who may have a good original story to tell may be cowed into silence for fear of criticism from literary autocrats . . . Who cares for Sanskrit grammar? Where is the Malayalam Grammar to say this is wrong?'[30] It is not only the defiance of classical prescription that is striking; one can also feel the presence of a desire for the autonomy of the vernacular, and the decisionist gesture of making it in one's writing. There is a sense that the rules of this new language occupy the temporality of the future anterior—that the writing will produce rules retrospectively to validate and legislate norms of intelligibility. *Dharmaraja*, when it appeared, attracted harsher criticism for the excessive difficulty and eccentricity of its language.[31] C.V. agreed that its style had taken after the diction of *Kirmiravadham*, a difficult Kathakali play; in *Ramaraja Bahadur*, the last in the trilogy, he tried to go back to an earlier, more lucid style, only to discover that it had left him, along with his youth![32]

[30] Parameswaran Nair, *C.V. Raman Pillai*, 166. Also cited in Venugopalan, '"Martandavarma": Srshtiyum Swarupavum', 26. C.V.'s notes are in English.

[31] Ramakrishna Pillai, 'Dharmaraja'.

[32] Raman Pillai, Preface to *Ramaraja Bahadur*, 7. C.V. justified his attempt at an elevated style in *Dharmaraja* as based on a false estimate of the progress

While citing a royal edict from the eighteenth century, the narrator of *Ramaraja Bahadur* places it in an unwritten history of Malayalam prose, usually mistakenly traced to the introduction of Western education in the nineteenth century.[33] This understanding of literary history privileged a vernacular strand of sovereign performative force over idioms of modern discursivity and the prominence of description and pedagogy.

Classical, scholarly uses of Sanskrit may therefore not help us much in understanding C.V.'s language; we may be better served by placing it alongside contemporary stylistic innovations in Malayalam prose. We noted earlier the existence of a long non-Brahminical history of Sanskrit learning in Kerala.[34] The tendency to incorporate Sanskrit locutions into Malayalam to produce effects of elegance, gravitas, or virtuosity was quite common in the early twentieth century. S. Guptan Nair observes that astrologers and Ayurvedic physicians were well known for their infatuation with *girvanam* (the language of the gods), and lawyers in lower courts tended to inflate their submissions with a generous sprinkling of Sanskrit.[35] These uses of Sanskrit must be differentiated from trained usages of the language in scholarly circles and from survivals of a pre-modern literary heritage. They occurred mostly in prose where the norms of composition were not entirely set, and form part of a popular and non-Brahminical usage where the linguistic signature of Sanskrit invoked the resonances and pleasures of cosmopolitan authority. C.V.'s inflated language, in spite of his scholarship and literary excellence, is arguably closer to this mode than to the restraint and correctness claimed by classical scholars.[36]

---

made by the Malayalam language on account of the new initiatives of the Travancore government in the field of education.

[33] Raman Pillai, *Ramaraja Bahadur*, 99.

[34] Muthulekshmi, 'Samskrtapadanam Keralathil'.

[35] S. Guptan Nair, *Gadyam Pinnitta Vazhikal*, 88.

[36] Sanskrit scholars too engaged in such usage. Guptan Nair cites as an example the playful correspondence between Chattampi Swamikal and some

The nature of this language turns out on a closer look to be even more complex: E.V. Krishna Pillai recounts in his autobiography how he transcribed C.V.'s oral dictation of the first draft version of several passages of *Ramaraja Bahadur*. C.V. was, he says, in the habit of dictating important descriptive passages in the novel first in English! Later, the English manuscript would be translated and reworked into the high Sanskrit-tinted style that became the signature of the novel's diegetic passages.[37] The language of C.V.'s later political essays, often written in an elevated and seemingly Sanskritized register in Malayalam, sometimes shows signs of having been translated, indicating a possible derivation from political thought and journalism in the English language. His style was tied to a modern multilingual condition in which English, Sanskrit, Tamil, and Hindustani were vital elements. The 'vernacular' in his work was marked by innovative transactions with local and cosmopolitan idioms and languages of earlier and newer epochs.[38] It is in this linguistic space that C.V.'s novels fashioned their idioms for commemorative acclaim.

We hinted at a subterranean current of mourning in C.V.'s heroic sagas. This strand symptomatically surfaces, for instance, when in *Dharmaraja* Pavati Kochi recounts the heroic lamentation of a mother whose valiant son sacrificed his life to Dutch cannons in the service of Martandavarma.[39] The incident is only tangentially connected to the story of the novel but works as a powerful narrative performance in its own right. Told in a register of unadorned native discourse elevated through grief and adulation, the story has at its core an act of intense mourning which unites the king and the

---

of his disciples, an exercise in virtuosity where the Guru and *sishyas* vied with each other in complexity and obliqueness. Ibid., 88–9.

[37] Krishna Pillai, *Jeevitasmaranakal*, 708.

[38] C.V. was not alone among Malayalam writers in using English in personal compositions and correspondence. We saw above that his marginal notes on Keralavarma's letter were in English. So was the letter itself. Kumaran Asan kept a diary in English, a habit that was not unique.

[39] Raman Pillai, *Dharmaraja*, 231–3.

Nayar soldier's bereaved mother in virtual kinship. The king pledges that he will be her only son from now on, and she accepts, celebrating this grand gift of maternity and filiation. Later she breaks into an inconsolable lament, addressing her lost son as the minister of the king. The alliance between the king and the Nayar minister, forged in blood and sacrifice, is the space of intensely avowed affect. As we saw, the tie between the sovereign and the Nayar minister was of special importance in C.V.'s imaginary. A new model of manly subjectivity, proposed through the figures of the king and the dewan, deftly measures its proximity and distance in relation to earlier normative models of masculinity. The community's heroic past, inscribed in the subject's body as a habitus of valour, is modulated and elevated to a higher register by the idioms of ministerial loyalty characterized by maturity, restraint, and administrative astuteness.

Parallel to this is a process of disavowal—a careful, invisible exorcism of some elements from the community's historical inheritance. C.V.'s trilogy is replete with symptoms produced by this unacknowledged rejection. We noted a principle of displacement in the very plan of the trilogy: ostensibly about kings, the latter two novels are actually about the Nayar dewan. We may still be mistaken in taking this at face value. The shift from king to Nayar minister may be standing in for another, unacknowledged shift—from the Nayar minister to the Nayar families who led the revolts against the king. In each of the later two novels, *Dharmaraja* and *Ramaraja Bahadur*, the destroyed Nayar power sprouts again from a branch in spite of repeated setbacks. What was to hold together the projected trilogy may not be only the Nayar dewan; it may equally be the Kazhakkoottathu house of Nayar lords who rise up repeatedly to confront royal power.[40] And, who knows, in the unwritten novel on Raja Kesavadas' last days, these strands would perhaps have merged with each other in affective terms.

[40] For a nuanced reading of C.V.'s novels that foregrounds these complexities, see Bhaskaran Nair, *Daivaneethikku Dakshinyamilla*.

The heroic-tragic strain of mourning in C.V.'s novels is directed not so much at foregone kings as at figures of Nayar sovereignty. This power, in its guise as the minister—the executive hands that operate the king's rule—was the explicit object of celebration in C.V.'s world. The Nayar lords who rose against the king and tried to murder him were unavowable objects of veneration and mourning. C.V.'s historical novels produced a literary apparatus that paid homage to erstwhile Nayar power in both these guises. Even as the Nayar minister, glorified as an image of responsibility and restrained power, occupies the centre of the field of events and actions visibilized in the novel, the heroic images of an older Nayar sovereignty, discarded as treason (*rajyadroham*), find their consecration in occasional tremors of affect felt beneath the level of narration. Tripura Sundari, the sister of Kazhakkuttathu Pillai, living incognito in her old age, asks Nanthiyathu Unnithan, 'Did my elder brother bear the executioner's sword with strength befitting our clan?' Unnithan replies: 'Sister, please don't ask about all this. That was a time of high waters. Let bygones be bygones.'[41] The unspeakable moment of execution, invoked momentarily but abandoned, controls and heightens the affective tenor of the novel.

K. Vinod Chandran, in an engaging study of early-twentieth-century Travancore, has argued that C.V.'s discourse of Rajya worship ought to be distinguished from modern forms of nationalism.[42] He makes a similar argument about Nayar identity, contrasting it with modern, enumerative forms of caste identity. Chandran argues that modern identity formations such as the nation and caste emerged in Travancore in the context of colonial rule and missionary work, and that in contrast with them the discourses on Rajya and the Nayar in C.V.'s work contained a dimension of sublimity which exceeded or escaped enumerative, governmental logic. Chandran is right to invoke the figure of sublimity; an element of the unrepresentable marks the invocation of disavowed inheritance. This should not

[41] Raman Pillai, *Dharmaraja*, 266–7.

[42] Chandran, 'The Counter Narratives of Power and Identity,' 49–114.

make us identify C.V.'s work with tradition: we see in it rather the invention of a tradition, and its use as a prop to stage a difficult, conflicted relationship to the past. This process took shape through an encounter with new technologies of power and new forms of identification prevalent in late-nineteenth and early-twentieth-century Travancore.

The stories told in C.V.'s historical novels share their idioms of sovereign power with the post-nineteenth-century historiography of Travancore. However, in the interstices of this narrative is inscribed a notion of Nayar sovereignty that is not centred on the king. This ought to be distinguished from the Nayar as minister, as dewan or Dalawa, which formed the kernel of C.V.'s political campaigns. In the pre-eighteenth-century conception of political power, the Nayar lords or Madampimar were actual bearers of sovereignty with their own militia and the power to administer justice and to kill. P.K. Balakrishnan suggests that even punishments awarded by the state were in all likelihood regularly carried out by them.[43] The story of the seventeenth century as it unfolds in histories of Travancore is replete with what are presented as challenges to the king or the queen from the Nayar lords. If we take the changes in the configuration and idioms of sovereignty in the eighteenth century seriously, these conflicts may well have been intrinsic to the divided, contestatory nature of sovereign power during that period. Martandavarma's rule put an end to this situation and began consolidating the state's position as the sole arbiter and monopolistic dispenser of legitimate violence.

However, we also know that the acquisition of kingliness—the transformation of Trippapur Mooppu into the Travancore king—was accomplished with the help of the English East India Company. The exemplary alliance between Raja Ramavarma and the native Nayar minister Kesava Pillai celebrated in C.V.'s novels was indeed the regime that took on financial obligations in return for English military support to Travancore. The much praised victory over Tipu Sultan, which is seen as having ensured Travancore's survival as an

[43] Balakrishnan, *Jativyavasthayum Keralacharitravum*, 159–60.

independent state, also marked an irreversible erosion of Travancore's economic and political autonomy. The honorofic 'Raja' was conferred on Dewan Kesava Pillai by the English East India Company after Tipu Sultan's defeat, making him known as Raja Kesavadas.

How are these paradoxes about sovereignty and autonomy produced and negotiated in C.V.'s fiction? I suggested earlier that answers to this question are to be sought less in ideological attitudes than at a plane of the aesthetic work performed in these novels. I use the word 'aesthetic' on account of its etymological alliance with perception: a quasi-mythic experience of history is generated in C.V.'s novels through a careful determination of how persons, objects, and spaces are made to appear in the fictional world, and how people exhibit themselves in action and speech. In order to understand this, we need to look closely at his character system, the organization of discourses, and the orchestration of spaces and perceptual modes.

III

Readers familiar with *Indulekha* and other early novels set in modern times will immediately notice two significant differences while entering C.V.'s fictional universe. Firstly the light changes: we are greeted by dramatic variations of obscurity and effulgence. An equally striking difference is in the language: C.V.'s novels are dominated neither by educated ordinary language made newly respectable for entry into the field of literature, nor well-known *slokas* from Sanskrit *kavyas* offered for the trained *sahrdaya*'s delectation. The language of these novels displays a variegated, exaggerated, and stylized performance, delivered not just to the faculty of understanding but to the entire sensorium.

Martandavarma opens in the recesses of a jungle, with the first sentences mimicking with sound and syntax the harsh intricacies of the landscape:

> The events being narrated at the opening of this story took place in a jungle. The word 'jungle' should not make the readers think that it was

> a fearsome forest resonant with roars and reverberations, and frequented by ferocious felines of prey. It was rather a patch of wilderness, rarely visited by humanity, overgrown with shrubs and spattered with thickets. Devoid of rocks and rivulets, not a single sweet-scented flower lent its fragrance to the dank forest atmosphere. Here and there, a few superannuated trees towered against the sky in solitary grandeur, but the rest of the ground was covered by a redundant growth of noxious weeds. Huge palms stood in the dark, alone and in clusters, like giant umbrellas held up in the procession of some jungle god.[44]

The English translation sounds inadequate, missing the original Malayalam's aural richness, typified in the resonant verse cited from Ezhuthachan's *Adhyatma Ramayanam*: '*jhillijhankara nadamanditam, simhavyaghra salyadi mrgagana nishevidam*'. The description accumulates detail over detail, blocking clear perception through a sense of obscure excess. This dark prelude gives way to the baffling appearance of a resplendent wounded body—of an unrecognized, radiant young man soon carried away from the scene by an unknown group of men in strange attire. The narration guides the reader's gaze over an abundance of particulars, suggesting possible explanations but denying certainty to any of them.

Dramatic scenes shrouded in mystery open *Dharmaraja* and *Ramaraja Bahadur* as well. They, as in *Martandavarma*, serve not only to whet narrative curiosity but to produce the past as a distinct space of dark, mythical intelligibility. A skilful concatenation of seemingly realistic detailing and an opposed orientation towards schematic signs holds out the promise of meaning but withholds or deflects it through destabilizing moves. The temporal and spatial coordinates are carefully calibrated: timings are indicated with precision, and nights of the full moon and the new moon are carefully calculated in descriptions of nocturnal scenes.[45] The narration, on the other hand, moves back and

[44] Raman Pillai, *Martandavarma*, 57. English translation, amended, from C.V. Raman Pillai, *Martandavarma* (*A Historical Romance*), 1.

[45] C.V. was not alone in using such calculations in fiction-writing. Such accuracy seems to have come as no surprise to A.R. Rajaraja Varma who, in his Preface to Ramavarma Kochu Thampuran's detective novel *Bhaskara*

forth in time, suppresses crucial intervals, and denies the apprehension of linear causal connections.[46] The unexpected eruption of a dramatic event on a scene is sometimes succeeded by a chapter where the story traces its steps back in time to present an earlier sequence of events which fills gaps in the narration.[47] Such timely satisfaction is not always offered; the unravelling of mysteries is often postponed to later moments. Transformational strategies in the presentation of objects, persons, and movements add to the impression of uncertain visibility and unstable orientation. This is how the habitat is constructed to house the quasi-mythical figures of C.V.'s novels.

A first step in understanding his grammar of figuration may be to look at schematic resemblances which connect human characters to animals. P. Venugopalan's annotations on *Dharmaraja* note how, in relation to physiognomic description, Chantrakkaran is modelled on the buffalo, Kalaprakkottu Thampi on the elephant, Ummini Pillai on the water snake, and Hari Panchananan, as the name suggests, on the lion.[48] These correspondences draw on schemata used in

---

Menon, notes: 'The author has determined not only the dates described in the novel, but also the lunar day for each of them. I did not calculate and verify the accuracy of the lunar calendar. Even though the story is set in the early days of the month Tulam, the seasonal rains are already fierce in the novel.' Kochu Thampuran, *Bhaskara Menon*, 8.

[46] It is said that C.V. did not write the chapters of his novels sequentially. The oral dictation of *Dharmaraja* apparently began with chapter 18, indicating that C.V. had conceived the novel in its entirety and its division into chapters before he began the actual processes of dictation and revision. This may also account for the apparent ease with which the novel moves its temporal and spatial coordinates from chapter to chapter. Balakrishnan Nair, *Sakshal C.V.*, 233.

[47] For instance, in *Martandavarma* the sudden appearance of the mad Channan and his force, to save the king from impending death at the end of chapter 5, is explained at the end of the following chapter. Both these chapters cover the same temporal span but are located in two different places. The figures who make a dramatic appearance at the end of chapter 5 are identified as the Channan and his force only in the later chapter.

[48] Raman Pillai, *Dharmaraja*, 122, n.77.

traditions of physical culture, such as Kalarippayattu, where bodily stances and postures are named after animals. Animal images suggest interpretative clues about the *swabhavam* (innate disposition) of characters.

The exteriorization of character is not confined to schematic resemblances in bodily features; actions and gestures are also sites of schematic stylization. C.V. was a great enthusiast of Kathakali, and the spectacular schematism of appearance and gestures in this form seems to have been a major influence in his novels. Kathakali characters are presented through a typology of costume (*vesham*): *pacha* (green costume) is used in the representation of gods and heroic protagonists, *tadi* (beard) for superhuman characters, *kathi* (knife) for villains, and *minukku* (radiant) for women. In C.V.'s novels, characters in conversation or action often appear as if they are on stage, absorbed in a dramatic, stylized performance. Major characters are usually introduced through a detailed description of their appearance, which incorporates schematic elements. Interestingly, the influence of performance forms like Kathakali is more evident in the visual imaginary of his novels than in his farces, which dealt with contemporary times.

The stylized descriptions transform his characters into larger-than-life images. Manikya Goundan, shocked by the disappearance of his family treasure, 'falls on the ground like Kumbhakaranan mutilated by Rama's arrows, emitting blood through his mouth and nostrils.'[49] Similarly, Thrivikrama Kumaran, on hearing the pledge made by Kesavan Unnithan, 'felt as if the earth had turned upside down. As a hallucination of darkness rendered him blind, he stood immobile on the ground for some time. Sweat, streaming down his body from his crown, inscribed the contours of his feet on the ground.'[50] A narrative inset in the novel rehearses the visual grammar of such dramatic transformations. In the story of the Yakshi Neeli told to Parukkutty by her mother, a pregnant woman killed by her Brahmin

[49] Raman Pillai, *Ramaraja Bahadur*, 122.
[50] Ibid., 40.

spouse reappears as a beautiful seductress, only to transform herself into the Yakshi Kalliyankattu Neeli, 'filling the forest and touching the sky, with terrifying teeth and a blood-dripping tongue reaching the ground, with a cavernous mouth and huge, round eyes which scatter sparks of fire, and enormous hair standing up like trees . . .'[51] The narration in C.V.'s novels often enacts similar transformations of character images.

Lines from Kathakali librettos or Attakkathas float through the novel, producing an atmosphere appropriate for stylized appearances and performance routines. In *Dharmaraja* and *Ramaraja Bahadur*, the delightful palace cook Mama Venkitan frequently breaks into bouts of Kathakali singing. Aurally resonant textual allusions sound a keynote while introducing some characters: Tripurasundari Kunjamma's initial appearance in *Dharmaraja* along with her granddaughter Meenakshi is accompanied in the description by allusions to Sri Sankara's 'Tripurasundaristotram', a composition in worshipful praise of the goddess.[52] Later in the novel, at Tripurasundari's deathbed, her granddaughter Meenakshi recites the same *stotram*.[53]

Schematic presentations of characters, as we saw in the previous chapter, may pose difficulties for interpretation, since schemata, which involve predetermined taxonomies and formulaic associations between signs and meanings, are open to deceptive reproduction. The stylized, performative presentation of characters foregrounds this threatening possibility. Can an appearance be trusted as genuine, or could it be the clever use of a formula aimed to deceive? C.V.'s work does not often draw on oppositions between the inner and the outer, between a private interiority and a public performance: the domain of the inner itself, as we saw, is presented through exterior, performative elements.

Disguises are particularly useful for clarifying the way unreliable exterior descriptions work in theses novels. Consider the initial appearance of Prince Martandavarma:

[51] Raman Pillai, *Martandavarma*, 78.
[52] Raman Pillai, *Dharmaraja*, 100.
[53] Ibid., 422.

> About two years after the events described in the first chapter, one morning, a Malayali Brahmin was found sitting on the eastern verandah of this house. His age might be somewhere between twenty and twenty-five. One might think that he is a Nambutiri or a Potti from Tiruvalla. The profusion of his hair and moustache indicated that he is perhaps observing some austerities. However, his face had hardly any ascetic aura (*vaidika tejas*). It is valour (*veera rasam*) that predominates. His complexion was very fair. One needs to be cautious in praising the beauty of his face since his nose is unusually long and somewhat thick. Apart from the deformity of the prominence of this organ, no defect can be found in his countenance. On careful examination, all other parts of his body appear as formed to perfection. His arms extend below his knees. Although the attire is that of a Brahmin, his high round shoulders, straight neck, arms strong like iron, his broad firm chest, and his gaze like that of a lion which has sighted an elephant—all these signs may make the observers decide that he belongs to the race of Kshatriyas. However, apart from a poor Brahmin's dhoti and shawl, he did not have any of the ornaments or expressions of the virile Kshatriyas.[54]

C.V. probably modelled the description on a portrait of the king found in Padmanabhapuram Palace. This apparent attempt at verisimilitude is offset by a careful deployment of schematic elements, probably adopted by the portrait painter as well. The epigraph of the chapter refers us to the appearance of Arjuna disguised as a Brahmin in the Sabha Parva of the Mahabharata. C.V.'s description of Martandavarma places, in a careful overlay, Brahmin and Kshatriya attributes. Martandavarma's disguise as Brahmin stands for C.V.'s transfiguration of the king's image: it combines the battle-readiness and courage of the *veera* with the protective kindness of the king as *prajavatsala*, the tenderly affectionate guardian of his subjects.

Disguises play several crucial roles in the novels. We can begin by noting some of the effects produced in the novel's order of visibility. Apart from its thematic significance, the prince's disguise protects him from becoming the object of a direct, non-sacral gaze. In the passage cited, empirical description slides into the schematic, re-

[54] Raman Pillai, *Martandavarma*, 62–3.

vealing the resplendent royal body only indirectly, tempered by the austere Brahmin attire. The king's body commands a ritualistic and reverential gaze, conceived in analogy with the worship of the deity. Just as the devotee's gaze does not confront and appropriate the deity's image, but rather submits to it in ritual obeisance, the royal body is available only for a reverential, oblique gaze, an ocular prostration. Appearance in the king's presence, as with the darshan of a deity, is less an act of perception than the devotee's entry into a relationship of ecstatic obeisance.

A passage in *Ramaraja Bahadur* shows this clearly, when Azhakan Pillai, a loyal peasant from south Travancore, has darshan of the king's body:

> When he surmised that the king was inside the building [watching his performance in the wrestling bout], Azhakan Pillai's soul bathed in an ocean of delight. Immediately he straightened his dhoti, adopted the posture of ritual obeisance by folding one arm over his chest and covering his mouth with the other. Standing with his feet folded inwards, he placed his fingers on his shoulders according to the old custom of the southern parts, and bent down to see clearly the king's sacred body and to bow down before that only god visible to the eye, protector to him and to his country.[55]

This loyal peasant had earlier chatted with an old man near the palace gates without the least suspicion that it was the king he was speaking to with bold familiarity. Ignorance and misperception resemble disguise in hiding the true nature of the object. Later, when Azhakan Pillai recognizes the features of the old man in the quasi-divine personage accepting his obeisance, he is terrified by a sense of violent transgression.

Ritualized acts of looking produce spectators as worshipful subjects. Vision here operates in excess of its cognitive functions as a fuller corporeal experience. Seeing is a way of approaching and making contact: certain sorts of vision may result in pollution or in the violation of limits. The practice of caste pollution reproduces a

[55] Raman Pillai, *Ramaraja Bahadur*, 53.

similar approach to spaces and objects. In C.V.'s novels the king's body occupies a limit of this codified perceptual space. As a special figure unavailable for direct, full vision, its role is to authorize and guarantee the stability of the visible universe and its schematic meanings. But can it fulfil this function? The stability of perceptual and moral universes is threatened in the course of each of the historical novels, even if it is restored at their conclusions.

If at one end of C.V.'s visual spectrum stands the oblique, devotional vision of the king's body, at the other end we encounter two extreme instances of its defiant negation: one of them summons overwhelming, apocalyptic powers of darkness, and the other an explosive conflagration of blinding light. It is in *Dharmaraja* that we find their most dramatic apparitions. Chilambinayethu Chantrakkaran, the illegitimate son of one of the executed Nayar lords, is defiant in his defeat, and apostrophizes the contra-sacral powers of the dark before disappearing from the novel:

> 'You, darkness!', he cries, 'open your mouth, take me, this dim-witted fool, in. What is time, which is the end, if not you! You alone are the god of death, the creator of all time . . . For me, the darkest of the dark, sown in the dark womb of a mother, grown in the pitch dark night of human pretence, ending in this unrelenting dark pit, for me, you alone the path, you deep, dreary dark.'[56]

This is succeeded by the last moment in the novel's denouement, when Hari Panchananan, the descendant of the most persistent of the defeated Nayar lord families, disguised as a *sanyasi*, sets ablaze his stupendous armoury:

> Then, amidst the loud exclamations of swelling crowds at the fire's spreading branches, a humongous universe-shattering noise—as if from Viswakarma's earth-shaking artillery—shook the camp—no, the whole earth—right to its deep subterranean foundation. From the centre of Haripanchananan's mansion a tower of light made of a thousand apocalyptic fires rose with an elephantine roar.[57]

[56] Raman Pillai, *Dharmaraja*, 418.
[57] Ibid., 452.

The invocation of the infinite dark and the detonation of an apocalyptic conflagration, these counterperformatives, mark the outer limits of the organized world of vision guaranteed by the king's body. One might even say that the colourful and variegated world of C.V.'s fiction unfolds between these opposed poles. Things appearing in this field of vision are from the outset contaminated by an ambivalence which opens them to hermeneutic or performative transformations. How do characters inhabit this uncertain field of vision? A closer look at the deployment of disguise in C.V.'s work offers some preliminary answers.

As mentioned earlier, disguise is one of C.V.'s favourite fictional strategies: a range of characters, from the king to his strongest enemies adopt it: Chantrakkaran, Veluthampi, Bableswaran, Perinchakkodan, Anantapadmanabhan, Haripanchanan, the list is long. Chantrakkaran, who made an apocalyptic exit into the dark in *Dharmaraja*, resurfaces in *Ramaraja Bahadur* as Kaliprabhava Bhattan, and then again as Manikya Goundan, playing a crucial role in the manoeuvres against the royal house in both these novels. Haripanchananan's disguises are even more fascinating. The deepest of his masquerades are not the personas adopted; they are to be found in the very unity of his character. The figure of Haripanchananan turns out to be the ultimate disguise: it conceals identical twins with contrary attributes: Ugran (fierce) and Santhan (calm). Their contrast finds expression in other schematic binaries: their names—Trivikraman and Janardanan—manifest a Saivite/Vaishnavite opposition. The narrative unity of Haripanchananan makes the twins appear as contrasting moods of the same person. Here too, the performance technique of *pakarnnattam* may have shown C.V. the way to conceiving this character.[58]

[58] For a discussion of *pakarnnattam*, see Arya Madhavan, *Kudiyattam*, 122–45. *Pakarnnattam* literally means the play of multiple transformations. *Pakarannu* means one to the other and *attam* means performance. Combined, *Pakarnnattam* means "performance by transferring from one to another"' (122).

Disguise is a favourite tool of spies: Kandirava Rayar, who appears at the palace as a famous wrestler from foreign parts, turns out to be a spy in Tipu Sultan's service, and attempts twice to assassinate the king. On the second occasion he is slain by Kunjikkutty Pillai after a one-to-one combat.[59] Ramavarma Raja, an invisible witness to Rayar's death, sighs remorsefully at this sinful killing of a Brahmin or *brahmahatya*; but Kunjikkutty Pillai reveals that Rayar's Brahminical appearance was a disguise: he was from the lower castes. This is true of the evil Sundarayyan who is killed in *Martandavarma*. The last chapter of the novel reveals that he was a half-caste born of a liaison between a Brahmin and a low-caste Marava woman.[60] The anxiety about *brahmahatya* may be double-edged: while the narrative ensures that no Brahmin is actually killed by the king's party, the use of disguise allows a repeated staging of *brahmahatya*; the world of appearances allows a fictional dissolution of the impunity of the Brahmin, even as the plot trades in the dispensable lives of the lower castes.

The most elaborate disguises deployed in the service of the king are used by Anantapadmanabhan, the hero of *Martandavarma*. After his supposed death in a jungle in the opening chapter of the novel, he reappears again and again, adopting different appearances and personas to save the king from his enemies, before he ultimately discards his disguise at the end of the novel and is reunited with his beloved Parukkutty. All other characters, including Martandavarma, pale in comparison before Anantapadmanabhan's resourcefulness. However, this hero is not only the ultimate in skills of warfare; suppressed anguish about his love marks him with a private, affective sense of interiority. The novel presents this through quickly controlled gestures of emotion: tearful eyes, voice choking with emotion, caresses without revealing one's identity. This character's external aspect, in comparison, is variegated and flamboyant:

[59] Raman Pillai, *Dharmaraja*, 203–7.

[60] Raman Pillai, *Martandavarma*, 333–4.

Anantapadmanabhan appears as a mad lower-caste vagabond who displays outstanding skills in swordfight and hand-to-hand combat, as the handsome interpreter from the Muslim trader's camp, as a mendicant who carries intoxicating substances, and as a beggar. Anantapadmanabhan's characterization is the obverse of Haripanchananan's: it is as if a number of independent characters are strung together to make up this figure. Especially, Shamsuddin and the mad Channan are developed as characters in their own right, with some degree of internal coherence and consistency.

I pointed out earlier that C.V.'s conception of sovereignty was built around a valorized relationship between the king and the Nayar minister, and that history did not supply such a figure for *Martandavarma*. Anantapadmanabhan, the fictional substitute that supplements this lack in history, presages the new subject in C.V.'s work. He, along with his half-sister Subhadra, displays qualities developed further in the figure of Raja Kesavadas in the two later novels. Anantapadmanabhan's disguises move across caste and religious divisions to draw on idioms of heroism from lower-caste Channars and the Muslims. Subhadra on the other hand works mainly through an astute ability to gather information and interpret misleading signs with accuracy. Unlike her half-brother, the master of disguises, she is the hermeneuticist, the decoder of all disguise. It is in these two figures that the colourful and misleading spectrum of visibility in *Martandavarma* finds its resolution. Raja Kesavadas inherits Subhadra's intelligence as well as Anantapadmanabhan's adeptness and valour, but does not use the flamboyance of disguise, especially in his later years. An idiom of restraint is privileged in his characterization. It is to this less dramatic idiom that we shall turn now.

IV

I suggested that movements of displacement play a vital role in the making of C.V.'s novels. We saw that the centre of these texts, in spite of their apparent focus on the kings announced in the title, in effect shifts to the minister, or the king's favoured Nayar lieutenant. The sacralization of the king's image and its apprehension through an oblique, reverential gaze may in turn function as a screen at a deeper level, deflecting direct attention from the thematic centrality of the Nayar minister. Interestingly, this initial displacement in turn works in tandem with another, more complex displacement, in which the apparent valorization of the king and his Nayar supporters and the denigration of the Nayar chiefs who rise against them seems to reveal—in spite of efforts to conceal—a current of unavowable reverence for the latter. This makes one wonder if the centrality of the state—the king and the Nayar minister—in the architectonic of C.V.'s works needs to be re-estimated: is this a device to simultaneously hide and make possible a strand of difficult mourning in relation to the past?

The Nayar chiefs who militated against Travancore kings in the seventeenth and eighteenth centuries represent an earlier configuration of sovereign power. Does the celebration of the new, exclusive sovereignty of the king hide a deeper longing for earlier forms of sovereignty exercised by Nayar chieftains? If this is indeed the case, how are these opposed impulses reconciled or allowed to coexist in C.V.'s narratives? What sort of aesthetic work is performed by his historical novels to hold these complex and conflicting allegiances and emotions together in an affective economy?

C.V.'s techniques of characterization play an important role as props for this aesthetic work. In the main, his novels differentiate between two kinds of characters, marked by distinctive ways of acting and inhabiting discourse. These indicate different forms of political existence, if the political is conceived, following Arendt and Ranciere, as a distribution of the visible, and as a field where people exhibit themselves to each other in action and utterance.[61] In this sense the aesthetic organization of stylized appearance, action routines, and

[61] See Arendt, *The Human Condition*, 180; Cavarero, *Relating Narratives*, 20; Ranciere, 'Ten Theses on Politics', and idem, 'Politics of Literature', *Dissensus*, 27–44 and 152–68.

speech in C.V.'s novels create a specific literary form of political intervention.

The speech of characters, as with bodily appearance and gestures, quite often obeys a logic of performance. It has been suggested that Martandavarma's first interior monologue reads like a verbal equivalent to the movements used in Kathakali performances to represent the act of gazing at a mountain.[62] Performing arts and performance routines are a model not only for movements and gestures, but also for speech.

C.V. is justly renowned for his command over the oral registers of southern Travancore and for the dexterity with which he differentiates characters on the basis of speech.[63] Critics have tended to see in this a sensitivity to the individuality and uniqueness of each character. However, a closer look shows that distinctiveness of character is constructed from trans-individual resources and locations, be they those of region, gender, or caste. Speech in C.V.'s novels is a site of excess and exaggeration, of inflections and eccentricity: they come across less as adequate expressions of carefully sketched interior lives than as conspicuous events that take place on language's surface and its outer thresholds. The utterances of Perinchakkodan and Chantrakkaran come across as flamboyant aural spectacles; they assume the presence of a large, rapt audience, even when they occur in quiet contexts of private conversation or inner monologues. Chantrakkaran's address to the night at the end of *Dharmaraja* is as much a ritual of inverted acclamation as a marker of the outer limits of the visible world.

Alongside these performances of excess, C.V. presents characters who adopt pronounced self-restraint in speech. The utterances of characters like Raja Kesavadas, Anantapadmanabhan, Subhadra, and Meenakshi show discipline and thrift in expression. Decorum in

[62] Raman Pillai, *Martandavarma*, 63, and Venugopalan's notes, 342, n.12.

[63] The best example of this is a stylistic study of conversations in C.V. Raman Pillai's novels by N. Krishna Pillai, *Pratipatram Bhashanabhedam*.

their speech is produced by moderation, by exercising control over expression as a sign of respect for the occasion and the addressee. This stands in opposition to elaborately ritualized forms of expressing respect. Mankoyikkal Kurup, a peasant Nayar lord, does not follow the protocols of speech and action in front of Prince Martandavarma in disguise fleeing his enemies: he offers him unsolicited advice and criticism, but before he speaks he performs ritual gestures of obeisance in all sincerity even if they deviate from the proper routines of respect. Raja Kesavadas' conversations with Ramavarma Raja, as the young Kesava Pillai in *Dharmaraja* and as dewan in *Ramaraja Bahadur*, combine ritual speech with gestures of holding back, offering hints and suggestions that the king is able to decipher. The culmination of such restraint is found in the exchange between the king and the dewan before the latter sets out for war. The exchange has no content, and through a ritual of vocatives ('Kesava!', 'Adiyan!') enacts the mere form of interpellation and submission between the sovereign and his devoted subject.[64]

Controlled speech is not merely a matter of decorum or urbanity. Through visible signs of self-restraint, utterances point to processes of silent deliberation and the presence of an inner domain of individuated memories and sorrows. Dewan Raja Kesavadas, Meenakshi, and Subhadra are probably the best examples of this in C.V.'s work; a sense of personal grief is denied expression in all of them but allowed to mark all speech as incomplete and suggestive. Elite lineage is not an essential prerequisite for this: Kesava Pillai's humble origins are foregrounded in the opening of *Dharmaraja*, and his close blood ties with Perinchakkodan come up in a dramatic confrontation between them in *Ramaraja Bahadur*. The dewan's utterances are marked by restraint, reflectiveness, and a control of emotions, even as conflict reaches its highest pitch.

These registers of restraint are distinguished by the absence or at least the subduing of signs of regional origin or blood belonging in

[64] Raman Pillai, *Ramaraja Bahadur*, 163.

caste or religious community. N. Krishna Pillai, who studied the styles of conversations in C.V.'s novels in detail, regards Kesava Pillai's language—in his boyhood, youth, and middle age as dewan—as unique in its freedom from regional markers.[65] Unmarked language is the new mark of dignity. It is only a few Nayar characters who qualify for this unmarked subjecthood, which most of the others continue to display in the speech signs of their region and origins. The use of an unmarked language was quickly becoming a sign of good breeding in C.V.'s own time, in educated urban interaction and in the emergent public sphere, in print and debate. A normative insistence on restraint in expression had gained ground in political debates, gradually replacing the supplicating idioms of royal petitioning by a dignified language of political criticism, moderated by respect for royalty. The emergent political public sphere, however, was not entirely a domain of stable peace: excess was present at the borders, as K. Ramakrishna Pillai's expulsion from Travancore showed.[66] C.V.'s own political essays in *Videshiyamedhavitvam* tried to bring into the controlled domain of public speech the energy and resonance of a self-consciously high register. Interestingly, if we look for its antecedents in C.V.'s novels, we may arrive at the political speeches of figures like Haripanchanan rather than the more pronounced self-restraint of Raja Kesavadas. The characters who show control in gesture and speech anticipate the language of public expression of the future. They combine a sense of individual integrity and selfhood with unstinting, taciturn loyalty to the country and its symbolic embodiment in the king. It is then not surprising that communication in the royal presence is the typical extreme of rarefied discourses in C.V.'s novels, as the king occupies the apex of a system of characters sketched according to strategies of self-control. However, the king's parsimony in speech does not

[65] Krishna Pillai, *Pratipatram Bhashanabhedam*, 40–1.

[66] For a discussion of K. Ramakrishna Pillai's language of criticism and his public interventions, see Kumar, 'The Public, the State and New Domains of Writing'.

refer us to a personal interiority of private affective memories. As in the case of visibility, the king marks the inner limit for the world of discursivity as well. This tells us why kings do not appear as the real protagonists in any of C.V.'s novels, in spite of their prominence in the titles. Individuated lives of turbulent emotions, painful attachment, suppressed grief, and the joys of love belong to the new subjects; the role of the king is to allow and authorize idioms of subjectivation through which individuated heroes are forged.

Since C.V.'s novels by and large rely on techniques of exteriority, individuation, and identification also are matters of external signs. These may be based on objects handed down in noble Nayar families: the ring that Tripurasundari from the destroyed Kazhakkuttam house sells to the gold merchant Annavayyan plays an important role in *Dharmaraja*, as does Kesavan Unnithan's stylus discovered on Annavayyan's corpse. But heirlooms or objects with personal inscriptions are not the only bearers of lineage, ownership, or memory; the more privileged signs are inscribed on the body.

C.V.'s novels, especially the later ones, are preoccupied with a particular kind of bodily marking: the delicate inscription of family resemblances on faces. The puzzling opening chapter of *Martandavarma,* the unconscious wounded body of Anantapadmanabhan is carried away by a group of Muslim traders at the instance of a young man in the group who was struck by the resemblance in countenance between the victim and his former wife. The momentary sensing of natural inscription holds the key to hidden kinship relations vital to the novel and puts in motion the narrative with which C.V. supplements Travancore history. This is not the only instance where an imprecise sensing of family resemblances is experienced by characters as inexplicable elective affinity.[67]

Physiognomic similitudes acquire momentous narrative significance in *Ramaraja Bahadur*. Kesavan Unnithan's suspicions about

[67] Karthiyayani Amma in *Martandavarma* is drawn to Subhadra by such an unknown sense of resemblance; Subhadra turns out to be the daughter of Karthiyayani Amma's brother Tirumukhathu Pillai.

his wife's chastity and his daughter Savitri's actual parentage are decisively reinforced by the daughter's facial features which suggest a different, unidentifiable lineage. Towards the end of *Dharmaraja*, Anantapadmanabhan trains the young Kesava Pillai to recognize the similarities between Savitri's and her grand-uncle Haripanchananan's facial features by using the yogic exercise of *trotak*: this helps him bring two distinct visual images before his mind's eye for comparison and analysis.[68] Family resemblances, the novel tells us, obey nature's laws of iteration, which skip a generation in manifesting antecedents.

Physiognomy is only the most apparent level of transmission within the family; one's character—inner propensities and emotional makeup—also bears the family's signature inscribed in blood. Importantly, it is in the rebel lineage of the Kazhakkuttam house that this finds its most exquisite development. Tripurasundari admonishes a tearful Meenakshi for lacking the steadfast courage of their family. Even destructive royal punishment—the horrific execution of men (*kazhuvettam*) and the selling of women and children to fisherfolk (*thurakettam*) are matters of glory for the lineage with unflinching hearts (*vadakkaralkonda kulam*). C.V.'s later novels are deeply invested in signs of such natural transmission in body and inner mettle. They are a matter of difficult decipherment, but they unveil a banished, precious inheritance of Nayar valour. The survival of the Kazhakkuttam house in the face of royal rage commands respect from the elders on the king's side as well. The seeming stigma of execution and destruction only serves to add 'a kind of glory', conferring on the lineage an aura of counter-sacrality. Women are the bearers of this difficult inheritance: Tripurasundari, Meenakshi, and Savitri assume it with a pride and a courage that is almost involuntary.

But there are other sorts of external marks too: those that do not come from the inheritance of blood. Raja Kesavadas is again the best example of this: of humble origins, he possesses no heirloom or regalia as talisman; it is the scar of a humiliating wound received

[68] Raman Pillai, *Dharmaraja*, 348.

as a boy from Arathamappilla Thankachy, the mistress of the house where he worked. The scar in some sense stands at the opposite end of signs of lineage; it marks a beginning, not an end: the humiliating incident is the commencement of Kesavan's subsequent self-made life and rise to glory. In later years, the dewan will touch this scar at moments of crisis in order to control his turbulent emotions, and inspire himself with strength and resolve. Unlike schematic signs that connect characters to exterior elements, the scar is a private personal mark, an automnesic external signifier deriving its force from an individuated life history.

Among autobiographical talismans are usually found gifts and souvenirs of a beloved or a dead friend, memory markers that refer to close personal connections. However, unlike in *Indulekha* or other novels invested in modern idioms of intimacy and domesticity, objects do not frequently appear in C.V.'s historical novels as bearers of a personal, intimate signature: no equivalent of a knit cap or a fiddle in his fictional eighteenth century. Of course there are exceptions to this: Trivikrama Kumaran in *Ramaraja Bahadur* presents the *veerasrnkhala* he received from the king to his beloved Savitri. Schematic and personal economies intersect here: the royal reward belongs to a system of ceremonial objects but, turned into a lover's gift, it enters a space of personal intimacy. This intersection is not accidental: it points to a deeper reliance on royal authorization for affective individual lives, underlining the close links in C.V.'s fictional universe between sovereign authority, personal lives, and the articulation of affect.

The preceding pages have tracked the ways in which the perceptual universe in C.V.'s novels is laid out and how characters appear in them. Schematism, performance routines, techniques of disguise, and a variegated and unstable field of visibility are central to the making of their distinctive world. Events from only a hundred years distant from the time of writing appear here as if they took place in a different epoch. Past-ness is not a matter of chronology; it is experienced as a modal difference, and its most apparent sign in the novel is the mythical attenuation of realism. The improbable postures and styles of visual representation which Chandu Menon carefully tried to avoid are brought back by C.V. and given a prominent aesthetic function. Their aim is not to document ways of living and thinking in the past, but rather to produce the past as a divided, conflicted inheritance.

Our point of departure was the differentiation between two sorts of characters: those who appear in dramatic idioms of excess and exteriority and those sketched in attitudes of restraint in speech and action. The difference between them regulates their relationship to the present, their modal proximity and distance. Excess produces fear and awe at its most grandiose instances and contempt or condescension at its low ebb. Chantrakkaran and Ugra Haripanchananan, resurgent remnants of Ettuveettil Pillamar, evoke much of this spectrum of affects. The Pillamar themselves appear in *Martandavarma* in their secretly held confabulations. C.V. drew on Shungoonny Menon's history and other royalist accounts in presenting them as cruel and violent in their murderous deeds against the royal family. T.K. Velu Pillai has subsequently argued that this picture of the Nayar lords was historically inaccurate and that many of the horrific deeds attributed to them were contradicted by historical evidence. Critics have suggested that C.V.'s more respectful treatment of the Kazhakkuttam house reflects a change in his estimate of the Pillamar. Kazhakkuttathu Pillai, however, was presented in positive terms already in *Martandavarma*: he was shown opposing the proposal to support Thampimar's claim to the throne and suggesting, instead, reconciliation with Prince Martandavarma, provoking a hostile reaction among other Nayar lords. His steadfast commitment to the group in spite of his disagreement is perhaps the most significant element in his valorization; from later novels we understand that he kept his word and faced his execution with unflinching courage. Kazhakkuttathu Pillai's speech and dignified restraint in behaviour single him out in the Pillamar *sabha*.

Restraint, in contrast with excess, inspires a dimension of respectful adoration in narration. Nuanced biographical elaboration of characters finds its place within this strand. One may say that Raja Kesavadas is not just the best example of this; he is arguably the only object of properly biographical investment in C.V.'s novels: *Dharmaraja* and *Ramaraja Bahadur* track his life from its childhood and show him at different points in his life and achievement. More importantly, the experience of a life lived in its extensity with memories, emotions, and a self-conscious inhabitation of relationships—is important in his presentation. A space is created for all this, often obliquely and by suggestion, in C.V.'s aesthetic procedures of exteriority. We get glimpses in Meenakshi and Subhadra of a reflective relationship with personal life. Subhadra is introduced through a description of her physical beauty, noting her resemblance with Raja Ravi Varma's portraits of women, but features are filtered through a semiological reading aimed at deciphering her inner nature.[69] A brief biographical summary follows, which converts the details of her life as publicly known into potentially significant, uninterpreted traces. Her character unfolds temporally through subsequent events and suggestive snatches of her inner reflections which we are allowed to overhear. Kesavan Unnithan's life is sketched in fuller terms but does not form a biography in this sense: defined through a fundamental failure at understanding, he is exteriorized as an object of condescension rather than respect.

The legacy of the Ettuveettil Pillamar was the difficult core of historical inheritance in C.V.'s novels. The unspeakable treason mentioned in royalist histories also represented an earlier form of sovereignty exercised in ties of honour and kinship. Kazhakkuttathu Pillai, while leaving the *sabha* of the Pillamar refers to the twenty-four idols of Sastha installed on the hills to protect the region. They mark the territory as bound not just by geography; the Pillamar as protectors are bound by this originary institution of sovereignty. It is not accidental that the myths of *Keralolpathi* surface repeatedly in this chapter. These foundational rituals combine Vaishnavite and

[69] Raman Pillai, *Martandavarma*, 172.

Saivite elements, as also local forms of worship of the goddess. The oath of secrecy administered at the Pillamar *sabha* begins by invoking Sree Padmanabhaswamy but swears also by the fierce Kali who reigns over the clan (*ikkulamalum karunkaliyane*) not to reveal their common resolve.[70] The Tamil phrasing of the oath embodies a form of sovereignty distinguished from the language of royal exchanges in the novel.

The only Pillai family to survive was the Kazhakkuttam house; that too because a branch of the family escaped destruction by leaving the country. The distinction made in *Martandavarma* between Thevan Vikraman Pillai of the Kazhakkuttam house and the other Nayar lords reappears as a division within the next generation. While Ugra Haripanchananan represents the violent assertion of the claims of an earlier sovereignty, Meenakshi and Savitri—and to an extent Tripurasundari and Santhan—are inheritors of the valour and self-control of Thevan Vikraman. While inheriting their lineage with pride, they do not see themselves as enemies of the king's sovereign power. Meenakshi thinks about her family's old conflict with the royalty: 'Were they evil acts? Could those valiant antagonists of royalty not be considered as the whetstone which through friction against the rock of royal power revealed the magnificent light of the precious diamond within?'[71] The king and his Nayar lords are united by this contestatory relationship: the inner worth of sovereign power is revealed only in moments of intense agonistic extraction.

Anantapadmanabhan and Raja Kesavadas displace the contestatory model in favour of a unified one. The king and the Nayar minister are united not in a relationship of domination and subservience, but in a fusion of sovereignties. The attenuation of Martandavarma's *veeryam* is not accidental: the king's belligerent qualities are displaced on to the physical courage and tactical acumen of his Nayar lieutenant. In *Dharmaraja* and *Ramaraja Bahadur* the gentle,

[70] Ibid., 163.

[71] Raman Pillai, *Ramaraja Bahadur*, 117.

compassionate king rules through the Nayar dewan in whom warlike qualities are turned into dignified, resolute authority in governance. 'In those days,' says the narrator of *Ramaraja Bahadur*, 'the engine of Vanchi Rajyam worked calmly like a submarine steered with skill by two experts in the art of governance, united as master and disciple in a single soul.'[72] Nayar sovereignty is detached from its contestatory exhibition of violence. A disciplined containment of violence, which can erupt in situations of conflict, defines it. Submission to the king is the external sign of this containment. Worship of the king is a ritual affirmation of the martial quality of the Nayar. Raja Kesavadas' exchange of vocatives with the king epitomizes this new configuration. Under the quasi-sacred countersignature of the king the Nayar legacy of sovereign violence finds its new, disciplined expression.

His preoccupation with the magic of royal endorsement distinguished C.V. from the Nayar reform novelists of Malabar. Chandu Menon's *Indulekha*, for example, attempted a reconciliation of English and Indian virtues of femininity by redefining and redeeming Nayar custom and by investing it with a modern affective dimension. *Sambandham* is transformed through the affective supplement of monogamous love into modern matrimony.[73] Self-fashioning in the Malabar Nayar reform novel drew substantially upon the world of English education. A colonial space of possibilities, involving a new territorial imagination, forms of domesticity, and styles of appearance and behaviour marked in these novels the space of the new subject. C.V. caricatured these contemporary styles in his farces (*prahasanam*) and in his satiric social novel *Premamrtam*. The comic mode of *Premamrtam* arises from an application of the literary apparatus of C.V.'s historical romances to contemporary society.

[72] Ibid., 88.

[73] Chandu Menon's note of dissent to the Malabar Marriage Commission report expressed a view about *sambandham* which the Nayar reformers of Travancore would have agreed with. C.V., C. Krishna Pillai, and other Nayar reformers aimed at a legalization of *sambandham* as marriage while introducing no substantial change in the system of inheritance.

The schematic dimension of the historical novels here becomes pure and arbitrary form without any foundation in a quasi-sacral moral universe. Techniques of gigantism and stylization serve only to produce the effects of farcical incongruity. The Western-educated new Nayars of *Premamrtam* are shown as incapable of negotiating the delicate relationship between custom and innovation. Their inability to interpret the objects and signs of a complex universe of custom lead to erroneous projections. *Premamrtam* presents this as a problem in negotiating the distance between Indian and Western models of perception—identified in the novel with *adhyaropam* and empiricism. In the affective universe of the novel, this is no less than the question of negotiating a harmonious equation between Indian ideas of *pranayam* and Western ideas of love.[74]

C.V.'s formulation and narrative resolution of the problem in *Premamrtam* remained inadequate, and this may be considered a sign of the unviability in his own times of the narrative model he developed in his historical romances. No countersignature from the sacred realm could validate a novelistic representation of contemporaneity. For novelists from Malabar, the modern institutions of marriage, family, and the law court held out the promise of restoration and validation in the modern world. In C.V.'s work the vocabulary of law remains inadequate, based as it is on evidence gathered according to an empirical organization of perception.

However, the royal decrees which could split structures of Nayar power no longer existed as moral resources in C.V.'s time. A pronounced colonial presence had hugely reduced the sovereignty of the king. The politics of the court hinged on the relations between the king, the resident, and the dewan—who was very often a non-Malayali Brahmin. The significance of the Nayars as a *jati* began its decline, and attempts to consolidate their political presence took the form of forging a Malayali identity through the notion of the Nayar *samudayam*. C.V.'s historical romances offered an aesthetic working

[74] See, for a discussion of the problem of interpretation and misprision in *Premamrtam*, Kumar, 'Seeing and Reading'.

through of the conflicted inheritance of the Nayars in relation to state power. On the countenance of the new disciplined Nayar subject prepared to sacrifice her life in battle appear the facial features of Ugran Kazhakkuttathu Pillai, the fearsome embodiment of older Nayar sovereignty. Political time is not only the time of state forms, institutions, and rightful claims by communities; it is also the time of the iterative transmission of bodily features and inner propensities. It is in its layers and interstices that C.V. found idioms for a contemporary formulation of historical inheritance.

In turning to C.V.'s historical novels in detail, we have been concerned with the idea of the human subject that they seem to presuppose. It may be a mistake to identify this with specific characters valorized in the novels. The figure of the subject should rather be sought at an anterior level, in the mechanisms by which characters are differentiated, made intelligible, and endowed with their performative potency. C.V.'s character system, as we saw, is dependent on an orchestration of modes of visibility, performance, and speech. These work by a continuous negotiation between flamboyance and restraint, performative exuberance and controlled gestures, and diverse idioms of exteriority in the interstices of which a space is carved for individuation and inner feelings. The forms of subjectivity that underlie C.V.'s novels ought to be sought precisely in such negotiations. The difficult tensions between the old and the new is the stuff of this subject. The old is simultaneously valued and renounced: it is praised as a glorious age worthy of emulation in the declining present; however, the past can be praised thus only after it is subjected to a transformation which involves the suppression of vital dimensions. A narratable past emerges by the excision of inheritances that cannot be directly assumed and inhabited. Ties of blood that do not obey the rules of individual autonomy are surrendered in favour of new allegiances to the king and the state. The disciplined Nayar minister emerges from the sacrifice of rebels and their claims. It is on the ashes of a community of earlier obligations that the new state is erected. C.V.'s subjects are produced at that difficult intersection where mourning for the old meets eulogies of the new. These cannot coexist on the same plane of the fictional world. C.V.'s challenge was to find an aesthetic procedure for allowing them to coexist by occupying two different levels in the subject's existence.

One form of the subject's relation to the past is oriented towards narration. The other remains unavailable for direct avowal or articulation, manifesting indirectly in forms that appear archaic within the fictional world. This induces a complex temporality: while the actions and events narrated in the novel are already distant in time from the present of the reader, an even older, seemingly mythical world makes its spectral presence felt in the atmosphere the novels powerfully conjure up. The latter is an object of explicit disavowal, but it holds a secret attraction within the fictional world, making the narrative turn to its charged proximity time and again in rapt fascination. The iteration of rebellion and its suppression—the repeated sacrifice of one form of sovereignty for another—is a sign of this movement in C.V.'s plots. In the intimacy and disjunction between these two impulses we may find the figure that C.V.'s novels put forward as the subject of historical inheritance. This figure stands at the junction of two strands: on one hand, narratable, avowable histories linked to the state with its new forms of subjection and identities; on the other, a less articulate, archaic past which inheres in the intensities of affect. Therefore, the subject of C.V.'s novels can narrativize its historical location only by paying an unavowable homage to the turbulent forces that reach out to it from the past. History is both narration and passion for this subject; the prominence of performance routines and forms of lamentation in C.V.'s work is not accidental.

His historical novels articulated this complex structure of inhabitation of the past through an aesthetic work of fictional organization. Later, writers of autobiographies would engage the relationship between individual lives and their historical dimension more directly. They too faced difficulties in narrating their inhabitation of history in its conflicting dimensions, but their solutions were different from C.V.'s. It is to them that we turn in the next chapter.

6

Incomplete Inhabitations

History's Autobiographical Signature

In a novel from early-twentieth-century Kerala—V.I. Mannadiar's *Kamalam* (1924)—the protagonist Venugopalan decides to suppress his love for the beautiful Kamalam, a difficult but necessary task, since he is unsure whether she reciprocates his feelings, or perhaps even rebuffs them. Further, her caste status is superior to his, and her family has thus far only made alliances with Brahmins and members of the royal family. Venugopalan's is an anxiety familiar from many of the romantic novels of Kerala at the turn of the century (including *Indulekha*):

> After his conversation with his mother, Venugopalan's resolve became even firmer. He vowed not to let such perverse intelligence possess him. He got up, went and had lunch. Instead of going back to his room to lie down again, he walked about in the verandah. After some time, he went into his room and picked up an old copy of an English book famous by the title *The Biography of Napoleon*. He opened the doors and the windows well, sat down upright in a chair and began reading.[1]

Time and time again in early-twentieth-century Kerala we encounter biographies, mostly from the Western world, serving as models for thinking through one's personal dilemmas and living out one's social

[1] Mannadiar, *Kamalam*, 180.

and interior projects. Such use has an obvious relationship with the spread of modern education and movements for social reform. An unusual example can be seen in the following episode from the autobiography of the Nair reformer Mannathu Padmanabhan:

> It was around that time that C. Krishna Pillai's sixtieth birthday (*shashtyabdapurthi*) was celebrated . . . On occasions like these and for other religious ceremonies the practice among the Nairs was to read the *Ramayanam* or the *Bhagavatam* over a period of seven days. This was known as the *Saptahaparayanam*. However, the social reformer C. Krishna Pillai called a few people and some of his friends some days before his birthday, lit a ceremonial lamp (*nilavilakku*) and arranged the recitation—instead of the *Ramayanam*—the biography of that great negro leader Booker T. Washington.[2]

The use of a modern autobiography from English in a Hindu ritual recitation captures the paradoxical space of life-writing here; Krishna Pillai's time saw a growth in genres of life-narration such as biography, autobiography, the personal diary, and letters with a biographical or autobiographical intent.[3] By recounting individual lives, these forms contributed to the setting up of new normative models for personal conduct and community service; they also participated in the making and modification of historical memory.

In 1939, at the age of seventy-five, K. Kannan Nair, a well-known figure in the Nayar reform movement, decided to write his autobiography. At the outset, he reassured his readers about the sources on which he had based his account:

> As advised by my teacher Sri Selvanayakam in 1879 when I was a student of Class Five—the Fifth Form of today—I took up the habit of writing 'my diary' regularly from 1888. This practice continued till 1932. My teacher felt that it would be a good means of literary training on an easy

[2] Padmanabhan, *Jeevitasmaranakal*, vol. 1, 68.

[3] An example of the biographical use of personal correspondence from the mid-twentieth century is seen in a letter addressed to his young son, written by Moorkothu Kunjappa, to transmit an account of his father, the famous writer and social reformer Moorkothu Kumaran (1874–1941). Moorkothu Kunjappa, *Moorkothu Kumaran*, 55–61.

> subject matter. On some occasions, conversations were also recorded in the diary, in the respective languages. The details included in this autobiography (*swajeevacharitram*) for the period from 1888 to 1932 are summaries of those diary entries. Those for later years have been written on the sole basis of memory.[4]

Kannan Nair belonged to the first generation of the few Malayalis who adopted the new habit of committing their daily experiences to paper and ink. As his case shows, the practice of diary writing, in its early days, was often linked to new projects of education. In addition to its usefulness as a mnemonic aid, the diary helped cultivate literary competence and prompted a disciplined survey of one's everyday activities. Some of the new writers, the poet Kumaran Asan for example, wrote their diaries exclusively in English, while others like Kannan Nair used primarily Malayalam.[5] These diaries were hardly a space for intimate confessions: Asan's mainly recorded ordinary events from his daily life; others recorded amusing incidents from real life to entertain themselves and potential readers.[6] In the latter half of the nineteenth century coherent autobiographical narratives began to be written in Malayalam, leading to the development of a distinctive genre in the twentieth century. Like the novel, the autobiography too appeared on the literary scene as a new expressive form associated with modern public-print cultures.

I begin here by examining two early autobiographies in Malayalam. One of them is a rudimentary autobiography, or *Atmakatha*, written by a traditional Brahmin scholar, Vaikkathu Pachu Moothathu

[4] K. Kannan Nair, Foreword to *Karuthodi Kannan Nayarude Atmakatha*, v. Interestingly, in an article published in *Bhashaposhini*, Kannan Nair wrote about the importance of a 'sense of individuality' (*pratyekabhavam*) for all action. K. Kannan Nair, 'Keraliya Samudayam', 195.

[5] See Kumaran Asan's Diary. For a discussion of entries from Asan's diary, see Prabhakaran, *Asante Diarikalilude*.

[6] Manjapra Ramunni Menon published a selection from his diaries for 1921–2 as a record of amusing real events. In the Introduction, the well-known writer K. Sukumaran, B.A., bemoaned the absence in Malayalam of accomplished diary writers like Samuel Pepys and John Evelyn. Manjapra Ramunni Menon, *Rasakkatta*, iv.

(1815–83), while the other is a text prepared for a public reading at a religious function by an upper-caste convert to Christianity, Yakob Ramavarman (1814–58). Pachu Moothathu was a renowned Sanskrit scholar, grammarian, poet, and Ayurvedic physician, and the author of one of the first histories of modern Travancore.[7] His autobiographical narrative begins with an account of his birth, an event that normally defies first-person recollection. For Moothathu, however, this poses no problem, as he begins by adopting an external, supervening perspective:

> Written by Parameswaran, according to remembrance . . . Birth on 25 Edavam in the year 989 of the Kollam Era [Malayalam calendar; CE 1814] at the convergence of *Suryavaram* (Sunday), *Pooradam* [Purva Ashadha—twentieth *nakshatra* in the Indian astrological system], *Aparadwiteeya* (in the *Candrapaksham*) [the second day of the lunar fortnight] and *Shubhranama nityayogam* [based on calculations of longitude of the sun and the moon] at *Kuleeradi drekkana samayam* [based on divisional charts of the zodiac sign] in Vaikkam Padinjaredathu house. *Upanayanam* [ritual initiation to *brahmacharya*] in 999 Edavam. *Samavarthanam* [ritual conclusion of *brahmacharya*] in Edavam 1000. Until then, due to negligence, only the alphabet could be learnt.[8]

The individual's life is plotted on a larger astrological map: appropriate, one might say, for an autobiographer who was also a renowned astrologer. Astrology was an integral part of Ayurvedic practice in Moothathu's time: both these systems treated the individual's location in time and place as vitally significant. It has been suggested that astrology, in offering a partial cosmology, 'projects the individual

[7] See, for a biography of Pachu Moothathu, Moosad, *Vaikath Pachu Moothathu*.

[8] Moothathu, 'Pachu Moothathinte Atmakatha', 55. Moothathu's autobiography is presumed to have been written after 1872 as it mentions events that took place till that year. It was first published in *Samastha Kerala Sahitya Parishad Traimasikam* in 1937. It was also reprinted in Naduvattom Gopalakrishnan's *Atmakathasahityam Malayalathil*. See Moothathu, 'Atmakatha'.

into an open future; but it is a future in which every individual has a determinate place.'[9] Moothathu's autobiographical account pointed to a truth that could not be articulated solely in terms of the individual's experiences. His personal remembrance did open a gateway to the truth about himself, but it would still need validation from a source that exceeded individual—or even human—lives.

We see an instance of this in his account of an illness that almost stole his life. While in his mid-twenties, Moothathu was afflicted by an illness attributed to vitiated blood (*raktadosham*). Various remedies were tried and physicians consulted, to no avail. Finally, he undertook a year-long routine of ritual austerities known as *valiya bhajanam* (the major devotional offering) at the Siva temple at Vaikom. Moothathu gives a detailed account of this demanding routine: divided into nine mandalas of forty days each, *valiya bhajanam* prescribed elaborate austerities whose strictness forced many devotees to abandon it midway.[10] Pachu Moothathu successfully completed it but the ailment was not entirely cured. On the contrary, he found himself afflicted by the far more dangerous smallpox.

> At a time when there was no smallpox anywhere around, I contracted the disease in 1020, and it became steadily worse. Those who saw me felt that recovery was impossible, and I fell into an unconscious state for three days. Some people insinuated that my illness was the result of mistakes I made while performing the *valiya bhajana*. On the third night, in the fourth *yamam*, I saw the figure of Shiva next to me, with a bright glow and with four arms and the signs mentioned in the puranas. With him was a short and beautiful young figure with a stick in his hand, with the *bhasmam* (sacred ash), the *rudraksham* beads and some ornaments. Even now I feel blissful whenever I remember the joy I felt while seeing these figures. He sprinkled some *bhasmam* on me. Immediately I saw some horrifying and ugly shapes running away from near me. Then the figure faded away after sprinkling some *bhasmam* around my bed . . . Since then, the illness began to lose its intensity.[11]

[9] Kemper, 'Time, Person and Gender', 754.
[10] Moothathu, 'Pachu Moothathinte Atmakatha', 56–8.
[11] Ibid., 59.

This is an exceptional moment of vindication for Moothathu: an act of divine intervention confirms the truthfulness and rectitude of his devotional practice against public misperception. The mode of veridiction invoked here has some tropological similarities to the ordeal, where the purity of the person is revealed through a difficult or unusual outcome in a trial. P. Bhaskaran Unni has listed several instances of the ordeal—such as *satyapariksha* (trial of truth), *jalapariksha* (trial by water), *agnipariksha* (trial by fire), and *thukkupariksha* (trial by weight) used in Kerala in the nineteenth century.[12] The incidence of smallpox, seen by others as punishment for laxity in the performance of austerities, is presented in Moothathu's autobiography as a variant of the ordeal. The vision of Siva and Subramanian remains private for the narrator, but the abatement of the illness is for all to see.

However, for all its power, the moment of divine intervention—as in the case of miraculous outcomes in ordeals—reveals nothing new to the narrator about himself; nor does it transform him in any significant way. When Pachu Moothathu continues his narrative, it is to speak again about journeys, patients, and remunerations, about more deaths and marriages in the family. It is about rise and fall, fortune and misfortune, without integrating them into an account of his own evolution or growth. Moothathu's account of his ordinary business of life conveys a strong sense of repetitiveness at the level of the everyday, even though this allows for individuated variations. The places one travels to are different, the illnesses, the patients, the students—all are different; yet they turn out to be minor variations when mapped on a deeper plane of time, that of planetary positions and stages in a person's life. The temporal scheme, which renders human life intelligible, remains outside the purview of human action and reflection. We must, however, be wary of seeing in this a simple denial of human agency. Divine intervention, as we saw, appeared

[12] Unni, 468–72. See also Joseph, 'The Hand Dipping Ordeal', 110, for a writ issued in 1627, granting permission to a Nambutiri Brahmin to perform the ordeal.

in Moothathu's narrative precisely to vindicate the human agent. An astrological or religious explanation of events may enable or endorse a particular way of performing actions in the world. The encounter with the divine in an exceptional moment of oneiric veridiction, however, does not mark in Moothathu's account any significant personal transformation or any substantial alteration of his relations to the world.

However, by the time Moothathu was writing his autobiographical text, efforts were already being made in Malayalam to write the story of one's life as a narrative of transformation. This strand appeared prominently in narratives of conversion to Christianity. In fact, the earliest modern autobiography in Malayalam is an account of his conversion by Yakob Ramavarman, written in 1856, published first in the journal *Keralopakari* in 1874, and subsequently printed as a book in 1879 by the Basel Mission Press in Tellicherry.[13] Ramavarman's autobiographical account was written for a public reading on the occasion of his *hastarpanam* (ordination as a preacher) in 1856.[14] Samuel Hebich and Hermann Gundert, the most prominent figures of the Basel mission, were present on the occasion.[15] Ramavarman's story finds mention in biographies of Samuel Hebich who was probably the most active missionary at work among the poor and in their conversion.[16] Gundert's biography, published by the Basel Mission,

[13] The Basel German Evangelical Missionary Society, the only Protestant mission at work in Malabar in the mid-nineteenth century, established their earliest mission station in the district in Tellicherry in 1839. The Basel Mission started printing books in Malayalam in Tellicherry from 1847.

[14] For a brief discussion of Ramavarman's life and of the position of his autobiography in the history of the genre in Malayalam, see Manalil, 'Malayalathile Adyathe Atmakatha'.

[15] Ramavarman sent a report of his ordination to the Mission Committee in Basel on 11 September 1856. I thank Matthias Frenz for making this report and other documents related to Ramavarman from the Basel Mission archives available to me.

[16] George N. Thomssen, *Samuel Hebich of India*, 135–43; *The Life of Samuel Hebich*, 176–7.

speaks of Ramavarman as one of the few converts of Gundert whose subsequent life as a Christian was a matter of joy for him.[17]

Ramavarman was the son of the Raja of Cochin, Veera Kerala Maharaja. He received a Sanskrit education as a child and soon demonstrated his aptitude for learning by mastering several *kavyas* and lessons in astrology at a very young age. His devotion to the Hindu gods was, however, shaken by a theft from the Trippunithura temple, seemingly by none other than the priest, who disappeared with precious ornaments used for decorating the idol. Another theft—this time that of the family idol used for worship by Ramavarman's father—conclusively destroyed his faith in idol worship: 'the idol is not God, it is a mere doll, bereft of life and sense.'[18] Disengagement from idol worship coincided in Ramavarman's narrative with his encounter with a new kind of sacred object, the Gospel. Gifted a copy of the Gospels he was, despite his sense of wonder at seeing a printed book in Malayalam for the first time, put off by the unfamiliar names used in the Biblical narrative.[19] There is also at this time an interesting change in Ramavarman's taste in reading—he avidly turns to the treatises on the erotic, to *Kamasastram*. This is accompanied by a reckless amoral posturing in everyday life: 'I should obtain whatever takes my fancy; this is the true *purushartha*.'[20] However, this new faith—or the lack of it—also receives a jolt: death appears as a frightening spectacle before Ramavarman to shake him out of the certitudes of sensual indulgence. The premature death and agony of the last moments of his young niece come to him as a wake-up call. Using the vocabulary of the

[17] *Life of Dr. H. Gundert*, 56.

[18] Ramavarman, *Yakob Ramavarmante Atmakatha*, 30.

[19] The first Malayalam translation of the Bible, based on the Syrian version, was published in 1811. Church Mission Society Press, Kottayam, published a translation of the New Testament in 1829 and of the entire Bible in 1842. These translations were prepared under Benjamin Bailey's supervision. Hermann Gundert's translation of the Bible, published by the Basel Mission, Tellicherry, was not published until 1868.

[20] Ramavarman, *Yakob Ramavarmante Atmakatha*, 31.

Hindu puranas, he begins thinking about the four hundred hells in which he will languish after his death. Around this time he is given a second copy of the Gospel. He opens himself to this unfamiliar narrative, largely in response to the favourable impression made on him by the missionaries and their message: he identifies readily with their criticism of idol worship.

A desire for conversion to Christianity begins to take root in Ramavarman's heart through a process of identification. Once, listening to a sermon on Isaiah, 53—'he bore the sin of many, and made intercession for the transgressors'—he begins to feel that the verse is addressed to him: 'It showed me clearly that I was that transgressor, that Jesus Christ prayed for me, that he continues to pray for me still, and that he offers eternal salvation to those who believe in him.'[21] Instances of the trial, similar to the one encountered in Pachu Moothathu's narrative, follow: a boat which carries Ramavarman is about to capsize and stabilizes upon his promise to convert; a painful abscess in his stomach is healed on praying to Christ. These events, protecting and binding the subject in promises of faith, lead to the moment of baptism, the final relinquishing of ties with family and community, and the adoption of a new way of life.

The acts of conversion and baptism, however, are not the *telos* towards which Ramavarman's narrative moves; they mark only the midpoint. There are further trials before he reaches the moment of *hastarpanam*, the occasion that the autobiography bears witness to. These new trials are primarily about the subject's conscience, indicating the emergence of a new kind of self-relationship. The silent prayer as an inner practice is a crucial site where this is explored:

> At that time I neither knew nor had heard of praying by heart. Since I was not satisfied with reading the ordinary prayer book and the book of family prayer printed at Kottayam, I talked to my friend Joseph Fenn about this. He told me that God looks not at the book but at one's heart.

[21] Ibid., 34.

> I could look at the prayer book when I go to the church, like everybody else. I began following this advice from then on, and began feeling much happier about it.[22]

The discovery of prayer by heart took time: as on earlier occasions of self-transformation, it alters the relations in which the subject is embedded. Ramavarman's narrative speaks about a sin committed by him while living in Belgaum: 'At this time I committed a grave sin (*kathinamaya oru thettu vannu*).' The syntax of the Malayalam is interesting: a literal translation would read 'a grave wrong came to me'. The subject is implicated in a mode of passivity, which is carried through in the ensuing passage:

> All of a sudden I became like a madman. Recalling that I had not been through such misery in the past ten years, I pleaded remorsefully before God, sweating and shivering, but I did not get any peace or joy. A few days later, when the white missionaries (*sayippanmar*) came to know and asked me about this, I boldly contradicted them. When they asked me to leave, I left with much pride and anger. Although some enemies of the mission asked me to stay, I did not relent, on account of my shame and anger.[23]

Madness, misery, remorse, shame, and anger: these are the initial affective stations on Ramavarman's path towards the act of self-revelation, which marks the climax of his narrative. Among these, shame occupies a crucial position, for it works as the trigger or cause of the other affects. Shame has a crucial relationship to visibility and exposure. It has been regarded as an experience of improper exposure where the subject wishes to escape from the domain of visibility but is unable to. As we saw in chapter 1, Levinas considered shame as arising 'from the radical impossibility of feeling from oneself to hide from oneself, the unalterably binding presence of the I to itself'.[24]

This reading of shame is important for Ramavarman's autobiographical account as the trope of shame works within an ensemble of

[22] Ibid., 38.

[23] Ibid., 42. See also *The Life of Samuel Hebich*, 176–7.

[24] Levinas, *Of Escape*, 64.

acts of exposure. It was some years later, in 1847, that Ramavarman confessed his sin and opened his heart to a new relationship with God and himself. This crucial incident is presented over two moments. At a sermon, some members of the congregation publicly confessed their sins. Ramavarman was deeply affected by this and retired to the missionary's room to weep in solitude. When he returned to the congregation he heard a voice within, admonishing him: 'You tough one, open your heart too!' In the evening he made a public confession before the congregation, though remaining silent about the shameful incident in Belgaum.

> Next Sunday when I was sitting in the church and listening to the sermon, I felt something hitting me in the heart like a fireball. In a moment, it burned my entire heart down. It descended to my bones and burned them down. My entire body began glowing in the fire and a fountain started all on its own from my eyes. Certain that this was the fire of hell, I wailed aloud and decided to vomit the poison inside me. However, I desisted thinking that this would interrupt the sermon. After the sermon . . . I went to lunch and began eating but unable to bear it any more I rushed towards Hebich Sayippu with unwashed hands and cried aloud: I am being destroyed; in Belgaum I committed such and such a sin; when they asked me I got angry and lied. I also spoke about many other sins which came to my memory then. God opened my eyes immediately: I saw for myself Jesus on the cross in Golgotha, shedding his precious blood for me through his five wounds. He granted me grace to throw my burden beneath his cross and to bathe in his stream and to wear his shroud.[25]

This experience of self-dissolution serves as the true moment of initiation into the practice of prayer by heart, which appears here as an unseating of the heart from its habits, a moment of dramatic opening to the divine in an unabashed act of public self-exposure. The state of being riveted to oneself inescapably in oppressive self-exposure is turned into the positive act of public confession.

In Ramavarman's autobiographical narrative several concentric circles of self-transformation lead to this final moment of acknowledging one's past and freeing oneself from it. Each circle involves

[25] Ramavarman, *Yakob Ramavarmante Atmakatha*, 45–6.

the appearance of a new semiological object, an attempt to come to terms with it through a new mode of reading, and then finally a disavowal of the object in favour of a more expansive horizon. This took the form of learning the Hindu puranas, rejecting idol worship, reluctantly reading the Gospels, and finally, disavowing the exterior experience of reading for an infinite and dramatic opening of the heart. Autobiography, for Ramavarman, is the record of these moments of rupture, which are also the points of new beginnings.

I have referred to the autobiographical accounts of Pachu Moothathu and Yakob Ramavarman to indicate two idioms of speaking about the self available in autobiographical writing in Kerala at the turn of the nineteenth century. Both accommodated personal and everyday experiences within a framework of larger, divine coherence. For Moothathu, the personal and the cosmological in their momentary encounter left each other largely unaltered. Ramavarman was concerned precisely with the nature of this encounter and the irreversible transformation it effected on him. The divine might be manifested in miracles in both narratives, but Ramavarman's aim was to measure himself against his experiential knowledge and examine the mark it left on his heart. The realm of the inner, hidden from others and at times even from oneself, is produced through strategies of concealment and confession: the 'grave fault' at Belgaum both refuses and incites speech. The public, autobiographical narrative read out on the occasion of Ramavarman's ordination is not the same as the act of confession: we do not know the nature of the grave sin committed at Belgaum from Ramavarman's account. The autobiography records his acts of confession and redemption rather than the primary experience of sin. The theme of the autobiographical narrative is an interior drama—that of concealing sinfulness and the final letting go which alters his relationship with truth and God.

These personal narratives of Pachu Moothathu and Ramavarman show different examples of the autobiographical truth-game. Though both invoke the divine as the ultimate source of veridiction, Ramavarman's account converts the experience into a rupture in the fabric of the subject. Stable structures of subjectivity are torn apart, and it is in destruction that the new truth of the subject is apprehended. This is mirrored in Ramavarman's almost involuntary act of self-articulation, the public, theatrical ritual of confession. Unlike Pachu Moothathu's narrative of continuity countersigned by the divine, Ramavarman's autobiography seeks to develop a narrative frame for the temporal experience of rupture. Life is sliced irremediably into a past and a present by the event of interruption.

The experience of a self-transforming moment of rupture reappears in the autobiographies discussed below. The pivotal event, though, no longer assumes forms of divine veridiction. Ruptured personal lives reveal, hereafter, a historical space—the zone of intersection of private experience and processes of social change.

II

I look closely now at two texts which conceive the autobiographer's task in relation to experiences of historical and social change. Both were written by Nambutiri Brahmins. Our first author, Kanippayyur Sankaran Namboodiripad (1891–1981), was born in a renowned and wealthy Nambutiri household in Kunnamkulam near Trissur. A well-known Sanskrit scholar and astrologer, Kanippayyur authored a Sanskrit–Malayalam dictionary and texts on traditional conceptions of architecture and the rituals of the Nambutiris. He also wrote several books on Kerala's history as well as a three-volume autobiography entitled *Ente Smaranakal* (My Reminiscences). V.T. Bhattatirippad (1896–1982), our second author, was probably the most prominent leader of the Nambutiri reform movement in Kerala. He was born in Mezhathur in Ponnani. Severe financial difficulties made V.T. (as he is popularly known) take on work as a priest in a temple near Shoranur in 1913; eventually, through much hard work, he also managed to get himself a further education. He became active as the leader of a radical youth faction within the Nambutiri social movement in the 1920s. V.T. appears as a major figure in the narrative of critical modernity in Kerala, which traces its origins to social-reform movements and evolves towards nationalist and the left-secular forms of cultural politics in the state. He wrote several well-known stories and essays, a historically significant reform play, and a series of autobiographical texts. His self-narratives, especially the first volume, *Kannirum Kinavum* (Tears and Dreams, 1972), has acquired canonical status in discussions of the autobiographical genre in Malayalam.

In spite of their shared caste and regional locations, it is difficult to think of two more contrasting authors or autobiographical narratives: while Kanippayyur appears as a traditionalist who justified caste differentiation and untouchability in terms of an earlier system of societal harmony, V.T. occupies an emblematic position within movements which challenged and transformed orthodox practices. These differences appear symptomatically in the way they saw their respective autobiographical projects. Both begin by posing a curious problem—the difficulty of narrating the life of a Nambutiri Brahmin. Kanippayyur's *Ente Smaranakal* locates this in the ordinariness and monotony of his own everyday life:

> Shri. Kuttippuzha Krishna Pillai demanded that I write my autobiography. I felt like laughing. Would anyone like to read autobiographies by ordinary people and not by great personages? . . . Therefore, I wrote in my reply to him: 'It is not difficult in the least to write my life history. Bathed in the morning, had breakfast, lunch, a coffee in the afternoon, and dinner at night, slept: now the history of a day is complete. If you change the date, and write 'ditto', the history of the following day is done. I am now sixty-eight years old. If you write down the dates in all these years and a ditto against each of them, my life history will be complete. However, I do not have the audacity to publish this. If some friends are ready to print and circulate it, I will happily give away the copyright for free.'[26]

V.T. resorts to a similar image at the outset of *Kannirum Kinavum*. It is not the reassuring predictability of everyday life, but the monotony of the drab, uncreative life of Nambutiris that poses a

[26] Kanippayyur Sankaran Namboodiripad, *Ente Smaranakal*, vol. 1, 1.

problem for life-writing: it was all too easy to narrate the life of a Brahmin, especially an Apphan Nambutiri. The term 'Apphan' referred to younger male members of a Nambutiri family, who, at the beginning of the twentieth century, were not entitled to marry within the caste and inherit family property. The ease of narrating their lives also meant that the project was not worthy of effort:

> There is no job easier than writing the biography or the autobiography of an Apphan Nambutiri who lived half a century ago. Born on such and such a day of such and such a year under such and such a star (*nakshatram*). Named Vasudevan, but was nicknamed 'Ittyasu' at home. At an auspicious moment, priesthood hunted him down, opened his mouth and inscribed with the ritual stylus the fifty-one letters of the alphabet on his tongue. Opened the rusty door to knowledge and made him enter. There he passed inside a golden cow (*hiranyagarbham*) called *upanayanam* (the ritual of wearing the sacred thread) and transformed into a *brahmachari*.[27]

V.T. goes on to sketch further landmarks of a typical life: tasteless Vedic training, the ritual *samavarthanam* that marks its conclusion, a faint whiff of freedom, nocturnal love relationships, meaningless years of adult life, then death. 'A Nambutiri's life is so uneventful that no author can really stretch it beyond half a page.'[28]

We can see similarities between Moothathu's account of his life and V.T.'s poignant caricature. The repetitiveness of the traditional Nambutiri way of life, which we saw in Moothathu's summary account of his childhood, made it difficult to stretch a Nambutiri's life narrative beyond a paragraph. The avowal of difficulty was not a constraint on the project of autobiography; in fact, it functioned as the essential productive condition of self-narration for Kanippayyur and V.T. Both wrote voluminously in the mode of self-narration. The autobiographical gesture of these writers comprises moves that turn the sense of impossibility into a ruse for autobiographization.

[27] V.T. Bhattatiripad, *V.T.yude Sampurna Krtikal*, 131.
[28] Ibid.

For Kanippayyur, the principal contrast is between extraordinary persons—makers of history—and ordinary people such as himself whose lives do not merit public narration. Writing up one's life to provide an account of well-known events in the past has been most common among people who played an active role in public life. Prominent bureaucrats, political leaders, and social reformers have justified their autobiographies in this vein.[29] Kanippayyur, however, overcame these hurdles posed by his unremarkable life: he wrote three volumes of his memoirs and published them from a press of his own, the Panchangam Book Depot. His strategy was to turn the uneventfulness of his individual life into the space for a different kind of memory-work. Kanippayyur's lifetime had been witness to enormous 'changes and transformations . . . in the lives of the Malayalis—especially the Hindus, the upper castes in particular, and more specifically the Nambutiris.' This meant that 'almost everyone below the age of forty or forty-five' had no idea how their predecessors lived. The older generation, along with the Kerala they inhabited, would soon disappear from collective memory, making it necessary to 'record, at least as history, those practices and traditions and the changes that happened to them.'[30]

It is this project of historical documentation that brings Kanippayyur back to the possibility of an autobiography. 'If I write my life story, some of these historical facts may be brought into it. And, writing in an autobiographical mode will be more convenient for

[29] For example, see the autobiographies of figures such as C. Sankaran Nair, K.M. Panikkar, K.P.S. Menon, Mannathu Padmanabhan, K.P. Kesava Menon, and Joseph Mundassery. Sankaran Nair has this to say: 'To be an octogenarian in a land where this species has become a rarity, and to have spent over half a century in the front ranks of public life, form, perhaps, a sufficient excuse for recapturing one's memories; but to have been in the citadel of the Government during the most formative period of recent Indian history, namely the Great War, and to have played a not inconspicuous part in launching "reformed" India on its course make it almost imperative to pass on one's experiences to the public.' Introduction to *Autobiography of Chettur Sankaran Nair*, xiv.

[30] Kanippayyur Sankaran Namboodiripad, *Ente Smaranakal*, vol. 1, 7.

describing them adequately.'[31] Nonetheless, Kanippayyur felt that his humbler labour of documentation should keep its distance from the grand aspirations of nationalist autobiographies; he decided not to use the title 'Autobiography' and chose 'My Reminiscences' (*Ente Smaranakal*) instead.[32] Studies of nationalist autobiographies in the colonial world have sometimes seen an allegorical relationship between the individual and the emerging nation, often with a paradigm of progress and development linking the two.[33] Kanippayyur's unremarkable life did not claim such parallels; but he had his own perspective on the times of change that he had lived through.

The basic compositional impulse in *Ente Smaranakal* is descriptive rather than narrative; accounts of rituals, caste practices, objects of everyday use, attire, and jewellery fill its three volumes. Documenting practices ranging from the gesture with which a Nayar greeted a Nambutiri to the details of the ritual trial of Nambutiri women charged with adultery, *Ente Smaranakal* has become, over the years, a standard reference in discussions of nineteenth-century Kerala. Kanippayyur's descriptions are often accompanied by photographs or drawings. Many of the pictures, like those that accompany colonial ethnographic texts, have a staged quality to them: people from the present are dressed up in anachronistic attire to play the role of 'proxy-witnesses' from a lost world. Autobiography is turned into an 'auto-ethnography' of the past, and the life of the author-subject, bereft of interest or significance in its own right, is reconfigured as the site of a historical rupture.

The witness, as a character, observes himself: not in his uniqueness, but in his community, in his immersion and engagement in the

[31] Ibid., 7–8.

[32] Kanippayyur also clarifies how the structure of his narrative will be different from autobiography proper: 'In this book, I may speak not only about my life but also about many other related things, sometimes according to the context and sometimes even without such connection. I wish to inform my readers that this is due neither to sloppiness nor stupidity; this is by design.' Ibid., 8.

[33] See, for example, Holden, 'Other Modernities'; Arnold, 'The Self and the Cell'.

world. This seemingly modest move of auto-witnessing is not for the great heroes who make history: the passion for history belongs to the ordinary. These gestures of humility may appear odd in Kanippayyur, the famous head of a grand Brahmin family renowned for its riches and scholarship. However, non-uniqueness grounds the subject even more firmly in the domain of tradition. In fact, for Kanippayyur, the less unique you are, the greater your access to the truths and the authority of tradition, especially at a time when those truths are changing. The autobiographer's task is to write a narrative of the non-unique: to make his life the object of an auto-ethnographic description.[34]

Unlike the usual ethnographer, Kanippayyur does not refer to a present, but to a world which has almost disappeared, and which can only be re-presented through the images of his memory, sometimes laboriously reconstructed in photographs and drawings. The photographs used in Kanippayyur's text show people wearing ornaments or attire no longer worn by later generations or enacting gestures or simulating customs and clothing from an earlier time. These are masquerades of the past, with the naturalism of the photograph conferring a sense of immediacy on the simulated postures of the figures represented. They serve as illustrations, but also claim a greater approximation to the ethnographic register by virtue of their 'reality effect'.

Kanippayyur's autobiography is made possible by the transformation of the ordinary details of his life and world into elements of a historical discourse. Not accidentally, his historical texts repeat the same inaugural gesture as his autobiographies. His four-volume book on early Kerala history, *Aryanmarude Kutiyettam* (The Aryan Immigration), has this to say while describing the details of everyday life in a Nambutiri house:

[34] For a discussion of 'auto-ethnography' and its use in anthropology, see Reed-Danahay, ed., *Auto/Ethnography*. I use the term 'auto-ethnography' to highlight the convergence of the projects of autobiography and ethnography in Kanippayyur's work.

> What is discussed in the first eleven chapters of this book (all except the last two chapters) has not yet entirely become history. I have been familiar with most of these things from my youth. Not only the heads of families, but also those belonging to Sudra castes like the Nayars who served in Nambutiri households, the people of the villages, and members of prominent Nayar taravads were all familiar with these. If I had set out to write about them at that time, it would have appeared foolish. This is because these matters were considered mere everyday activities at that time; they had not become history. 'Got up in the morning, brushed one's teeth and bathed, had breakfast. Maidservants swept and swabbed the floors, and cleaned the courtyard. Menservants cut firewood'—does anyone write these everyday occurrences down? Is there any need to do that? Would it not appear foolish if one did this?[35]

Both autobiography and history arise out of a break in time, a fading away of custom and practice. For a practice to become history, contemporary society has to begin to forget it; its reappearance, or reminding, will then be accompanied by a sense of unfamiliarity and wonder. 'What happened here?', Kanippayyur asks when he begins his self-narrative, inquiring into the nature of the event that made it necessary. World wars, natural calamities, epidemics—no such spectacular event took place in Kerala; then, what was the momentous event that came to pass?

> The response to this question is interesting. Human beings began to interact with one another as man and man rather than like men and animals (e.g. temple entry). Growing or removing one's hair and beard became matters of personal preference in which others could not interfere (e.g. the cutting of the *kuduma* or the customary tuft of hair indicative of caste). The Government stopped the practice of preventing women from entering public places if they had covered their breasts (the wearing of blouses) . . . Are these what we call revolution! . . . On closer examination, these revolutions turn into storms in a teacup! People differ from each other in their views as in their looks. The world has immense variety. That is all we can say.[36]

[35] Kanippayyur Sankaran Namboodiripad, *Aryanmarude Kutiyettam*, vol. 2, i–ii.

[36] Kanippayyur Sankaran Namboodiripad, *Ente Smaranakal*, vol. 1, 9.

Kanippayyur discounts the magnitude of the transformation, even as he seems to endorse the legitimacy of the changes. His narrative does not propose a simple anti-reformist subject; his aim is to inhabit the past through recollection, while accepting the changes that brought in his own era.

Historical change is not merely a break in custom and practice, in lived experience; it is also the site of a production: that of a new relationship to one's past, a new mode of remembrance tinged with wonder, the experience of new sorts of emotions. 'Now I shall describe the daily routine of Nambutiri women folk at that time,' Kanippayyur announces, 'not only strangers but even young Nambutiri women and girls will be struck with wonder if they listen to this.'[37] However, wonder does not belong solely to the onlooker from the modern world: within the foreign territory of the past too, there is space for the marvellous. This arises in relation to the new objects encountered in the past for the first time. 'At that time travelling on a bicycle was more dignified than travelling in a car nowadays. People used to feel such wonder and respect for it. It must have been difficult to ride bicycles then. [Unni Raja] used to struggle for breath after getting off his bicycle. However, the bicycle was a rare and wonderful vehicle and inspired too much respect to make one notice that difficulty.'[38] These dual senses of wonder, one emerging from the past and moving towards its future (which is the present of writing) and the other coming out of the present and gazing at a past that one never lived (as in the case of the younger generation), are the coordinates of temporal experience in Kanippayyur's theatre of historical reminiscence.

The wonder felt by the subject of his autobiography when he meets modern objects is mirrored in another emotion that appears several times as its structural counterpart—a feeling of unease (*vallayma*). Novelty, instead of leading the subject to a state of pleasure, can also threaten his sense of stability. While innovations in the material realm offer the experience of wonder to Kanippayyur, transformations in

[37] Ibid., 159.

[38] Ibid., vol. 2, 55–6.

the social realm—in caste practices—are recognized as a source of deep unease:

> [It was in a friend's house that] I saw for the first time Nayar women wearing blouses (*ravukka*) while working in a Brahmin household . . . I have not forgotten the unease (*vallayma*) I felt then. It was similar to what I felt later when I saw young Nayar men and Nambutiris with cropped hair, without the traditional tuft (*kuduma*). I had felt as if all this was an insult to us . . . It is normal to feel a sense of discomfort or displeasure when you see unfamiliar practices for the first time. Would anyone agree to people entering a temple for worship wearing trousers and coats and hats?[39]

The opening of *Ente Smaranakal* had attributed a sort of natural legitimacy to many of the changes in customs, including the wearing of blouses. However, the rational acceptance of change comes up against a difficulty in the affective sphere: change may appear natural to reason but may still remain unacceptable in the light of what is felt as natural by virtue of habit. The sense of unease arises from an unconscious, embodied realm of memory, and experiences innovation as an 'insult to us'. Here the individual autobiographer merges into a collective: The 'we' of Kanippayyur cannot be defined in the abstract as custodians of tradition; it refers more specifically to the self-identity of the Nambutiri Brahmin.

Events that announce modern transformations in histories of Kerala—changes in legislation and institutions, and the emergence of community organizations and political parties—are not directly discussed in Kanippayyur's text. Instead, *Ente Smaranakal* teems with descriptions of customs, rituals, and objects of use in the past. These also provide silent testimony to an empty space in the present world created by the disappearance of all that is described. This sense of emptiness is constantly matched by the irremediable promiscuity of modern spaces: Kanippayyur finds new multitudes of people and things crowding into the world. He notices this newness at times

[39] Ibid., vol. 3, 290–1. Translation slightly amended.

with fascination; but they are not the proper objects that he wishes to describe and document.[40] 'Nostalgia' may be too simple a word for his attitude, if it is understood as a longing to return to the past and occupy a space that the work of time has made unavailable. Kanippayyur saw transformation as inevitable. In fact, he took advantage of opportunities created by modernity, as his ventures in printing and publishing clearly indicate. What preoccupies this Nambutiri Brahmin in changing times is a problem of unredeemed debt in contemporary memory. The principles of coherence that shaped the old world, he feels, are all too easily forgotten; what appears to the present as absurd and unjust belonged to a coherent, meaningful world in the past. Kanippayyur's aim is to re-present the past world of Kerala from the perspective of an insider.

This raises a question of right: who is entitled to give voice to shared historical memory? When Kanippayyur wrote his autobiography, a powerful critique of Nambutiri dominance in Kerala was being made by scholars such as Elamkulam Kunjan Pillai.[41] In a series of publications, Elamkulam claimed that the Nambutiris, who came from outside Kerala, were responsible for instituting an inegalitarian and exploitative caste society in the region. After acquiring considerable economic and effective political power by the fourteenth century, Elamkulam argued, they imposed new practices that allowed them sexual access to women from non-Brahmin upper castes. These contentions must be seen in the context of shifts in power relations between communities. From the late nineteenth century, the practice of *sambandham* (customary marital alliance) between Nambutiri men

[40] Two sorts of fascination come up repeatedly in Kanippayyur's text: his encounter, as a child, with modern objects such as the bicycle (his adult experience of air travel does not match this in excitement), and a grudging engagement with new social spaces such as coffee clubs and tea shops, which provides opportunities for him to reflect on how others, as well as he himself, negotiated them.

[41] See, for example, the following works of Elamkulam P.N. Kunjan Pillai: *Keralacharitrathile Iruladanja Edukal, Chila Keralacharitra Prasnangal, Keralabhashayude Vikasaparinamangal,* and *Janmisampradayam Keralathil.*

and Nayar women had become a flashpoint in discourses of reform.[42] Nayar social reformers, advocating a shift from a matrilineal to a patrilineal form of inheritance, had sought a redefinition of the sexual mores of their community, and rejected *sambandham* arrangements with the Nambutiris as primitive, claiming that a morally degenerate Nambutiri caste had imposed such 'uncivilized' practices on other castes in Kerala. From the 1920s, the Nambutiri reform movement also began criticizing *sambandham*, seeking to limit marital relations to one's own caste. Although the Nambutiri and Nayar communities moved to new arrangements for marriage and inheritance by the middle of the twentieth century, making *sambandham* a thing of the past, the issue continued to possess much symbolic value in the historical imagination of Malayalis. Elamkulam, in his studies of medieval Malayalam literature, noted a preponderance of erotic versification and attributed this to the moral turpitude of the dominant caste, the Nambutiris.[43]

For Kanippayyur, Elamkulam's criticisms were symptoms of a modern inability for historical understanding. The normative frames of the present impeded entry into the past on its own terms. Kanippayyur's autobiography and his historical accounts were aimed at remedying this problem and establishing an alliance between autobiography and the writing of history. In one of his volumes on Kerala's history, Kanippayyur proposed an analogy between history and biography:

> Generally speaking, the biography of an individual is written in order to provide information . . . on his qualities, how he came to acquire them, what sorts of difficulties he encountered, and how he overcame them.

[42] In the late nineteenth century, according to custom, only the eldest son in a Nambutiri household was allowed to marry within his caste; the younger sons entered into *sambandham* alliances with women from the non-Brahmin upper castes, especially the Nayars and the *ambalavasis* or temple-serving castes. For a discussion of *sambandham* arrangements among the Nayars, see Arunima, *There Comes Papa*.

[43] Elamkulam P.N. Kunjan Pillai, *Sahityacharitrasamgraham*, 51–2.

> Therefore, the task of writing a person's biography is usually entrusted to friends who have affection and esteem for him and had opportunities to interact closely or live with him . . . Nobody would appoint as biographer an enemy who tries to humiliate and malign his protagonist . . . Now let us examine those who have set out to write a history of Kerala . . . The people of Kerala have few everyday practices that are not linked to religion. An accurate history of Kerala, then, can only be written by those who have seen the core of these rituals and practices, and who—even if they do not hold these in respect—are not hostile towards them. In this light, all will agree that many of the educated Nayars are not qualified to write a history of Kerala.[44]

History, therefore, is like the biography of a society, and the best biographers are those who know their protagonists from the closest proximity. Biographies are here judged from the vantage point of autobiography where external observation and self-perception merge. The ideal biography should in this view coincide in content and tone with the autobiographical mode. Kerala's history is best written by the protagonists of Kerala's social past, since they alone possess the insider's knowledge of the principles of coherence that shaped caste society in Kerala. In Kanippayyur's view this position belongs solely to Nambutiri Brahmins.

This clarifies for us how Kanippayyur could turn his personal autobiographical project into another sort of life-narrative: his new project was to write the biography of the society which he had lived in and known from within, and which he thought he could describe intimately as an insider. Thus, the biographical and the autobiographical referred to distinct but interrelated levels of authorship: the biographer Kanippayyur was a Nambutiri from the Kerala of the past; as an autobiographer, he was the subject of an unremarkable personal life. The author-subject of *Ente Smaranakal* was located at the point where these two planes intersected. In order to write an autobiography, Kanippayyur had to assume the roles of

[44] Kanippayyur Sankaran Namboodiripad, *Aryanmarude Kutiyettam*, vol. 4, xii–xiii.

biographer and obituarist in relation to Kerala's past. This explains the strand of mourning that runs through his text. However, it moves alongside a less prominent narrative of his personal enchantment with new artefacts and technologies. A complex intermingling of wonder and discomfiture marks the affective landscape of *Ente Smaranakal.*

On rare occasions, intimate experiences make a hesitant entry into this narrative, as when Kanippayyur comments on his first *sambandham* to a lady from the royal family of Kochi.[45] Life at her Kovilakam in Trippunithura afforded him new comforts, as also opportunities to study Sanskrit and English. However, Kanippayyur also felt a growing disparity between this new life and his own ways (*sampradayam*), leading him eventually to end the relationship and leave Trippunithura. In a rare personal vein, he notes his sense of pain at ending the *sambandham*, there having been no conflict between him and his spouse; in fact, they were very fond of each other. Intimate personal grief appears fleetingly as a minor detail in a story of changing life practices. Although this is entirely in tune with Kanippayyur's narrative principles, it is important to note that the displacement of the personal by the historical, promised by him in the Preface, is never final; a new sense of the personal, which derives its value from the 'historicality' of one's experience, is produced by his narrative. This is different from the 'historical' interest possessed by the autobiographies of great national leaders.

Yet, interestingly, Kanippayyur's attempt at countering the amnesia of modern historical consciousness led him to new forms of analysis. He argued that two levels of difference were to be taken into account in dealing with caste: one is the level of customary nomenclature—the categories of caste (*jati*) differentiation that have come down to our times through history. These categories, in Kanippayyur's opinion, have no natural validity. There is another level, though, where distinctions are 'natural'—this is the level of

[45] Kanippayyur Sankaran Namboodiripad, *Ente Smaranakal*, vol. 1, 339–44.

racial (*vargam*) difference. The distinction between the Aryan, the Dravidian, and the Mongoloid racial types is for him an instance of natural difference. An anthropologist, says Kanippayyur, will not be able to differentiate between an Ezhava and a Nayar, but he can perceive a clear natural distinction between a person of Aryan racial stock, such as a Nambutiri Brahmin, and a person of Dravidian stock. Races are primordial, natural, and indestructible; 'castes are imaginary creations; they can also be destroyed through imaginary activity.'[46]

Kanippayyur equates race (*vargam*) with varna, as mentioned in the *Gita* and the *smrtis*. He argues that there are only four races in Kerala, in spite of the contemporary differentiation of Malayalis into a large number of castes: they are the Aryans, Nagas, Ezhavas, and Adivasis. The first three groups—all except the Adivasis (the indigenous tribes)—are immigrants: they have come in from outside the region. Kanippayyur argues that while Brahmins are undoubtedly the Aryan immigrants, the Nayars, the carpenters, the blacksmiths, and some of the temple-dependent castes (Ambalavasis) belong to the Naga race brought to Kerala by the Nambutiris as their attendants during their immigration. Ezhavas are later immigrants from Ceylon who entered Kerala after the Aryan settlements and the new political system were well established.[47] Nagas, according to Kanippayyur, include castes that occupy widely varied positions of status in contemporary Kerala. He explains this variation by the degree of mixture of Aryan blood in various castes, which in turn is referred to the polyandrous marital practices of the early Nagas. A contemporary anthropologist, Kanippayyur argues, will place all these castes in the same racial category. In fact, he cites the *Malabar Gazetteer* and Thurston's *Castes and Tribes of Southern India* to argue that it has become difficult to distinguish in physical terms the Nambutiris from those of the Naga race who intermarry only with the Nambutiris. The rich admixture of Aryan blood in these castes

[46] Kanippayyur Sankaran Namboodiripad, *Aryanmarude Kutiyettam*, vol. 1, 102–3.

[47] Ibid., pp. 104–6.

marks them apart from the Dravidian population of the Eastern districts.[48] In his *Nayanmarude Purvacaritram* (The Early History of the Nayars), Kanippayyur states this argument in even stronger terms: 'What is the present status of [the Nayars]? Nowadays, "Nayars" has come to signify "Keralites" and "Keralites" means "Nayars". If we think about it, [we can see that] the governance of Kerala takes place largely according to their interests . . . The Nayars reached this high status solely because of their racial mixture (*vargasankalanam*) with the Nambutiris.'[49] Kanippayyur now makes an interesting move by interrogating the cultural capital of various castes in Kerala. He compiles a 'census' of well-known writers from different castes between 500 and 1087 ME (CE 1325–1912) and plots them against caste groups arranged according to their varying distance from pure Aryan stock, ranging from the Ezhavas who have no Aryan admixture to the Nayars, Ambalavasis (temple castes), and Kshatriyas, in an ascending order of Aryan hybridization.[50] The results range from 2 writers for every 100,000 people for Ezhavas, to 10 in the case of Nayars, 688 for Ambalavasis, and 786 for Kshatriyas. These figures, Kanippayyur claims, demonstrate the predominance of the Aryan element in the cultural realm.[51]

In this apparently naturalizing argument, Kanippayyur seems to move away from his earlier account of caste as a harmonious system of mutual dependence. His own construction of caste categories reflects typically modern tendencies that had a major role in the production

[48] Ibid., 132. The same argument is also made in Kanippayyur Sankaran Namboodiripad, *Nayanamrude Purvacharitram*, vol. 1, 247.

[49] Ibid., 246.

[50] Kanippayyur makes a similar comparison between these castes on the number of historical personages (*charitrapurushanmar*) to reach similar conclusions, in ibid., 239.

[51] Ibid., pp. 132–3. Kanippayyur even proposes a systematic study of the races of Kerala, to identify their typical innate characteristics. He argued that this should involve the segregated nurturing of samples from each race for a few generations, and can be carried out only with state support. See *Aryanmarude Kutiyettam*, vol. 1, 137–8.

and consolidation of caste identities in India—ethnography, anthropometry, and census as a system of enumeration of populations. Studies in recent decades, beginning with the work of Bernard Cohn, have investigated the role of technologies of colonial governmentality in producing modern caste and community identities.[52] In fact, the transformation from caste as hierarchy and interdependence to caste as identity cannot be understood without reference to these technologies and their impact. In the context of the Nambutiris of Kerala, a clear example of anthropometric research can be found in a monograph published by Fred Fawcett in 1900. Using measurements of the nasal index, Fawcett argued that the Nambutiri Brahmins of Kerala are the clearest approximation to the Aryan racial type to be found in southern India: 'he is perhaps, as his measures seem to prove, the truest Aryan in Southern India, and not only physically, but in his customs, habits, ceremonies, which are so welded into him that forsake them he cannot if he would.'[53] Thurston's *Castes and Tribes of Southern India* also combined an ethnographic account of the customs of various castes with anthropometric information.

Kanippayyur's reliance on a 'census' of literary authors is no less modern. Census categories and data became very important instruments in the campaigns mounted by non-Brahminical castes in Kerala from the early twentieth century for adequate representation in government employment and access to education. Following submission of the Malayali Memorial to the Travancore Government in 1891, census data was used by social groups for grounding their claims. Ezhava campaigners like Dr Palpu, as we have seen early in this book, drew on census reports for evidence of official neglect and upper-caste prejudice.[54] Kanippayyur's histories belong, in spite of their apparent celebration of premodern social coherence, to the very sites of negotiation of modern caste identities.

[52] See Cohn, *Colonialism and Its Forms of Knowledge*; Dirks, *Castes of Mind;* and Samarendra, 'Anthropological Knowledge and Statistical Frame'.

[53] Fawcett, *Nambutiris*, 33.

[54] See Unni, 755–68; Panikkasseri, *Do. Palpu*, 23–46.

What then is the relationship between these two registers in Kanippayyur's narratives of selfhood and memory? Is *Ente Smaranakal* meant to provide an affective supplement to the arguments of Kanippayyur's historical narratives? We need to take full cognizance, of course, of the complex nature of a supplementarity that always exceeds its brief. The narrative of *Ente Smaranakal* produces locations and spaces of an impossible inhabitation. In the real world they bear the marks of irreversible present-day usage that transforms inhabitation into acts of possession, access, and appropriation, tainted irremediably by ways of classifying, managing, and organizing castes as modern social groups. It is only in the recollected life of these spaces and events that Kanippayyur can hope to carve out a space for caste as ethos, the affective coherence of which he had to sacrifice in his historical speculations. The tensions between these two idioms animate Kanippayyur's memory project in *Ente Smaranakal* and confer on it a rare poignancy. Its narrator—autobiographer and historian at the same time—is divided between the unselfconscious habitus of an old world of caste practices and new narrativizable caste identities. The task that *Ente Smaranakal* sets itself, without stating this explicitly, is to bring the former into the world of narration without shame and self-consciousness. Nonetheless, the passage between the two worlds appears in the text in affective flashes of wonder and discomfiture, in losses that cannot be adequately acknowledged and conflicts that sit ill at ease with harmony and conviviality.

III

Unlike Kanippayyur, V.T. Bhattatiripad embraced the project of autobiography with readiness: the transformations over the past half-century had, in his view, given Nambutiri Brahmins unique personal lives to narrate. V.T.'s autobiographies celebrate this change as a shift from the meaningless monotonous rhythms of an impoverished life to a temporality of newness and vibrancy. From decay and repetition to purposiveness and innovation: *Kannirum Kinavum* (Tears and Dreams), his first major self-narrative, was structured along these coordinates. V.T. placed at the centre of his story a vignette saturated with affect. It recounted his first encounter with alphabetic writing. Like other members of the elite subgroup of Aadyan Nambutiris who had a right to Vedic learning, V.T. had trained in Vedic recitation as a child. This practice of learning, known as *othu padikkal* (the learning of Vedic recitation) comprised repeating after the master verse after verse of the Rg Veda, thus preparing oneself for the innumerable incantations that mark an Aadyan Nambutiri's adult life. In spite of acquiring intricate skills in recitation, V.T. was not taught to read and write Malayalam or any other script. This was not unusual. E.M.S. Namboodiripad recounts that even after he had been trained to read Sanskrit texts extensively, he was not at all adept in writing: at the age of fifteen, when he was appointed secretary of a community group, he found it difficult to write out notices and keep records in spite of several years of education.[55]

V.T. began to learn the Malayalam alphabet from a schoolgirl of the Tiyyadi caste who was a regular visitor to the village temple where he had found employment as a priest. He helped her with her sums, and she in return began teaching him the alphabet. One day, as he was looking at bold typefaces printed on newspaper wrappings, he realized all of a sudden that he could read:

> When there was no one else in the temple, I began reading a piece of newspaper in which jaggery for the *payasam* had come wrapped . . . While looking through that torn scrap of paper stained by jaggery, I saw an advertisement with the picture of an animal standing with head raised. When I read with difficulty the words *maan-marku kuda* (Stag Mark Umbrella) printed in large letters beneath it, an echo of joy escaped my mind. I cannot say how many times I repeated the sounds *maan-marku kuda*. My eyes become moist with gratitude when I recall that it was this everlasting flame lit by that Tiyyadi girl in the surroundings of that Ayyappa shrine which became the bright light that guided my later life.[56]

Initiation into reading and writing is the decisive moment of rupture in V.T.'s narrative. The acts of reading and writing—which led

[55] E.M.S. Namboodiripad, *Atmakatha*, 127.
[56] V.T. Bhattatiripad, *V.T.yude Sampurna Krtikal*, 189.

eventually to the act of autobiographical writing—replace earlier forms of inscription based on ritualized learning. The training in Vedic recitation is presented in V.T.'s narrative as an instance of earlier, pre-literate inscription. Both he and E.M.S. Namboodiripad recall in their autobiographies the training in Vedic incantation (*othu padikkal*) as monotonous, repetitive, and intellectually vacuous. Competitions such as the Kaduvangattu *anyonyam* tested the skills of young Nambutiris in the recitation of the Vedas; there were contests in reciting the verses forward and backward (*jada* and *ratha*), requiring advanced mnemonic skill.[57] However, understanding the meanings of the Vedic verses did not figure as part of the training.[58] V.T.'s famous Nambutiri reform play, *Atukkalayilninnu Arangathekku* (From the Kitchen to the Stage), opens on a Vedic lesson in progress where the master dozes off and the students trick him by imitating the incantatory tone of Vedic recitation and carry on a conversation about other, more entertaining things.[59]

Incantation as against reading for meaning: are we to see in this a simple opposition between an ignorant repetition that teaches nothing and an intelligent decipherment aspiring progressively towards total comprehension? Or are we dealing with two histories and idioms of teaching and learning? V.T.'s account stands at the cusp of a change in practices of learning and writing, where age-old techniques gave way to new processes. The lesson in Vedic incantation stands alongside other cultural practices that do not aim at training the learner to articulate what he or she has learned: a self-conscious discursive grasp of the object is outside its scope. Training in traditional performing arts illustrates this clearly: lessons and techniques do not primarily focus on producing an articulate, discursive subject.

[57] E.M.S. Namboodiripad offers an account of the *anyonyam* competition in his *Atmakatha*, 101–7. For a discussion of details of Vedic recitation and training, mainly in the context of ancient India, see Scharfe, *Education in Ancient India*, 212–51; Wood, *Knowledge Before Printing and After*.

[58] For an account of his experience of learning to recite the Vedas, see E.M.S. Namboodiripad, *Atmakatha*, 28.

[59] V.T. Bhattatiripad, *V.T.yude Sampurna Krtikal*, 347.

At issue here are modes of embodied knowledge that may be differentiated from those that nurture self-reflective explanation. Learning by rote had a similar role in education until recently, and perhaps some of this has survived even to the present day. This was prominent in arithmetic classes, where one was trained to do 'sums in the mind' (V.T. could help the Tiyyadi girl with her sums even though he was unfamiliar with alphabetic learning). V.T.'s account does not pay attention to the embodied dimension of Vedic recitation; there is no recognition of the 'habitus' produced by this training. When Marcel Mauss proposed the term 'habitus' to refer to 'techniques and work of collective and individual practical reason', he insisted: 'there is no technique and no transmission in the absence of tradition.'[60] V.T.'s narrative is about the experience of an unavailability: it regards the tradition on which the habitus of Vedic training was predicated as absent or ineffective in his time and circumstances. Vedic incantation and alphabetic learning in vernacular Malayalam indicate, in V.T.'s account, two contrasting models of inscription. He recounts how ritual initiation into Vedic incantation led to an inner inscription of Sanskrit as a caste marker: 'Malayalam was uncivilized (*mlechham*); it was Sanskrit, the language of the Gods, which was appropriate for the Brahmins. Even if imbibed along with mother's breast milk, Amma and Acchhan [the Malayalam words for 'mother' and 'father'] were contemptible (*nikrishtam*), and I began using the Sanskrit words *mata* and *pita* instead.'[61] *Upanayanam*, the initiation rite of the Brahmin when he is given the sacred thread to wear, transforms V.T. into a *dvija* (twice-born) and introduces a split in his conception of himself, one that is projected onto his picture of the world: 'Another "I" was born inside me. I felt that this second "I" was superior to and wiser than the first. This venerable second "I" was a Brahmin and the other a mere Sudra. It was thus that I began looking at people as belonging to two categories—superior

[60] Mauss, 'Techniques of the Body', especially 73 and 75.

[61] V.T. Bhattatiripad, *V.T.yude Sampurna Krtikal*, 154.

and inferior. It must be thus that I acquired the thought of caste discrimination—*sudram aksharasamyuktam duratah parivarjayet*—which forbade the alphabet to the Sudra.'[62] The 'inner', non-literate inscription of Sanskrit severs the subject from his natural first language as inappropriate, and differentiates the world around him according to caste. However, this symbolic and ritualistic access to the Sanskrit language does not provide anything but a rudimentary foothold; the initiate does not possess sufficient mastery over Sanskrit to form complete sentences or convey his everyday needs. He can mobilize the beginning of a solemn utterance, but he soon flounders, unable to complete the sentence. '[O]ur speech was dull with perverse usage, as in "*mata, alpam kudi bhojanam dehi*" (Mother, please give a little more food).'[63]

In contrast to this disconnect between the sacred language and the everyday, the second inscription—that of alphabetic reading and writing in Malayalam, received from the Tiyyadi girl and practised in the temple in solitude—leads to new experiences of language and time. The training in incantation enabled V.T. to recite the Vedas in fragments and in preset combinations (back and forth). Alphabetic learning also works with fragments (the torn piece of a newspaper, the isolated letter repeatedly inscribed or deciphered over and over at night). However, the fragment functions in utterly different ways in these two models. The learning of Vedic recitation in V.T. is oriented towards the repeated production of an identical corpus; it leads to ritualistic performative acts in accordance with a set of finite, preformulated rules. Learning to read and write Malayalam leads in his account to a new set of performatives directed at non-identical forms of repetition, as in the deciphering and production of texts. These new performatives presuppose an open-ended realm of possible utterances, which can even include a non-ritualistic repetition of incantatory phrases from the Vedas, as in the use of the Vedic lesson in V.T.'s

62 Ibid.

63 Ibid., 155. *Alpam kudi* are Malayalam words.

play. If the first form of performance has its example in *othu* (Vedic recitation) in his autobiography, the second finds its paradigmatic instance in the newspaper. While the first alludes in his text to the immemorial and repetitive time of the ritual, the second presupposes an open temporality where each utterance slides into the domain of memory as soon as it is deciphered.

This is evident in the way the notion of the 'day' works in the contexts of everyday ritualistic performance and the daily newspaper. Two economies of time are at work. Newness appears in the former schema only as external and contingent, as the perversion of the temporal scheme in *kaliyuga*, requiring an intensification of the practice of ritual. In V.T.'s play *Adukkalayilninnu Arangathekku*, the grandmother who admonishes young Thethi for delaying her evening prayers sees it as a sign of the bad time they live in.[64] Reform initiatives were seen by conservatives as a foolish attempt to aggravate an already doomed period: 'one can't resist the onslaught of bad times; but is it not foolish to invite danger and harm oneself?'[65] As against this conception of the present as the time of decay, the daily newspaper presents the 'day' as the valorized space of the present. The unique difference of the present validates the newspaper everyday and invalidates it the next day, making it waste-paper only fit for wrapping things, and at the same time adding it to an ever-expanding archive.

The second model of inscription—that of alphabetic learning in V.T.'s narrative—repeats the past through new forms of appropriation. Ritual is made part of a repertoire of used signs which one may decipher in relation to fresh experiences and use in innovative ways. The verses in the Rg Veda had remained meaningless for the young V.T. during his ritual training ('What is the meaning of *agnimile purohitam*, what is the purpose of learning it by heart? Neither the master nor the student was concerned about that.').[66] Later he would come to understand the meaning of the verse, not through textual

[64] V.T. Bhattatiripad, *V.T.yude Sampurna Krtikal*, 374.
[65] Ibid., 265.
[66] Ibid., 155.

hermeneutics but through the experience of erotic desire. 'In the temple kitchen the fire burned again. What excitement! The dry logs and the heat and glow of the fire ripened the illusions that arose in me. It was then that I really learned the first *sukta* of the Rg Veda, which begins "*agnimile purohitam*".'[67]

The new insight emerges from individual, personal experience; this mechanism—where personal affect illuminates the ritual text—was unavailable to Kanippayyur's autobiographical universe. In V.T.'s text the moment of new learning succeeds the ritualistic and the alphabetic, and includes all three within a realm of 'personal life'. The choreography of remembrance is new: it returns to the past, retrieves elements, and relocates them. This process effects changes in the nature of the verse from the Rg Veda for the subject—it is no longer an indecipherable verse in incantation, nor a marker that allows him to identify the sacredness of his present existence as a Brahmin, but a lens for deciphering the present—for understanding a secular, erotic experience in terms of the sacred.

A new form of access to tradition is made possible: it is retrieved as a chamber of resonances that echoes new experiences. The same move also makes tradition a ground of intelligibility for the present: in order to grasp their own location and meaning, new experiences insistently call in to this chamber for a response. However, tradition can offer a reply only by foregrounding an experience of rupture, an event that moves the subject away from the ambit of ritual and its corporeal habitus. It is only by discounting the body's synchronous carriage of tradition that a narratable personal life takes shape in V.T.'s autobiography.

Three modes of learning and three modes of remembrance: the first located in an experience of indecipherability, the second linked to learning the rules of combination for an open future, and the third to a domain of personal life experience. When V.T.'s autobiographical subject recognizes the meaning of the first verse of

[67] Ibid., 202.

the Rg Veda, he also grasps the secret strands that connect the lesson in Vedic incantation to the experience of erotic desire. The production and comprehension of this connection—the making of a narratable personal life—is the autobiographical work accomplished in V.T.'s text.

If this were all there was to his autobiography, we could set it aside as a naïve text of modernity. However, the story gains in complexity as it unfolds further. The signal addressee of V.T.'s self-narrative is the 'woman'. The preface to *Kannirum Kinavum* is unequivocal in foregrounding this figure who combines within herself the mother, the lover, and the sister: 'I know very well the heartbeats of she who followed me like a shadow as my mother, sister and spouse, occupying all levels of womanhood. I have understood her complaints and inadequacies. I have gazed at my own form in her tear-filled eyes. I have longed for the fulfilment of her budding sweet desires. In the firmament of life, in the dazzling glow of male power, this Arundhati bears witness to the creative universe; let her shine for ever in my afflicted eyes.'[68]

The woman is not a conventional muse for V.T: she is not only a source of inspiration, she is also the object of his transformative initiatives. On many occasions, he characterized his attempts to reform the Nambutiri community as efforts made in the name of Nambutiri women.[69] What is the status of the woman in his autobiographical project, then? Is woman the addressee or the interlocutor of his self-narrative? Or is the woman's life narrative summoned and deflected in the moves through which his autobiography finds its voice, holds its authority, and unveils its truth?

V.T. begins his autobiography by recording his birth which, unlike the auspicious births located in astrological schema, is presented as a non-event, having passed without so much as being noticed by

[68] Ibid., 126.

[69] V.T.'s most elaborate statement on this is perhaps his 'Nambutiripenkidangalku Oru Ezhuthu' (A Letter to Nambutiri Girls), first published in *Unni Nambutiri,* 19 January 1930. See *V.T.yude Sampurna Krtikal,* 556–65.

anyone. He explains this as a mark of the inconsequential destiny of younger male members in a Nambutiri household. In his time, the patrilineal Nambutiri community allowed only the eldest male member to marry within the caste. The younger members often sought alliances among the Nayars and other upper-caste non-Brahmins. Family wealth too was inherited only through the eldest male member; younger male members of not-so-affluent families led an inconsequential and sometimes impecunious existence. V.T.'s own account of his destiny as an Apphan (a younger male member in his household) highlights the impossibility of finding a life companion within his caste.

If these younger Nambutiri men condemned to bachelorhood within their caste form one side of V.T.'s portrayal of contemporary Nambutiris, the other side is occupied by the even sadder existence of the Nambutiri woman, who is often married to a man far older, and who generally has to share her husband with his other wives. The women and the younger men in the family share a common predicament of suffering and unfulfilment. V.T. writes about the warm proximities he shared with women in his house during childhood; these come to an abrupt end with the advent of adulthood, when the Apphan is banished from the interior of the household, abandoned to find fulfilment for his desires elsewhere. One of the principal objectives upheld by the young faction within the Nambutiri reform movement was that of *sajatiya vivaham* (marriage within the caste for all male members of the household); along with it we also find a trenchant criticism of *adhivedanam* (polygamy), practised often by the eldest male member of the family.

The desire for *sajatiya vivaham* in V.T. is not merely a matter of affect; it also involves a question of property inheritance, signifying the claim to a legitimate family life within the ambit of the community.[70] V.T. achieved this in later years and founded a new space of domesticity for himself after marrying Sreedevi Antharjanam in 1930.

[70] See, for discussions on the need to reform practices of marriage and inheritance among the Nambutiris, back issues of *Unni Nambutiri*, published

The new house, Rasikasadanam, to which he moved with his family in 1931, became a launching pad for his public initiatives, including widow remarriage and inter-caste marriage for Nambutiri women. His sister-in-law was the first widow to be remarried as part of his reform agenda, and his younger sister's marriage to a Nayar was the first inter-caste marriage he presided over.[71] The name that V.T. chose for his house is no less interesting than the activities that animated it. The notion of a *rasika*, a subject with the ability for tasteful aesthetic enjoyment not only of works of art and literature but of everyday practices of life, was at the heart of his conception of a desirable life. In the metaphorics of his autobiography, the opposite of the *rasikas* were the deformed, ugly, and awkward male figures who represented the decadence and sterility to which the Nambutiri community had descended.[72] In contrast to such infelicitous figures stood the *rasikas*, they the young Nambutiris who introduced innovations in

---

by the Nambutiri Yuvajana Sangham. The Madras Nambutiri Act of 1933 resulted in significant changes in Nambutiri practices of inheritance, conferring on all male and female members equal rights in family property. It gave younger male members in the family the right to marry within the caste, and enabled the progeny of such marriages to inherit family property. For V.T.'s own appreciation of the passing of the new bill by the Legislative Assembly, see his 'Malabar Billinte Maha Vijayam' (The Grand Victory of the Malabar Bill), *Unni Nambutiri*, 11 November 1932, reprinted in *V.T.yude Sampurna Krtikal*, 607–8. For a later assessment, based on the links between the economic problems of the Nambutiri community and its response to reforms in custom, see E.M.S. Namboodiripad's Presidential Address at the 34th annual conference of the Nambutiri Yogakshema Sabha at Ongallur in 1944: 'Nambutiriye Manushyanakkan', in *E.M.S.inte Teranjedutha Prasangangal*, 19–61.

[71] The widow remarriage took place in 1935, and the inter-caste marriage in 1940. For V.T.'s accounts of these events, see 'Vidhavayude Jeevitam Thaliraniyunnu' (A Widow's Life Blooms Again) and 'Misravivahaprasthanathinu Oru Mukhavura' (A Preface to the Movement for Intercaste Marriage), in *V.T.yude Sampurna Krtikal*, 295–300 and 307–11.

[72] The apparent image of this is the bodily blemish, the wart or *palunni*, which evokes disgust in the onlooker. V.T. invokes this image to signify the

their clothing or adopted unconventional modes of transport like the bicycle, or the friends that assembled at V.T.'s new household for a regular session of *vedivattam* (animated conversation). V.T. reflected on the unstructured, but cultured and even revolutionary energies of *vedivattam* in later years. He used this word as the title of one of his collections of essays, and reflected on this mode of sociality in the title essay:

> The immediate lookout of all *vedivattam* is simple entertainment. But, when necessary, it can turn into a pit of fire out of which a revolutionary movement may be forged. To speak more clearly, the revolutionary movement within the Nambutiri community developed from *vedivattam*. It will not be wrong to say that the Yogakshema Sabha and the Yuvajana Sangham emerged from the *vedivattam* at the southern veranda of Othanmarmadam in Trissur.[73]

In his journey towards the comforts of Rasikasadanam, V.T. was obliged to abandon other forms of desire and habitation. In his autobiography, he announces a confession:

> I respect the general rule that the life narrated in one's autobiography ought to remain loyal to truth. However, I cannot be satisfied that what I have written so far is truthful. Whatever the consequences, the autobiographer should gain the courage to speak out the entire truth. Do circumstances or one's inborn tendencies shape one's individual self? This question of biographical analysis is not relevant here. But man is a strange creature . . . There is something in him that allows him to rise towards ascetic heights or descend towards savagery.[74]

Against these speculations on the ambivalent prospects of human life, he presents the story of his first conjugal alliance (*sambandham*). His bride Madhavikkutty Varasiar was from an Ambalavasi caste. His narrative disowns responsibility for the alliance—a common friend

---

blind adherence to tradition in the decadent Nambutiri community. See V. T. Bhattatiripad, *V.T.yude Sampurna Krtikal*, 132.

[73] V.T. Bhattatiripad, *V.T.yude Sampurna Krtikal*, 491.

[74] Ibid., 283–4.

had arranged it without clear consent from V.T. and, once the wedding was announced, his refusal would have tainted the reputation of the bride for life. After entering the *sambandham*, V.T. stays away from his bridal home for a long time, at the end of which the young wife writes to him that it was time for them to take a decision about their future. He responds to her cultured and mature tone, and his next visit to her house inaugurates his conjugal life in a real sense. A delightful memory of intimacy recounted by V.T. shows Madhavikkutty dressing up in the traditional attire of a Nambutiri bride to make fun of V.T.'s avowed desire to marry within his caste. This gesture of mockery is also resonant with the erotic: the masquerade of the Varasiar creates a new, playful space of desire which fits well with V.T.'s own ideas of the *rasika*: 'She stands behind the door, shy, looking down. The attire of an *antharjanam* (Nambutiri woman). Earring, the small necklace, brass bangle, pleated dhoti, the mark of new moon on the forehead, bare breasts—laughter burst, an uproar. The dinner plate fell down in a rattle.'[75] V.T.'s account of their conjugality is fulsome: 'a disciple of tender devotion, a loving wife, a friend who captures you with wit and repartee—she behaved in all these ways, without reserve. Eventually, she bore a girl child for me.'[76]

A few years later V.T. is offered the opportunity that he had struggled for his community to allow—to overcome his constraints as an Apphan, obtain a share in his family property, marry within his caste, and set up a new home. He meets Madhavikkutty Varasiar late at night and presents her with an impossible choice: either she must leave her own family to set up a new home with V.T., or he will abandon her for a new bride from his own caste. We do not hear Madhavikkutty's reasoning in V.T.'s autobiography, but her response is eloquent: 'I am expecting another child. How I wish a Valmiki would appear to save me now.'[77] V.T. abandons her, marries Sreedevi Antharjanam, and sets up Rasikasadanam as his new home. We know from his narrative that Madhavikkutty meets him once again before

[75] Ibid., 290.
[76] Ibid.
[77] Ibid., 291.

she goes away with her uncle to Hyderabad, expecting the change of station to soothe her mind. She dies of cholera there, and V.T.'s response to the news of her death is mixed with guilt and anxiety: let this not be a suicide, he prays involuntarily when he listens to the tragic news. His self-deprecating confession emerges from a mixture of self-condemnation and a desire for exoneration:

> I am a great sinner who committed an act of betrayal close to murder. I am a cruel man who abandoned without fear my pregnant wife of unimpeachable conduct. The history of the world has recorded no such instance except that by Sree Ramachandra, the son of Dasaradha. But he was kinder than me. He did not remarry even when he performed the Ashwamedha ritual: he made do with a golden image of his abandoned wife. But I, even before the tears on her cheeks dried, I obtained for myself a Nambutiri woman brimming with youth and five thousand rupees as dowry.
>
> This incident, which took place in 1105 ME [1930], was buried in the dazzling fame that I acquired later. I can pretend to be a respectable in the guise of a social worker or a humanist. But I have no desire for such self-satisfaction. I will not be able to bear the prick of my conscience.[78]

A paradoxical autobiographical move: the gesture of self-condemnation is also that of self-redemption. In confessing his guilt and submitting himself to the reader's judgement, V.T. also performs an act of self-exoneration. The public revelation of one's tainted self attenuates the shameful mark under display. Madhavikkutty Varasiar can no longer be the addressee of V.T.'s discourse: death completes a process, already under way, of her evacuation from the autobiography. Affect in V.T.'s discursive world has found its new habitat in the drawing room of Rasikasadanam. The community's contemporary decay is interrogated and challenged by a new domesticity endorsed by the community's altered norms. It is indeed a home set up by an Apphan, but this younger male member has now become the new patriarch. His home—the space of a progressive Nambutiri family—is the new location of public discussion and private enjoyment. In this exchange between the family and the community, Madhavikkutty Varasiar's

[78] Ibid., 283.

masquerade and her cultured exchanges with V.T. do not find any room for survival. Like Ammukkutty who, against the glow of the kitchen fire in the temple in V.T.'s youth, demonstrated the meaning of the first verse of the Rg Veda for him, Madhavikkutty Varasiar can only have a figural role: it is to prefigure, rather than inhabit, the new world of conjugality. In V.T.'s autobiography the Nambutiri woman, whose proximity was lost to him along with his childhood and in whose name his own public initiatives are launched, is reclaimed in this new space of domesticity.

Into his project of reclamation, however, V.T. brings two female figures who resist and refuse reconciliation. One of them is Kuriyedathu Tatri, the accused in the last and best-known ritual trial for adultery, conducted by the Nambutiri community in 1905. During her interrogation Tatri is said to have named sixty-five sexual partners. The lovers, whose complicity in adultery had to be demonstrated by the accused recounting verifiable and intimate bodily detail, led to the excommunication of several well-established Nambutiri men. Tatri has become in later Malayalam writing the emblem of a female critique of Nambutiri patriarchy.[79] At the beginning of V.T.'s autobiography, soon after his invocation of the anonymous and all too easily forgettable lives of ordinary Nambutiri women, Tatri is brought in as a sign of the decay of Nambutiri society, and of the times in which V.T. seeks to refashion his own life: 'Let me ask, who was that Kuriyedathu Tatri who shook the entire Kerala [world] about half a century ago? Was she not born of the Nambutiri community? What was the background of that terrible event where sixty-five boys of the community were invited, disrobed and insulted to her heart's content?'[80]

In some of his other writings V.T. speaks of Tatri as the leader of a movement for cultural reform.[81] Here Tatri's sexuality and desire

[79] See, for instance, Lalitambika Antarjanam, 'The Goddess of Revenge'; and Madambu Kunjukkuttan, *Bhrashtu*.

[80] V.T. Bhattatiripad, *V.T.yude Sampurna Krtikal*, 132.

[81] V.T. Bhattatiripad, 'Kuriyedathu Tatri—Samskarika Navothana Nayika'

are set aside in favour of a social movement orchestrated by her. Her relationships cannot be explained as manifestations of lust or greed for money and should be seen as motivated by a desire for revenge against patriarchy. V.T. suggests that some of Tatri's so-called lovers may have slept with her maids, who were instructed to take her place, the lovers having gone off believing they had shared Tatri's bed. The idealization of Tatri as the pure spirit of social criticism allows V.T. to ignore her life after excommunication. Although she left unanswered questions before the Nambutiri community which he ponders over, her individual destiny ceases to matter. V.T. and his band of reformers carry forward the criticism voiced by Tatri in more effective and acceptable ways. Tatri becomes the sign of a potential danger that lies in wait for all Nambutiri women if the community does not reform itself.

Another female figure enters V.T.'s narrative with disturbing consequences and supplies a contrast to Tatri's redeemed rebellion. This is Uma Antharjanam, later known as Umaben. Her story of Umaben has no apparent relevance for V.T.'s story of his own life. He seems aware of this and offers a tenuous justification for its inclusion:

> I do not intend to retell an old history. My theme here is the story of a poor Nambutiri woman who floundered on her life's path. It is not my aim to praise or blame the individuals who find mention here.
>
> This is a part of my autobiography because I have lived on the banks of river Bharatappuzha. The greenroom and the stage of this tragedy too is Bharatappuzha . . . How many stories of rise and fall have taken place here. The events which I am going to narrate may also become part of this repertoire.[82]

This may appear poor reasoning to justify the inclusion of Uma's narrative in his autobiography. Nonetheless, Uma can be seen as supplementing the spectral destinies of Nambutiri women with

---

(Kuriyedathu Tatri: A Leader of Cultural Renaissance), *V.T.yude Sampurna Krtikal*, 626–7.

[82] V.T. Bhattatiripad, *V.T.yude Sampurna Krtikal*, 322.

which V.T. began his autobiography. Unlike Tatri, whose subsequent life story remained a matter of indifference to him, Uma's real existence is a disturbing reminder that needs to be spoken about and castigated.

What is the story of Uma? Uma is married to a man from a renowned and austere Nambutiri household and, even though her husband married again, she continues to be the favoured wife. One day, she is abruptly sent to her parental home; then it is discovered that she is a kleptomaniac. In V.T.'s narrative, Uma's unhappiness in her marital home had to do with her discontent over its austere routine. Her propensity for indulgence runs as an unstated thread in V.T.'s narrative. She creates a scandal by taking lovers, and in an attempt to reform her ways a Nambutiri social worker, Devaki Narikkattiri, takes her to the Gandhi Ashram in Wardha. This experiment fails; Uma resurfaces in Kerala after a year with a vague set of scandalous rumours trailing her. She tries to enter into a civil marriage with a non-Brahmin and seeks V.T.'s help, but he refuses, sensing a plot on the part of the bridegroom to rob Uma of her property. V.T. argues, interestingly, that for a ritually married Nambutiri woman there is no legal exit from marriage. Uma gets married to a driver called Muhammad and becomes a Muslim. V.T. has an ugly public confrontation with Muhammad, who speaks insultingly about his wife's inability to cook fish and meat. After a time Uma returns to her home, is taken to Lahore, and converted back to Hinduism through the Arya Samaj. She marries a Punjabi Brahmin and over the travails of Partition moves to Delhi and settles there. V.T.'s narrative of Uma concludes by suggesting parallels between her and Kunti of the Mahabharata, who bore children to different husbands.

V.T.'s retelling of Uma's life did not go uncontested. He received a letter from Uma's daughter-in-law, who criticized his insensitivity in raking up old wounds affecting other people. V.T. published his response but did not address the accusations, merely affirming the purity of his intent in writing about Uma. His narrative of Uma is characterized by a lack of generosity: while Tatri is presented as an avenging victim who sacrificed her identity as a Nambutiri woman, Uma is shown turning up, time and again, within the space of the community to create anxiety and shame. Uma lives with a Muslim man, and her children dress like Muslims and walk in the very neighbourhood where they had moved about as Nambutiris. This, bringing to mind alliances between Nambutiri women and Muslim men during the Mappila rebellion, creates a zone of unease in V.T.'s narrative. Although Uma does not directly make demands on the community, her very way of life, its unstable identity, poses a threat to his project of reforming and rescuing Nambutiri women for new ideals of conjugality. Paradoxically, V.T., whose discourse of freedom invoked Nambutiri women as its source, is forced by Uma's presence to uphold a doctrine of unfreedom for all Nambutiri women: for them, there is no legal point of exit from a ritually consecrated marriage; they are legally heteronomous spouse-subjects. While Tatri's voice—that of an accused in a ritual trial prior to her excommunication—can make its presence felt in the world of the reformer, Uma remains inaudible. Listening to her, taking her voice into cognizance, would involve an act of recognition that unsettles the links established in V.T.'s autobiography between the family and the community of reformed Nambutiris.

This second strand in the autobiography complicates the story of reform and apprenticeship we encountered. The thrust of my reading has been to see the second movement as intrinsic to the confident gestures of the autobiographer we analysed earlier. The autobiographer is also a new masculine subject whose desire gives him access to the truth of his historicality. The path of desire seemed easy in its reopening of tradition for a secular experience; however, on a closer reading the very logic of desire seems to be divided between its affective reproduction in the familial realm and a larger engagement with freedom and alterity. V.T.'s narrative relinquishes the latter in the name of the valued link between the domestic sphere and the public domain of the community. The figure of the woman occupies a special position in his story: she is the link between the private and the public, endorsing reform, submitting to its new rules, and countersigning and validating its new mores through affective reassurance as a companionate spouse within the domestic and community space. It is not accidental that one of the signal gestures made by V.T. as a writer of fiction is to reinvent the Nambutiri woman as the subject of affective-erotic investment. His early story, 'The Gift of Vishu', shows the heroine appear in the dissolving darkness of the dawn to imprint her lips on her young lover's face.[83] The aim of the story was to produce a new realm of intensity within the imaginative life of the community and redeem the erotic from the vengeful legacies of a Tatri and the ugly and infelicitous transactions of ageing polygamous patriarchs. However, in order to devise a language to express this intensity, V.T. needed to lean on the erotic practices from which he as a masculine subject drew sustenance—the world of Ammukkutty and more specifically Madhavikkutty Varasiar. In the conjuring of these worlds of the intimate and the erotic as part of a narrative of apprenticeship, and in their disavowal in a language of self-assured and self-exonerating confession, we can see the decisive gestures through which the autobiographical subject in V.T.'s texts takes shape. The life of this subject can no longer be told in a linear narrative of progressive self-realization. It weaves in memory and guilt, destitution and acquisition, intimacy and sacrifice, in ambivalent moves. The redeeming gesture of this project of recollection is entrusted to the act of confession itself which, initially directed at the woman in general, eventually ends up redrawing the boundaries of its audience.

IV

I return now to the use of autobiography as a historiographical tool. Kanippayyur's autobiographical account told us a story of privilege: it was his advantaged location in Kerala's caste society that made him eligible to undertake his memory-work. Around the same time, other writers lacking privileged status also began writing about their lives,

[83] Ibid., 55–8.

claiming that ordinary life experiences in changing times possessed historical value, this being reason enough for writing them down.[84] It is important to note the timing of these texts. Debates around the formation of Kerala state and the movements for its unification produced, in the 1940s and 1950s, a number of discourses on the social, cultural, and historical identity of the region.[85] E.M.S. Namboodiripad's influential history of Kerala, *Keralam Malayalikalude Mathrubhumi* (Kerala, Motherland of the Malayalis), and the writings of Elamkulam Kunjan Pillai, belong to this moment.[86] Quite a number of biographies and autobiographies which now appeared occupied the same field in their effort to forge connections between a modern Malayali identity and the differentiated pasts their authors or protagonists had lived through.

E.M.S. Namboodiripad's *Atmakatha*, initially serialized in magazines and first published as a book in 1969, is an example of this. Readers interested in Namboodiripad's personal life were disappointed by his narrative. Apart from the early chapters, which dealt with his childhood, *Atmakatha* focused almost exclusively on the social and political movements in which the autobiographer had played an active role. The personal element was often confined to a discussion of the positions he took on important issues. The 'I' of Namboodiripad's narrative was a political activist whose life outside the political domain had little relevance for the story. Neither was a detailed account of the author's political life offered: the narrative ended in the late 1930s, when Namboodiripad became a full-time activist of the Communist Party of India. In later editions of his autobiography a concluding

[84] T.K. Raman Menon, writing in the early 1960s, suggested that the lives of extraordinary figures were atypical and partial, and that there is no reason one should privilege the lives of rulers and politicians over those of peasants and singers. Vidwan T. K. Raman Menon, *Ente Ayushkala Anubhutikal* (My Life Experiences), 1.

[85] For a discussion of debates around the unification of Kerala, see Devika, 'The Idea of Being Malayali'.

[86] E.M.S. Namboodiripad, *Keralam Malayalikalude Mathrubhumi*.

chapter was appended, clarifying why the story ended there. He accepted the criticism that his *Atmakatha* lacked an adequate display of the self (*atmam*) and was more a political report than the emotional expression of an individual life:

> While acknowledging this weakness without any hesitation, I believe that this story—of how someone who was born into a 'world of gods and demons' and spent his boyhood in learning the Sanskrit language and the Rg Veda became a communist—will be useful to tens of thousands of readers who have no relationship with that life. Since the book has been written with this conscious aim, it is better not to narrate the subsequent tale of my life, which is inseparably linked to the story of the communist movement. Historians of the movement will also have to tell the story of my life from 1938 till my death. Leaving that task to them, I have been trying to spend the remaining part of my life in efforts to nurture the movement.[87]

As in Kanippayyur, the customs of his time found ample room in Namboodiripad's book; but they had a different narrative function. They supplied elements for building a framework for 'properly' historical explanation. *Atmakatha* showed the unreflective child of earlier chapters turn gradually into a self-conscious political subject by recognizing this frame. For Namboodiripad, autobiographical narration was, by its very nature, marked by the merits and flaws of a 'subjective approach'.[88] In terms of its value, an individual's autobiography was clearly subordinate to the history of the society he or she lived in. Once the story of the emergence of a self-conscious political subject was completed, there was very little to be told within the frame of an autobiography; political history then superseded the claims of personal narration.

[87] E.M.S. Namboodiripad, *Atmakatha*, rev. edn, 327–8.

[88] In his introduction to the autobiography of Cherukad, a communist novelist, Namboodiripad argued that the genre of autobiography involved a self-confessedly subjective description of how a rapidly changing society transformed an individual 'who was no more than a point within that society', and how this individual in turn contributed to social change. E.M.S. Namboodiripad, 'Avatarika', i.

A different way of linking autobiography and social history is seen in *Jeevitasamaram* (Life Struggle) in which C. Kesavan (1891–1969), a leader of the Ezhava movement and later of the Travancore State Congress, recounted his life experiences till the 1930s.[89] Unlike Namboodiripad, Kesavan intended to write about the well-known chapters of his active political life. He managed to publish two volumes of his autobiography; the third and final volume, which was meant to deal with the peak of his political career, remained unwritten when he died in 1969. *Jeevitasamaram* begins by introducing two interlocking temporal sequences—the chronology of a personal life, and regional and national history:

> I was born in Kollam-Mayyanadu in an Ezhava household that no one could call prosperous, on a day of the full moon, Saturday, 23 May 1891, under the star Anizham. It is startling to think about the enormous difference between the socio-political situation then and now. Those were the times when the tremor of political unrest spread all over India. The Indian National Congress was formed five years before I was born. The Malayali Memorial, which marked a new chapter in the history of Travancore, was submitted when I was one year old. It was the first instance of a political agitation in Travancore going beyond caste and religious divisions. *Malayala Manorama* began its publication in 1064 or 65 of the Malayalam Era [1889]. In 1067 [1892], the great scholar Paravur Kesavan Asan founded the Keralabhushanam Press and the newspaper *Sujananandini*. *Malayali* also started publication around this time: a turning point in history, marked by the emergence of class-consciousness (*vargabodham*).[90]

The narrative continues in this vein for another four pages, bringing into its ambit significant events from the political and social histories of Kerala, and India, in the first five decades of the twentieth century. For Kesavan, this is a narrative of democratization and increasing

[89] C. Kesavan, born in Mayyanadu near Kollam in Travancore, entered public life in Kerala as an activist in the Ezhava movement. He became a prominent leader of the Travancore State Congress and chief minister of Travancore-Cochin in 1950.

[90] C. Kesavan, *Jeevitasamaram*, 19.

egalitarianism; kings, Brahmins, and Parayas enjoy the same rights today, he says, a situation unimaginable five decades ago. The events of his lifetime form 'chapters of a wondrous and revolutionary half-century' and, in the making of this history, Kesavan admits with a modesty tinged with pride, 'I too was not without some small roles.'[91] The politically active life of the protagonist ensures the link between the principal events in his personal life and larger regional and national histories.

Yet the historical narrative which runs through his autobiography is not confined to events in which he played an important part. Much of what he has to say, especially in the early chapters, presents him less as an agent and more as an observer, and sometimes as a mere sign for comments on the larger social context in which he lived. A macro-narrative of public history is interwoven with the lesser narrative of events in his childhood and youth.[92] His first memories of schooling lead to a discussion of the establishment of a school for Ezhava children in Mayyanadu, and then to the history of the education of lower castes in Travancore. Kesavan is anxious to place his own experiences in a larger historical frame. On many occasions he cites official documents or earlier histories. Unconcerned with the originality of his historical account, he constructs it with elements from a public repertoire of texts available to him. This includes state manuals, missionary writings, and colonial ethnographic works. The passages Kesavan cites from these texts were used frequently by lower-caste writers before him. He also rehearses earlier accounts of

[91] Ibid., 23.

[92] In many of the autobiographies about changing times, accounts of childhood play an important role, by virtue of their association with practices that are clearly identified with a past that no longer exists. Childhood also is a narrative tool of defamiliarization, especially in criticisms of discriminatory caste practices. The child's perplexed encounters with untouchability and distance pollution (*ayitham*) orient the rhetorical organization of historical remembrance in many texts. This tendency is not confined to autobiographies by authors from lower castes like Kesavan. See, for example, B. Kalyani Amma, *Ormayil Ninnu* (From Memory).

the past written by prominent figures from his community, such as C.V. Kunjuraman and K. Damodaran. The sense of a public history of Kerala, and the position of the lower castes within it, forms a necessary part of his personal narration. In this sense, the larger history invoked by Kesavan is not entirely external to his autobiography; it is as if his personal story could not be told without it.

Throbbing with the energy of reminiscence, *Jeevitasamaram* is an exceptionally engaging autobiography. Although concerned with the disappearing customs of his society, a marked difference in spirit differentiates Kesavan's project from Kanippayyur's. This can easily be grasped if we consider the two strands in Kesavan's recollection. Firstly, his account of past customs belongs to a history of injustice: the sense of unfamiliarity that animates his narration is not wonder but incredulity and revulsion. The reader is asked to share a sense of moral unacceptability while listening to his account of traditional practices. Secondly, Kesavan's narrative consistently mobilizes an energetic relationship to life, even if the specific actions narrated may be morally open to criticism. While the first strand assembles as its discursive background a history of anti-caste writing, the second appeals to another register of virility and spontaneity that does not justify itself by appeal to principles. Kesavan's narrative negotiates its passage between a moral criticism of injustice and the celebration of a natural response to life. His project of shaping his life and speaking about it is but another name for this process of negotiation.

Kesavan's early memories are tinged with two hues of injustice: the discrimination he suffered as an Ezhava boy in streets and other public places where he was forced to defer to upper-caste people, and the unjust exercise of authority by elders and the upper subdivisions within his own caste. Anecdotes illustrate this. The interweaving of a personal and historical narrative with larger political events and micro occurrences from the everyday locking into each other is enabled by the historically evolved self-consciousness of the Ezhava community, an awareness that Kesavan's own political positions would come to represent in later years.

The second strand in Kesavan's narrative emerges from the first: stories of his spontaneous rebellion against injustice provide the first glimpses of this aspect of his persona. His refusal to step out of the public street before arrogant upper-caste men and his confrontations with casteist teachers at school are examples. These acts of rebellion are presented as emerging from more fundamental personality traits: a refusal to submit to authority, a search for pleasure, and a sense of personal integrity built on an unwavering attachment to the vital energies of life. Kesavan's amoral adventures, sometimes indolent and ignorant, but at other times knowing and calculated, range from playing truant at school to causing grief in his early youth to young women in the village. His account of these events is often celebratory: even when they are admittedly indefensible, they receive acceptance on the alibi of innocence. A sense of unaccountability accompanies them. Kesavan recognizes this and makes a plea for what theorists of autobiography would call the claims of 'epistemological solitude' at the outset of his narrative.[93]

> I have a heart which quickly becomes turbulent with emotion. Forbearance is not part of my nature. Therein lie the sources of my few abilities and my abundant weaknesses. Injustice is unbearable for me; I cannot reconcile myself to it. I am always ready to stick to the very end and suffer all consequences in this irreconcilable struggle with injustice. No one should misunderstand me; I am not flattering myself either. My heart and my head may have acted in confusion at times. But I alone—and no one else—has seen them really for what they are. Therefore, I have no complaints against those who have misunderstood me. My aim has always been constant, and my purpose pure. My own testimony is enough for me to affirm this.[94]

In his narrative the rebellious moral impulse is the source both of moral action as well as weakness and instability. There is pleasure in this weakness as it provides evidence for one's own impetuous and ultimately lovable masculinity. Kesavan's masculine self-image needs,

[93] For a discussion of the concept of 'epistemological solitude' in autobiography, see Cameron, 'Autobiography and Philosophical Perplexity'.

[94] C. Kesavan, *Jeevitasamaram*, 18.

for its validation, an appreciative spectator, an adoring gaze. In his early years, theatre and music provide two contexts for Kesavan to redeem himself before this gaze. The applause that greets his entries on stage, the widespread approbation of his songs, and the admiration he receives in his college—all these reassure him. As in the case of V.T., this is an aesthetic gaze: that of a *rasika*, although Kesavan's registers of the aesthetic are more energetic and wild. He does not appeal to classical traditions of taste; his claims are based on a memory of accomplished people within his community and an immediate recognition of talent, the recognition of a gift that marks him out as special. Kesavan's early participation in politics and his recognition as a popular leader continue this pattern.

The autobiography contains, however, a counterpoint to this impulsive strand in his life. A prominent example is the influence that a fellow teacher named Paul exercises on him. Paul's morally upright life and sense of integrity provide a new model in which solitude and reflection assume importance. Paul lives the life of a good Christian even though he has very little to do with institutionalized forms of religious practice. The encounter with Paul makes Kesavan reflect on the nature of his own religious consciousness: 'Paul became a question mark for me. Who is this man? Does religion have the power to entrance man? If this trance has been good for Paul, couldn't it be good for me too? Do I have any religion? I am considered a Hindu; I regard myself as one. But, am I really a Hindu? Do I know anything about that religion?'[95] Kesavan's introspection reveals that his own sense of holiness consisted solely in a few elements of popular religion. The obscene songs sung at the Kodungallur temple, some *strotras* learned by rote, and an engagement with local temples based on an intoxicated enjoyment of festivals and popular rituals—his religion added up to no more than these.

> Paul's conduct in life made me feel that religion is a *Gita* written for the edification of man, and that the text of this *Gita* can be found in the gospels. I was impelled to analyse and assess my past life. It was a vacuous

[95] Ibid., 194.

> life that I saw behind me. A life without purpose or seriousness, blown by the wind and dried by the sun. I felt as if I were waking from slumber. My heart felt a tremor, a sweat. I am sure it was Paul who caused this. That tremor and that sweat have not subsided. A sense of cool has not spread in my heart yet. I am still striving for that feel of cool.[96]

Kesavan begins to miss order and purpose in his life—a sense of form, of narrative coherence. Religion soon ceases to be the language for understanding this coherence: a quick study of Hindu and Christian scriptures convinces him that the admirable qualities of Paul's life cannot be reduced to the influence of Christian doctrine. Deeper than any divine command, it was a fundamental hostility to injustice that determined Paul's conduct. This takes Kesavan to an engagement with Hinduism; he reads the *Bhagavat Gita* and the writings of Vivekananda and finds short-lived inspiration in them. In his later years, Kesavan rejected Hindu religious practices centred on temples as inappropriate and harmful to the spiritual and political aspirations of the lower castes.

Kesavan's encounter with Christianity contains an interesting moment of engagement with biographical writing. He found most accounts of Christ's life contaminated by mythological accretions that portrayed him in the style of a character from the Hindu puranas. On removing this overlay of exaggeration, Kesavan found in Christ's life the story of 'a lover of mankind who was born as a poor carpenter boy, and whose life was sacrificed on account of his grand moral teaching.'[97] Ernest Renan's *Life of Jesus* answers Kesavan's expectations. He finds a plausible version of the story of Jesus there, which shows respect for his humanity. In Kesavan's autobiography the demythologization of the Christ story and the search for narrative coherence in his own life converge. These models are abandoned when he moves on to speak about his engagement in the caste movement and public life; we return to stories of misadventure and spontaneous moral outbursts. However, the strand of reflection

[96] Ibid., 195.

[97] Ibid.

introduced in the narrative of Paul does not altogether disappear. In spite of a continuing narrative of misadventures there is a greater stress on purposiveness and practicability in Kesavan's account of the later years of his life. When he becomes the secretary of the SNDP Yogam, his tries to introduce financial discipline among its branch secretaries and organize the community on principles of public responsibility rather than kinship.[98]

Kesavan's engagement with order and purposiveness is in tune with some of the ideals upheld by the Ezhava reform movement. Sree Narayana Guru's instructions to the Ezhavas covered not only their spiritual practice and customary rituals, but also the development of new material practices. When Sree Narayanan announced the pilgrimage to Sivagiri, he clarified that it should have some concrete material objectives. Agriculture, education, industry, and commerce were among them, and the pilgrimage would involve lectures on these themes.[99] Dr Palpu's initiatives, equally important for Kesavan's intellectual formation, involved a more direct avowal of the ideals of secular modernity. Palpu organized the first industrial and agricultural exhibition of the Ezhavas as part of the second annual conference of the SNDP Yogam in 1905. Kesavan visited this exhibition and remembered it for the marvellous modern objects he saw there, which included a manual typewriter that Palpu's younger brother operated with one finger![100]

A secular vision of modernity was an important strand in the discourse of reform among the Ezhavas in the early decades of the twentieth century. Unlike other idioms of community reform which stressed the loss of masculine valour and the restoration and cleansing of sanctified traditions, this strand foregrounded rational planning at the levels of the individual and the collective.[101] Democratic

[98] Ibid., 360–4.

[99] Balakrishnan, ed., *Sree Narayana Guru*, 148–51 and 163.

[100] C. Kesavan, *Jeevitasamaram*, 294.

[101] There were strands in the Nayar reform movement too which stressed planning and development. The work of M.A. Paramu Pillai, who drew inspiration from Booker T. Washington's experiments in vocational education,

organization of the community, concerted endeavours aimed at a better future, and attempts to orient individual life in terms of plans and projects—Kesavan's autobiography incorporates these as themes for reflection in the middle of his narratives of reckless misadventures and impulsive defiance.

What is distinctive about Kesavan's account, however, is the way he tells stories that capture the rich dynamic of popular practices. The account of his childhood provides examples. As a young boy he was invited to act in a play produced by C.V. Kunjuraman and his friends. Kesavan uses it as a context for describing the state of theatre arts in Kerala at that time.

> Musical plays had not yet arrived on the scene. Tamil drama troupes had not started rushing into Kerala from across the ghats. Nor was there any practice of an actor leaping with a song from the wings to centre-stage as the curtain rises. Malayalam theatre was entirely dominated by plays written in *manipravalam* (a mixture of Sanskrit and Malayalam) like Valiyakoyil Thampuran's *Shakuntalam* and Mannadiar's *Uttararamacharitam*. There were no songs; only *slokas*. But these *slokas* would be sung according to musical schemes. Perunelliyil Krishnan Vaidyar was then widely appreciated as a Venmani of the Ezhavas. Everyone could recite from memory the single *slokas* that he wrote in periodicals like *Vidyavilasini* and his intoxicating erotic songs like the *Maranpattu*. Several legends had formed around him. His play *Subhadraharanam* appeared around that time. Naturally, it attracted the attention of C.V. Kunjuraman and others.[102]

---

is a case in point. For an account of C. Kesavan's experience as a student of Paramu Pillai, see C. Kesavan, *Jeevitasamaram*, 129–49. Mannathu Padmanabhan's autobiography combines elements from both these discourses, in protesting against the emasculation of the Nayar and in thinking of communitarian economic initiatives. See Padmanabhan, *Jeevitasmaranakal*, vol. 1, 50–1.

[102] C. Kesavan, *Jeevitasamaram*, 35. Perunelli P.K. Krishnan Vaidyan (1863–94) authored plays such as *Subhadraharanam Bhashanatakam* and poems including *Kachacharitam Ammanappattu*. He was a fellow student of Sree Narayana Guru and a close friend of Chattampi Swamikal. For

Kesavan moves away from high-cultural accounts of this period to focus on popular initiatives in literature and theatre by Ezhavas, which combined the resources of *manipravalam*, popular musical performances, and a repertoire of erotic versification. This light-hearted and playful scene stands in interesting contrast with the literature commonly associated with Ezhava reform which was to reach its peak in the early decades of the twentieth century—the disavowal of sensuous eroticism in the poetry of Kumaran Asan and, indeed, Sree Narayana Guru. Kesavan's intimate engagement with the world of popular entertainment allowed him to adopt a 'double vision' towards the new idioms of cultural modernity Ezhavas were adopting in his time. This attitude extended beyond the world of literature. He was initially not an active participant in the SNDP Yogam's activities. Later he became its secretary and led the Ezhava community into electoral politics.[103] Although in his youth he supported the efforts of his community to create a new identity for itself, he also viewed some aspects of this process with scepticism. He had high regard for Sree Narayanan but not for his *sanyasi* followers, many of whom he thought lazy and covetous.[104] He was more at home in the popular political culture of virile combat than in idioms of reformed civil conduct: even as he adopted the ideals of the latter, his did not fully fit into their new disciplines. This lack of fit allowed him to observe and record not only the past customs that contemporary Malayalis were moving away from, but also the new practices they were embracing.

Like many autobiographies of its time, *Jeevitasamaram* contains

---

a detailed account, See R. Raman Nair and Sulochana Devi, *Chattampi Swami*, 108–9.

[103] C. Kesavan became secretary of the SNDP Yogam in 1933. He was one of the foremost leaders of the Nivartana Movement spearheaded by Ezhavas, Christians, and Muslims from 1932 to 1937. For an account of the politics of Travancore at the time of the Nivartana movement, see Ouwerkerk, *No Elephants for the Maharaja*.

[104] Kesavan, *Jeevitasamaram*, 235–40.

numerous discussions of the embodied technologies of caste. Kesavan provides interesting ethnography on distance pollution (*teendal*). Unlike many parts of Kerala, in Mayyanadu, the village in southern Kerala where Kesavan grew up, the Nayars did not generally regard Ezhavas as polluting. The Pulayas and the Parayas, much lower in the caste hierarchy, bore the brunt of practices of pollution. Kesavan has interesting anecdotes on casteism, including that of a teacher at his school who devised a new technique of punishment for lower-caste students: to avoid all polluting contact, he would throw his cane at them rather than hit them with it! Many of his stories evoke incredulity and disgust in the reader, in marked contrast to the wonder that Kanippayyur's descriptions had aimed at creating.

The practices of his own community occupy many of Kesavan's descriptions in *Jeevitasamaram*. Some of them are sarcastically critical accounts of features of community life: traditional roles performed by the *vatti* (the barber-priest), the oppressive behaviour of the elders, the false pride of *jatis* that claimed a higher status within the community, and the arrogance of the new Ezhava elite—all these become the targets of acerbic humour. Some of his other stories are more complex, like an account of *talikettukalyanam* (a symbolic wedding ritual performed before a girl child reaches puberty, strongly criticized by the Sree Narayana movement), and his pilgrimages to the Kodungallur temple. Kesavan's description of *talikettukalyanam* does not echo the reformists' rejection, but captures the exuberance of the celebration through the eyes of an enthusiastic insider. The perspective of childhood offers some justification for this, but the energies of the description arguably exceed the child's viewpoint. The domain of popular practices, irrespective of a rational, reformist assessment, seems to provide Kesavan with an energetic, even if unstable, space from which the setting in of modernity could be surveyed. When he writes about the *tirandukalyanam* feast, his gaze lingers not only on elements that have disappeared, but also on practices that were to appear. The main course at Ezhava feasts in Travancore at that time was rice alongside a fish curry made with tamarind and roasted coconut paste. Sambar was popularized among the Ezhavas by the SNDP Yogam.[105] Kesavan's autobiography documents the emergence of many such everyday practices that were subsequently naturalized among Malayalis.

His description of the Bharani festival at Kodungallur is another example of this. When Kesavan was seven or eight years of age, he accompanied some family members on a pilgrimage to the Kodungallur temple. Lower castes were allowed into the temple premises during the Bharani festival, and drinking and the chanting of bawdy songs (*purappattu*) formed a prominent part of the ritual celebrations. Kesavan and his companions observed austerities for ten days before they set out; he counts the boat journey to Kodungallur as among the most marvellous experiences of his childhood. As the boat approached Kodungallur, the pilgrims began singing *purappattu*. Kesavan memorized several of these songs and, in all innocence, took to singing them with gusto. Upon his return he tried one of them at home, but a stinging blow from his father put a quick end to his effort! The journey to Kodungallur was repeated a second time a few years later, during Kesavan's adolescence. His participation and enjoyment were now, as an adult, even fuller. Years later, when he went to Kodungallur a third time, it was to campaign against these practices of worship, which had come to be seen by Ezhava reformers as 'barbaric'. In the autobiography, Kesavan's language oscillates between his consciousness of relishing the festival over his childhood and youth, and a critical view of the same event as a reformer.

In the middle of his description of the festival with its animal sacrifice and unrestrained, sexually suggestive behaviour by men and women, Kesavan inserts his views as a reformer on the history of this practice, echoing the arguments of C.V. Kunjuraman and K. Damodaran that the rite commemorated the destruction of a Buddhist nunnery.[106] In the 1920s and 1930s several Ezhava writers

[105] Ibid., 90.

[106] Kunjuraman, 'Njan', 140–4; K. Damodaran, *Ezhavacharitram*, esp. 214–17.

had suggested that the community possessed a Buddhist past, using it as an argument in support of advocating conversion to Buddhism.[107] P. Palpu, as mentioned in chapter 2, had made this view the kernel of his petitions and campaign writings, suggesting that the lower-caste status of the Ezhavas was the result of a Brahminical usurpation of political power in a predominantly Buddhist Kerala.[108] The historical argument invoked by Kesavan is oriented towards a rational programme of collective endeavours; the remembered pleasures of his childhood, on the other hand, are grounded in what one may call a non-intellectual estimation of popular practices.

Kesavan was not unique in foregrounding this popular, non-intellectual strand. We find similar moments in the life stories of A.K. Gopalan from the Communist Party and Kumbalathu Sanku Pillai from the Travancore State Congress.[109] Their life narratives privilege spontaneous moral reactions marked by a good deal of physical courage and a strong sense of masculinity over rationally planned actions. Even their participation in new disciplinary programmes is mediated often by strong-willed masculine assertion. Both Sanku Pillai and Kesavan narrate strikingly similar instances in which they use physical force to control drunken behaviour.[110] Sanku Pillai was an enthusiastic practitioner of physical exercise and wrestling, even exhibiting his wrestling skills at Congress conferences.[111] A spontaneous masculinity, which prevents hiding or controlling just outrage and turbulent emotion, underlies the conception of ethical agency in these narratives. Kesavan and Sanku Pillai were known

[107] See, for example, Kunjuraman, 'Buddhamathavadangal' and 'Adhakrtarkku Buddhamatamanu Nallathu'.

[108] Dr P. Palpu's correspondence with colonial officials and his memoranda are replete with these arguments. See, for example, 'Memorandum: Some Additional Notes'.

[109] See A.K. Gopalan, *Ente Jeevitakatha*; Kumbalathu Sanku Pillai, *Ente Kazhinjakala Smaranakal.*

[110] See C. Kesavan, *Jeevitasamaram*, 145–6; Kumbalathu Sanku Pillai, *Ente Kazhinjakala Smaranakal*, 43–4.

[111] Kumbalathu Sanku Pillai, *Ente Kazhinjakala Smaranakal*, 99.

for the strong language of their public speeches. One such speech, delivered during the Nivartana agitation, led in 1935 to Kesavan's imprisonment by the Travancore government. These leaders, in contrast with the educated elite who dominated state politics, spoke in a language marked by intense indignation and enthusiasm. The strongest condemnation in *Jeevitasamaram* is reserved for some prominent members of the Ezhava elite. Kesavan was disgusted by their condescending and unfeeling attitude towards the poor of the community. He also disagreed with their style of politics, which for him was far too removed from popular sentiments and authentic moral passion.

The presentation of history in Kesavan's autobiography is informed by an ambivalent estimation of the disciplinary dimension of modernity. This allows him to make visible a level of popular practice irreducible to public historical accounts. An interesting incident reported in *Jeevitasamaram* provides a good example, and allows us to reflect on aspects of the link between autobiographical memory and social history. While discussing changes in the attire and appearance of men and women in his time, Kesavan writes about the introduction of the blouse (*ravukka*) and the upper cloth (*melmundu*). He draws on Nagam Ayya's *Travancore State Manual* and correspondence between British officials and the Travancore government regarding agitations around women wearing the breast cloth. This is followed immediately by a personal recollection from Kochikka—C.V. Kunjuraman's wife, also Kesavan's mother-in-law.[112] In a fascinating conversation recalled by the autobiographer, Kochikka remembers wearing her blouse for the first time. Two of her cousins from Trivandrum, visiting her at Mayyanadu, had brought it for her as a gift. She tried on the new apparel, felt it tickled her a little, but found it altogether quite nice. When she showed it to her mother, however, her mother warned her never to appear in public so obscenely dressed. Kochikka tried it on again the following day,

[112] C. Kesavan, *Jeevitasamaram*, 73.

and upon inadvertently emerging from her room was thrashed by her mother for dressing up like Muslim women and shameless stage actresses. It was a time when revealed breasts were the norm for the correctly dressed woman, a necessary aspect of the 'proper' appearance of Ezhava women as well as for women of other non-Brahminical castes; to wear a blouse was therefore to be scandalously obscene. Kunjuraman, the Ezhava reformer, however, rather relished his wife in her new blouse. Since her mother would not let her wear it outdoors, Kochikka would wait patiently for night to fall, and after her mother was safely in bed she would wear her blouse within her room, where she awaited her husband's arrival![113]

How do we understand this fragment from the past, which presents before us a complex field of visibility and an equally complex set of performative acts? In an insightful study of the transformations in female clothing in the context of caste-reform movements in the twentieth century, J. Devika highlights a tendency to clothe women with 'culture' and aestheticize them, producing them as providers of enjoyment for their modern spouses in monogamous arrangements.[114] She cites the testimony of Kunjuraman's wife to illustrate this movement, contextualizing it in a range of discourses from the time. The figure of the 'husband' in this passage, she argues, 'emerges out of a combination of the images of "Vasanthy's father", "*Vadhyar*" (teacher) and "*Gandharvan*" (celestial lover, seeker of beauty, favouring young virgins). It is for such a man—modern in tastes and inclination—that the woman in the account dupes traditional authority and wears the blouse.'[115] The act of wearing the blouse in the privacy of a conjugal space at night involved constituting oneself as the object of the tasteful, modern gaze of one's husband. This act was embedded in a range of disciplinary performatives which produced new forms of gendered identity in modern Kerala.

[113] For a translation of this passage, see Devika, 'The Aesthetic Woman', 478–9.

[114] Ibid.

[115] Ibid., 479.

Does Kochikka's recollection, as cited by Kesavan, possess a dimension that is not exhausted by this disciplinary paradigm? The passage also seems to bear witness to the pleasures of a new mode of embodied subjectivation. Indeed, this is not entirely separable from mechanisms that produce women as objects of domestic, marital enjoyment for their partners. The question is whether the acts of the subject—trying out this new piece of clothing which covers one's breasts and tickles one's body, turning and twisting to look at oneself in it, wanting to wear it everywhere, and, when it proves impossible, rebelliously deciding to confine it to the indoors at night for approbation by a husband—are all ultimately reducible to the desire for objectification before one's spouse's gaze. Or could it be that, alongside this, inseparably entwined with this, we can also discern a different, if closely related, gesture in the history of individuation and self-fashioning—a moment of subjectivation—at work? Is the gaze that we find Kochikka training on herself solely a disciplinary one, or does it create a new relationship to herself, the trajectory of which is not determined in advance nor in its entirety? These questions could be important for unravelling the relations between personal narratives and historical accounts. While embracing novel disciplines, the subject also performs a certain 'work' of improvisation in negotiating new forms of normativity, and a fresh set of analytical tools may be needed to understand them.

But how do we proceed from here? The problem is complicated by the nature of Kesavan's text and its mechanism of citation. It would be naïve to consider Kochikka's words as having been retrieved in their original authenticity. The documentary status of her utterance is produced by strategies of historical recollection at work in Kesavan's autobiography. This makes it difficult to correlate verbal moves in the passage securely with originary postures adopted by the subject. In some sense, the passage works as a typical anecdote in Kesavan's narrative, with its ironic reversal of public and private spaces at a time of change. Like his account of the changing fashions in the shape of women's earlobes—growing them long was the preferred practice earlier, and a modern set of aesthetic norms and new kinds of jewellery led to their shortening—the anecdote of the blouse appears as part of an ironic history of normative practices.

It is difficult to reduce the pleasures of ethico-poetic acts of self-making to normative prescriptions; in fact, such pleasures may arise precisely from a temporary suspension of secure normative frames. Judith Butler, following Foucault's work on 'technologies of the self', proposed a distinction between 'conducting oneself according to a code of conduct' and 'form[ing] oneself as an ethical subject in relation to a code of conduct'.[116] The latter involves a stylization of the acts and pleasures of the subject. The acts generated in the context of a new normative frame may involve forms of stylization at variance with the rules of conduct foregrounded by the frame. It is precisely this lack of fit that makes testimonial anecdotes important for autobiographies written in changing times.

Stephen Greenblatt and Catherine Gallagher touched upon a similar problem when they revisited the status of anecdotes and the possibilities they open up for historical understanding. They argued that some anecdotes compel us with a cluster of individualizing details that may not fit into the frame of the larger narrative within which they appear:

> [T]he undisciplined anecdote appealed to those of us who wanted to interrupt the Big Stories. We sought the very thing that made anecdotes ciphers to many historians: a vehement and cryptic particularity that would make one pause or even stumble on the threshold of history. But for this purpose, it seemed that only certain *kinds* of anecdotes would do: outlandish and irregular ones held out the best hope for preserving the radical strangeness of the past by gathering heterogeneous elements—seemingly ephemeral details, overlooked anomalies, suppressed anachronisms—into an ensemble where ground and figure, 'history' and 'text' continually shifted . . . Approached sideways, through the eccentric anecdote, 'history' would cease to be a way of stabilizing texts; it would instead become part of their enigmatic being.[117]

[116] Butler, 'What is Critique?', 310.

[117] Greenblatt and Gallagher, 'Counterhistory and the Anecdote', 51.

Autobiographies and other genres of first-person narration are major sites for the production and circulation of anecdotes: many a time, an autobiographical voice testifying to an odd detail supplies the unorthodox historian with a stimulating combination of eccentricity and authenticity. This produces two sorts of disturbances: a narratological disturbance effected by the little story on the big one, and the presentation of a new kind of subject on the scene. However, the use of the anecdote by the historian, for Greenblatt and Gallagher, also risked a certain paradox: 'the strong desire to preserve the energies of the anecdote by channelling them into historical explanation, which is followed by frustration and disappointment when the historical project stills and stifles the very energies that provoked it.'[118] This paradox underlies the peculiar pathos of anecdotalism: 'the (counter) historian clutches the life of the anecdote, but it expires in his or her grasp.'[119]

Greenblatt and Gallagher's analysis is relevant for the fortunes of the anecdote, not only within the writing of professional historians but also in Kesavan's own historical project in his autobiography. Nonetheless, as in the case of the blouse, some anecdotes in Kesavan's text, regardless of the apparent uses to which he puts them, do allow us some intimacy with the diverse ways in which modern identities were negotiated in Kerala. This owes something to the relationship that Kesavan's narrative maintains with the domain of the popular, which enables a suspension of strict normative disciplining. The popular and the anecdotal have much in common: popular memory offers a domain where anecdotes flourish; also, the popular, in manifesting the workings of a collective habitus, escapes rigid normative control. The anecdote makes visible odd moments in the inhabitation of norms and permits a glance into negotiations that cannot be adequately analysed as belief systems through concepts like 'ideology'. What we see often is not a difference in avowed beliefs but a distinction between affirmed norms and their inhabitation through practices of life. If 'style' is

[118] Ibid., 68.
[119] Ibid.

an adequate word to point to these inflections, the popular domain and the anecdote enable a stylistics of subjectivation. Kesavan's most profound intervention in historiography is in carving out a space for style between the diverse narrative strands of his autobiography.

V

Did autobiographical writing provide everyone with such eloquent and entertaining remembrance? Or did it also introduce for some a new relationship between solitude, silence, and self-narration? Lalitambika Antarjanam (1909–1987), one of the most important women writers of Kerala, did not write a full-scale autobiography, although C.V. Kunjuraman had encouraged her to write one even when she was young. She did not heed his advice, but three decades later brought out a collection of essays and fragments, some of them previously published, under the title *Atmakathayku Oru Amukham* (An Introduction to [My] Autobiography). A novelist and writer of short stories, Antarjanam explained her hesitation to write an autobiography in terms of the new set of demands that this genre placed on her talents. Novels might give room to the autobiographical element, but the fictive had no place in autobiography. In that genre, art had to give way to truth in all its nakedness. Antarjanam tells us that she regarded 'the hundred-headed serpent of the ego' as the worst enemy of self-narratives; as she was unsure of conquering it, she did not want to venture into this new form of writing. She also had a more immediately personal reason for her reluctance: decades after she turned down Kunjuraman's suggestion, once she thought of presenting herself in public through an autobiography she felt as diffident as a young Nambutiri woman stepping into the world without the protection of a veil or a covering umbrella.[120]

It is not accidental that the autobiographical act is so closely linked in Antarjanam's imagination with her difficult—and desired—entry into the public realm. In her youth, girls from Nambutiri families

[120] Antarjanam, *Atmakathayku Oru Amukham*, 9.

were not even allowed to exit the inner space of the household after they had reached puberty. In fact they were not to be seen even by most male members of their own household. Nambutiri reformers criticized this practice, and M.R. Bhattatiripad's play *Ritumati*, which focused on the plight of a pubescent girl, was performed as part of their campaigns in several places. Lalitambika was among the early Nambutiri women who shed their protective veil and umbrella.

The formative years in an Antarjanam's life, according to Lalitambika, were spent in the dark recesses of her house. Her sense of self, even her desire for freedom, was forged not in an open, collectively shared space, but in the solitude of her inner rooms. She recalls how, when she 'came of age', everybody at home wept, moved by the plight that awaited her. Her entry into adolescence signalled her death to the external world. However, Lalitambika says that her 'real' education took place in the two and a half lonesome years she spent in the inner rooms of her house. Her father had gifted her a copy of Tagore's *Ghare Baire* (Home and the World), in a recent Malayalam translation.[121] Her emotions were nurtured less by real-life contact than by literature and the experience of unfreedom. During this period she had even begun writing a story in the manner of Tagore's novel.

Entry into the larger public arena as a new woman put into crisis the very sense of self that had desired a wider world. Lalitambika's way of coping with this new world was to use the protective veil of her imagination, which enabled her to speak without speaking as herself. Fiction allowed a displacement of one's self by all that one spoke about: it was possible to reveal things without revealing oneself, except obliquely. This made autobiography a difficult genre for Lalitambika. She did not wish to rid herself of fiction's protective umbrella and, she believed, there would be no room for any trace of fiction in an autobiography. Her response to this was to incorporate the difficulty into the very form of her autobiographical text. Instead of an

[121] Tagore's *Ghare Baire* was translated from an English rendering into Malayalam by B. Kalyani Amma under the title *Veettilum Purathum* (Home and Outside).

autobiography, one could have only a Preface to an Autobiography, the use of a fragmentary form to speak about a difficulty.

This gesture of hesitation, which also became an act of speech, was Lalitambika's way of linking autobiographization with historical inscription. The very form of self-narration, in its intimacy with solitude and silence, revealed a historical moment in its amplitude. Her times entered her autobiography as solitude and diffidence, and enabled her fragmented self-narration. This configuration was of course not representative of all women writers in Kerala in the early twentieth century. Women from many of the non-Brahmin communities did not share Lalitambika's experience in the same way, and the repertoire of their personal expression from this period was far more diverse. Essays published in women's magazines as early as the first decades of the twentieth century show the emergence of strong autobiographical voices which draw upon a range of sources, including the rhythms of everyday life in the domestic realm.[122] Such forms of self-narration, used effectively by several Nayar and Christian women, were not easily available to Lalitambika. The subject that speaks in her writing displays an uneasy relationship with self-avowedly autobiographical performance. Her preface to an impossible autobiography suggests that her more elaborate practice of self-narration was in the 'veiled' mode of fiction. This aspect of Lalitambika's writing challenges historians of autobiographical practice to redraw generic boundaries and look more closely at the wider range of expressive forms used by emergent subjects in modern Kerala to write about themselves.

[122] For a fascinating selection from these writings, translated into English, see Devika, ed., *Her-Self.* Mantaraveetil Lakshmy Amma's essay, written in the form of a description of the author's daily routine at home, is a good example of the malleability and inventiveness of autobiographical forms at this time. Ibid., 10–21.

7

Style and the Subject

IN ONE OF HIS longest fictional works—though not long enough for critics to stop wondering whether to call it a novel or a short story—Vaikom Muhammad Basheer, the great master of first-person tales in Malayalam, presented a dream. The narrator finds himself lying on the bare ground under a dark sky, bearing witness to his own impending disappearance. The body's dismantling begins with the eyes: they are plucked out and fitted, like electric bulbs, on the 'sides of the sky's belly'. Suddenly there is a flood of light. Next comes the lighting of the pyre; except there is no pyre, the body is the pyre: 'someone set fire to the big toes. The body is burning like celluloid.' As the fire reaches the knees, a voice asks for the last words. The burning corpse responds with metaphysical formulae of benediction: Om, shanti, shanti. Then it is all over: 'All burned out. Some ashes in the shape of a body. The wind blew them away. The ground is empty.' But this is not the end yet, something persists: the two eyes continue burning against the belly of the sky. 'Suddenly a deep voice called: "The Next One."'[1]

Basheer's image of disarticulation, of the body and the voice, could serve as a point of arrival at the end of a book on self-articulation. Our expectations of a sombre funeral ritual are belied; we are in the

[1] Basheer, 'Mantrikappooccha', in *Basheerinte Sampurna Krtikal*, 1221.

presence of something machine-like, with plucked-out eyes serving as arc lights and the corpse a strip of celluloid to crackle quickly in the fire. God—or is it an assistant?—is now a booming voice making a routine announcement on the megaphone: Next, Please! Basheer's art strips down not just the body; the space of language where the self rules as author and narrator is taken apart, thrown away, until the ground is bare, empty. Still, the dream was but a moment in the twists and turns of Basheer's first-person storytelling.

This book has discussed the early moments in which a space was cleared in Malayalam writing for the 'I' to tell its stories; moments when the empty ground had acquired its initial population, of people and things, bodies, a world. Basheer's images of emptiness and a machine-like assemblage may help place this landscape under a different sky and permit us to listen with new ears to the early stutters of a language in its making.

When I began work on this book I was interested in scanning self-narratives for a distinctive clue to the specific formation of modernity in Kerala, an arrangement of things on the surface of which Basheer's cheerful laughter would come to fall later. As it has emerged, however, the book offers neither a map of the original site where self-narration began nor a narrative history of its evolution. Instead of a story or a gallery of portraits we have a series of snapshots; they slice into time to interrupt and isolate postures, gestures. These fleeting images do not even qualify as likenesses; they would find it hard to make it to official documentation as stable tools for identification. But they do make for a different gathering of traces, an inscription less vivid than the well-formed characters of alphabetic writing. The figures assembled in this book do not always demand or permit an activity of reading. They exist in an order of visibility which calls for description and documentation rather than interpretation. The compositional choices of this book have been shaped by a sense of these features; my aim was to seek arrangements which would expose these snapshots to the daylight of our present.

Forms of visibility have cropped up as a recurrent concern during work on this book. They initially appeared as a matter of tropology:

light and vision have been vital to the imagery in most of the texts studied here. Luminous bodies and spaces appear in Sree Narayanan's poems to suggest states of liberation, interestingly paralleled by his installation of mirrors in place of idols in temples, and his elevation of specular reflection as a paradigm for thinking about the divine. My discussion of early novels in Malayalam suggested that configurations of light play an advanced, form-giving function in them. This is true in a different way of C.V. Raman Pillai's historical fiction too, where dramatic contrasts between darkness, effulgence, and the misleading visibility of disguise predominate. Novels written by C.V.'s contemporaries show an obsessive preoccupation with the activities of seeing, looking, and reading, and track in their pages a spectrum of visual experiences ranging from the curious, engaged observation of new objects to feeling dazzled by the glare of the marvellous. Reading in varied forms—as decipherment of signs and as search for the right code—come up repeatedly, cutting across genres.

What does the prominence of orders of visibility, and of situations and actions defined in their terms, indicate? A response may be sought in the links between first-person utterances and structures of exteriority. This book has stressed that the public dimension ought to be seen as playing a constitutive role in autobiographical enunciation: self-narration carves out a space for the 'I' in the field of public utterances. Its grounds are to be found not in privately experienced moments of self-intuition but in the experience of being exposed in a field of perception populated by others. In the Introduction I pointed to strands in more recent thinking which argue that claims of singularity are made within this domain of shared visibility.[2] This insight prompted a shift in the focus of my analyses from an originary sense of the inner to the field of exposedness within which the inner emerges as a mark of certain statements and claims. Configurations of visibility prominent in the texts examined called for a closer engagement with this terrain.

[2] See Arendt, *The Life of the Mind, One: Thinking*; idem, *The Human Condition*; Cavarero, *Relating Narratives*; Butler, *Giving an Account of Oneself*; idem, 'What is Critique?' See chapter 1 for a discussion.

This book uses the figure of visibility in a range of senses: while it refers to specifically optical configurations, to acts of seeing and reading, and to states of being dazzled or being exposed, it also stands as shorthand for what I referred to as 'perceptual economies'. By this I mean the organization of perceptual relations within which various textual entities, such as objects or characters, images or descriptions, acquire their presence. The two chapters on the novel insistently brought the nature and mode of existence of perceptual economies into focus. Early novels in Malayalam were preoccupied with the activity of differentiation—making distinctions between communities, genders, emotions, and conceptions of history. Sometimes these distinctions crop up as topics of direct discussion between characters or invite commentary from the narrator. More importantly, they sometimes appear in the form of an 'aesthetic' work, determining the way people and things are presented in the narration and seen by characters. The use of the term 'aesthetic' should not suggest that we are dealing with a problem specific to the arts and that we need a theory of art for its resolution; our concern is with the organization of perception. The etymological lineage of the 'aesthetic', as we know, shows its early alliance with perception. Early novels make extensive use of perceptual relationships to delineate the orientation of subjects in the world and establish differences among them.

We saw, for instance, that the contrast between older and newer marital norms in the Nayar and Nambutiri communities resonated with two distinctive orientations of erotic desire in O. Chandu Menon's *Indulekha*. More interestingly, the novel's differentiation of modes of desire, as the discussion in chapter 4 showed, is closely tied to its presentation of objects and appearances. Collections of objects, ways of dressing, and the display of material riches all formed essential elements in an economy within which subjects of sensation and desire appeared. It may be tempting to see in this merely the outer manifestation of an inner, psychological difference: objects, etc., one may argue, are no more than mere instruments used for revealing character. This view treats objects as possessing essentially a metaphorical function: they are primarily extensions of character.[3] The analyses in this book suggest, however, that distinctions established between characters in terms of their identities rely on a perceptual logic which permeates the entire fictional world: its scope exceeds the framework of characters and affects narration and description. The very possibility of the novel as a discursive form seems to have emerged out of a new ability to configure perceptual relationships as a basic ground for the intelligibility of things, persons, and actions.

How did language acquire this new ability? We encountered in earlier chapters dissonances between schematic descriptions and attempts at verisimilitude, as well as between various schematisms. The emergence of print in nineteenth-century Kerala unmoored and put into circulation a range of schematisms from various domains of knowledge and practice. Most periodicals in the late nineteenth century were religious in nature, and secular news began making an appearance first as a section in religious periodicals.[4] The domain of print was closely tied to the emergence of new forms and practices of knowledge strikingly different from the older ones. The contrast between the old and the new was complicated by the differential access possessed by caste and religious communities to various kinds of knowledge. Autobiographies show that this was not only an intellectual difficulty; practices of knowledge acquisition involved modes of embodiment.[5] This has been recognized more clearly in the case of traditional knowledge practices; but new methods of instruction, even when seemingly not anchored in the body, produce their own distinctive forms of corporeal investment. Kesavan's autobiography, for instance, documents the strange newness of bodily experiences:

[3] For a discussion of the literary critical treatment of objects in novels in terms of their 'metaphoric' and 'weak metonymic' functions, see Freedgood, *Ideas in Things*.

[4] For an account of early print history in Malayalam, see Ramakrishnan, 'Varthamanappathrangaludeyum Achadiyanthrangaludeyum'. On early newspapers in Kerala, see Priyadarshan, *Kerala Pathrapravarthanam*.

[5] See Nedumpally, 'Ways of Knowing'.

of sitting on the floor with classmates from other castes, of the sense of shame produced by disparities in dress in the classroom, and of improvisation in techniques of corporeal punishment devised to ensure the maintenance of rules of untouchability. New discourses of knowledge, be they of science, geography, or history—in spite of their claims to factual truthfulness—acquired their own schematic, magical dimension. They became objects of marvel and fear, prompting simultaneously an admission of their powers as well as generating efforts at taming their newness.

Public discourses in Kerala at the end of the nineteenth century showed a diversity of norms and practices, with no settled authority to arbitrate over disputes or legislate norms. Practices of literary and religious expression moved out of their earlier habitats to enter into new, heterogeneous alliances. Compositions which demonstrated and appealed to literary virtuosity and specialized skills began losing their earlier addressees; their new publics were too diverse in their knowledge, judgement, and literary habitus. In spite of its small size and enormous exclusions, the print-public sphere emerged as a diverse and promiscuous space. Objects of discourses—literary, religious, or social—appeared incompletely formed, always in need of some form of supplementation. We saw how early novels presented female bodies through formulaic head-to-toe descriptions borrowed from the *kavya* tradition. This helped illustrate a point: realistic descriptions promised by the novel did not seem adequate in themselves and called for schematic supplementation. Earlier literary formulae too were inadequate or unconvincing in the new discursive space of the novel: often they functioned like a protective screen which allowed public uses of language to get closer to what they spoke about without dissolving social barriers and distinctions. The formulaic nature of head-to-toe descriptions permitted a new discursive intimacy with the female body. The preoccupation with perceptual economies was a symptom of literature's new status as public discourse; it revealed an impulse to regulate and at the same time permit access to all that appeared in literature's new space of exposure. Self-narratives fashioned not only their voices and their audience but also the selfhoods they spoke about, within this new space. I have repeatedly addressed questions of visibility to take account of the dimension of publicness that the language of self-articulation came to possess at this time.

In my brief discussion of K. Ramakrishna Pillai in the first chapter, I examined the complex and ambivalent manoeuvres through which borders between political and literary publicity were produced and negotiated at the beginning of the twentieth century.[6] Ramakrishna Pillai's use of scandal as a mode of political criticism demonstrates how exposure—proper and improper—and its consequences remained central to such distinctions. The political charge of exposure brings to light a deeper dimension of all public visibilization, even when carried out under the sign of the avowedly non-political activity of literary writing. Literature as a form of public utterance acquired the ability to cause individual and collective hurt and provoke claims for redress in this period. At the core of this new zone of sensitivity were caste and community identities and their relationship to public experiences of shame and humiliation. Ramakrishna Pillai's own use of scandal pivoted on issues of sexuality and corruption; but on a closer look these appear intimately linked to questions of caste: sexual improprieties around the palace and the dewan's office are implicitly felt in Ramakrishna Pillai's writing as offences to the dignity of Nayar women. This was anticipated in some of his early editorials, where Pillai had urged reform in a temple custom requiring Nayar women associated with the palace not to cover their upper torso while participating in ritual processions.[7] Pillai made a distinction between

[6] For a detailed discussion, see Kumar, 'The Public, the State and the New Domains of Writing'; idem 'Ambivalences of Publicity'.

[7] K. Ramakrishna Pillai, 'Tiruvitamkoor Maharajavu Tirumanassukondu Kalpichu Erppetuttenda Oru Samudayika Parishkaram' (A Social Reform that Needs to be Introduced by the Command of His Highness the Maharaja of Travancore), *Keralapanchika*, 27 September 1901, cited in K. Bhaskara Pillai, *Swadeshabhimani*, 40.

the devotional space of the temple and the streets through which the later phase of the procession progressed. The streets were a space of public visibility and the onlookers formed a promiscuous audience; Pillai described this public as including diverse communities, especially low castes (*hinajati*).

Caste matters had an ambivalent status in the public domain: glorious references to caste histories, produced by many communities at this time, provoked disputes when the claims of communities conflicted with one another, leading to satiric debunking and counterclaims. But the very mention of the caste identities of authors could be demeaning in a discursive space predicated on the disavowal of caste. There were frequent insinuations of the caste status of authors in the early twentieth century.[8] I mentioned controversies over the surnames used by lower-caste writers; some upper-caste critics saw the very entry of certain communities into the space of literary writing as presumptuous. Debates over the literary canon came to be coloured by claims regarding the cultural capital of communities, demands for inclusiveness, and disagreements on the quantum of representation of caste groups. Some of these debates were carried out in poetry: compositions such as *Kaviramayanam*, *Kavibharatam*, and *Kavipushpamala* adopted allegorical devices for formulating literary canons, by comparing Malayalam poets to characters in epics or to flowers in a garden. They provoked criticism and countercompositions from excluded caste groups.

The story that I have tracked is therefore also about the vital role that caste identities played in the production of a public domain which worked on the premise of its disavowal of caste. This had an affective dimension, with caste humiliation acquiring a new intensity and visibility in lower-caste writing, and a sense of caste offence beginning to be experienced by the privileged castes. Kanippayyur's autobiography, we saw, offers elements for a phenomenology of the caste offence felt by a Nambutiri Brahmin when the norms of public visibility changed. He felt *vallayma* (unease) at many of the changes,

[8] For a discussion, see Kumar, 'Shaping a Literary Space'.

which he felt were meant to insult the Nambutiris. Equality could become a source of hurt. The disappearance of external signs of caste difference, for Kanippayyur, did not signify the extinction of caste. It served, he felt, only to highlight the changing power equations between castes; he saw in it a public demeaning of the Nambutiri's status which drew attention to the incongruous combination of his high-caste identity and weak political power. As older caste markers began to disappear and discourses of *jati* gave way to those of *samudayam*, the language of caste began to signify the limits of the public domain. At the same time, through caste community movements, it also became the major propeller and even a paradigm for constituting a public. These ambivalences of visibility indicate the complexity of caste as a form of political existence in late-nineteenth and early-twentieth-century Kerala.

Political existence does not always involve organized collective effort. The autobiographies considered in the previous chapter show how deeply individual and familial experiences were marked by the tensions I indicated above. Instances of slippage have been noted, where dominant strands in self-narration were belied by elements that escaped its direct control. Such slippages need to be considered intrinsic to autobiographical enunciation, and, at a more general level, to the social life of identities. Hannah Arendt, who stressed the public appearance of human beings in action and utterances, valorized biographical writing—which reflected how others saw one—over autobiographies.[9] The distinction may not be entirely satisfactory: what is actually visibilized in self-narratives is often not identical with what the author-protagonist intended to project or avow. The figure of the subject engaged in the act of self-exhibition does not stay within the author-exhibitor's control or vision but forms a vital

[9] Adrianna Cavarero's comments on Arendt are instructive: 'The autobiography would figure, in Arendt's view, as an absurd exercise, since the identity revealed by its actions is the very thing that the agent does not master and does not know. Thus, it will be even more difficult for him to be able to know and master the story that such actions leave behind.' Cavarero, *Relating Narratives*, 24.

component of what is revealed in self-narratives when they appear in the public domain. Instances of slippage and incongruence are a part of the very conditions of possibility of self-narration; they manifest ambivalences inherent in political existence rather than a hidden, more authentic or substantial selfhood.

Judith Butler's insights into the performative character of identities and the possibilities of subversion they open up have been hugely influential in recent scholarship.[10] Her arguments are based on her claim that processes of identification remain necessarily incomplete, and thereby prompt constant performative iteration. The slippages we encountered in self-narration manifest this constitutive lack of closure in identities. The notion of 'inhabitation', as I indicated in chapter 1, offers a useful way of understanding the complex social life of identities. The texts that I looked at do not reveal subjects in stable occupation of their identities. This has compelled me to move away from a prominent strand in literary studies which uses representations of social identities as a privileged tool for interpreting texts. This book has focused, instead, on a far less stable presencing of the figure of the subject. As said earlier, snapshots of gestures and movements rather than portraits of identifiable faces: these indicate the book's trajectory.

As in photography, the snapshots were captured often through a process of interruption. Interestingly, such interruption took different forms, partly determined by the kinds of material we engaged and the habits of writing and reading associated with them. Narrative continuities and assumptions about the unity of characterization were at times set aside in my reading of novels, to move to a plane of analysis prior to them—that of economies of perception and utterance. This generated connections which cut through stories and characters to reveal other orders of fictional coherence. My choice was guided by a dissatisfaction with those modes of literary reading that see in plots and characters the primary location of a text's meaning. I found it useful to regard these and other components of literary fiction as

[10] Butler, *Gender Trouble*, 163–80.

machine-like elements in an assemblage; their status is rather like that of props in a theatrical production or in the performance of a ritual. They are not bearers of meaning on their own, although their presence is necessary for the work that takes place. This is not to suggest that narrative structures do not matter. I found them particularly useful while discussing Kumaran Asan's monologic poetry. Rubbing the narrative grain against the coherence of poetic language helped track the fleeting appearance of subjects caught in liminal moments: of destitution, infancy, or an incandescence of desire bordering on death.

This book has returned repeatedly to figures of the body. Their presence is evident in all its chapters, but they do not form a single coherent narrative. In my reading of Sree Narayana Guru's writings and actions the body appeared as a crucial link of transmission between his devotional, metaphysical, and instructional writings as well as the new practices initiated by him. This does not however mean that all his writings and actions can be synthesized and anchored in his conception of the body. Placing the body at the foreground of discussions, however, allowed new connections to emerge, for instance between Sree Narayanan's metaphysical works, his writings on caste, and his pronouncements on the community. This made possible a close consideration of some of his lesser-known writings and often unnoticed aspects of his well-known works. This allowed me, more importantly, to track fresh, oblique links between the distinct discursive events associated with Sree Narayanan and Kumaran Asan. The problem of the body does not offer a vantage point of privileged critical visibility; it impacted the analyses here in widely different ways. In the discussion of Kumaran Asan's poetry, a focus on corporeality brought into relief complexities of desire and encounters with limits and intensities. In the chapters on the novel and in the discussion on self-narratives, the body worked in several ways to open the discussion to questions of sensation, historical memory, and time.

This book does not try to write a history of the body in modern Kerala; the analyses offered here at times do touch tangentially the contours of such a project. The texts discussed emerged at a moment of major transformation in bodily practices and in the estimation of corporeality in Kerala. Could we use the body's figuration in literary articulation as a lens to re-view these transformations, singled out often as signs of Kerala's encounter with modernity? Recent scholarship, following Foucault's crucial insights, has often highlighted the moves through which the body was invested with a new regime of disciplinary technologies, revealing how our experience of individuation is produced precisely through a deployment of disciplines. Arguably, we are yet to generate adequate descriptions of the consequences of these transformations for a corporeal sense of the past. Modern subjects are also subjects of remembrance; how do they come to acquire an articulate language of recollection which also produces moments of slippage? And how, existing alongside the disciplinary production of corporeality and narratives of structured history, do less articulate orders of memory reveal themselves?

I have not sought answers to these questions in an account of inner selfhood; I have considered the space of the inner more as an effect, as produced by processes which in turn need to be understood and explained. The attempt in this book has been to see how the coexistence and overlap of different ways of configuring the body permits insights into forms of less articulate retention. C.V. Raman Pillai's novels present this in perhaps the most spectacular terms. However, this dimension is not unique to C.V. and appears in the other texts examined as well. The complicity between disavowal and retention may not have been hidden in the deep recesses of souls; it may be inscribed in the figuration of the body, in the different grids within which it is simultaneously placed. The double vision to be found in Kesavan's autobiography demonstrates an ability to see the body in different grids simultaneously. The sense of their immediate coexistence, the synchrony of bodily memory, sometimes interrupted Kesavan's narrative of evolution and progress to reveal complex dimensions of historical inhabitation.

We are back to the trope of inhabitation. And here perhaps my book can end: with a brief reflection of a concept crucial within it, though not made wholly explicit, namely 'style'. Style is but another name for the discursive presencing of the subject's inhabitation—of identities, of the body, of norms, of the world. Style has not been developed as a stable concept in this book, and has been seldom named in these analyses. However, it operates as a running thread, shaping the questions raised and the connections probed. One may say that style stands in several oppositional relationships: with respect to signs, representations, images, and stories. These oppositions do not acquire the predictability of stable binaries since style is made visible precisely in the working of the elements it is placed in opposition to. The word style has acquired in our times a late Foucauldian ring, from his studies on what he called stylizations of the self.[11] My use of the word leans also on the use of the term in ordinary language in relation to writing: a certain manner, a way of working with language or working language, that cannot be equated with what is being said or written, or with the tools chosen for the purpose. The space of style is distinguishable from ideologies and belief systems; by virtue of its complex materiality, style offers resistance to its reduction to ideas and representations. The fleeting movements visible in the snapshots offered in this book offer a point of entry into the realm of style. My aim is not to develop a theory of style or propose a new stylistics as method; it is rather to document the existence of style as a discursive figure for the subject's unstable and variable inhabitation of the self and the world.

[11] See especially Foucault, *The Use of Pleasure*.

Bibliography

Abu, O., *Arabimalayala Sahityacharitram* (A History of Arabi-Malayalam Literature) (Kottayam: Sahitya Pravarthaka Co-operative Society, 1970).

Achutan, K.R., *C. Krishnan (Jeevacharitram)* (C. Krishnan: A Biography) (Kottayam: Sahitya Pravarthaka Co-operative Society, 1971).

'Adikeralacharitram' (History of Early Kerala), *Vidyavinodini*, 1: 2–12 (1889–90).

Agamben, Giorgio, *Remnants of Auschwitz: The Witness and the Archive*, tr. Daniel Heller-Rozen (New York: Zone Books, 1999).

Aiyer, Ulloor S. Parameswara, *Kerala Sahityacharitram* (History of Kerala Literature), vol. 4, 4th edn (Trivandrum: University of Kerala, 1990).

Amma, Ammini, 'Streedharmam' (Duties of a Woman), *Mahila*, 13: 11–12 (1933), 346–9.

Amma, B. Kalyani, *Ormayil Ninnu* (From Memory), ed. K. Gomathi Amma (Kottayam: Sahitya Pravarthaka Co-operative Society, 1964).

Amma, G. Gomathi, *Mahakavi K.C. Kesava Pillai: Diarykkurippukalude Patanavum Pradhanakrtikalum* (Poet K.C. Keshava Pillai: His Major Works and a Study of His Diaries) (Thiruvananthapuram: Prabhatam Printing and Publishing Co., 2012).

Amma, K. Padmavathi, 'Bhartrsusrusha' (Care of One's Husband), *Sarada*, 1: 9 (1905), 2–5.

Amma, P. Bhageerathi, 'Vyayamam' (Physical Exercise), *Sarada*, 1: 4 (1905), 2–3.

Amma, T. Ammukkutty, 'Streevidyabhyasam' (Women's Education), *Sarada*, 1: 3 (1905), 10–11.

Amma, T.B. Kalyani, 'Streedharmam' (Duties of a Woman), *Sarada*, 1: 3 (1905), 1–3.

Antarjanam, Lalitambika, *Atmakathayku Oru Amukham* (An Introduction to [My] Autobiography) (Kottayam: Sahitya Pravarthaka Co-operative Society, 1979).

———, 'The Goddess of Revenge', tr. Gita Krishnankutty, *Caste Me Out If You Will* (New York: Feminist Press, 1998), 18–30.

Aquil, Raziuddin and Partha Chatterjee, eds, *History in the Vernacular* (Delhi: Permanent Black, 2008).

———, 'Introduction: History in the Vernacular', in Raziuddin Aquil and Partha Chatterjee, eds, *History in the Vernacular* (Delhi: Permanent Black, 2008), 1–24.

Arendt, Hannah, *The Life of the Mind, One: Thinking* (London: Secker and Warburg, 1978).

———, *The Human Condition* (Chicago: University of Chicago Press, 1998).

Armstrong, Nancy, *Fiction in the Age of Photography: The Legacy of British Realism* (Cambridge, Mass.: Harvard University Press, 2002).

Arnold, David, 'The Self and the Cell: Indian Prison Narratives as Life Histories', in David Arnold and Stuart Blackburn, eds, *Telling Lives in India: Biography, Autobiography and Life History* (Delhi: Permanent Black, 2004), 29–53.

——— and Stuart Blackburn, eds, *Telling Lives in India: Biography, Autobiography and Life History* (Delhi: Permanent Black, 2004).

Arunima, G., *There Comes Papa: Colonialism and the Transformation of Matriliny in Kerala, Malabar, c. 1850–1940* (Hyderabad: Orient Longman, 2003).

———, 'Glimpses from a Writer's World: O. Chandu Menon, His Contemporaries, and Their Times', *Studies in History*, 20: 2 (2005), 189–214.

———, 'Imagining Communities—Differently: Print, Language, and the Public Sphere in Colonial Kerala', *The Indian Economic and Social History Review*, 43: 1 (2006), 63–76.

Asad, Talal, *Formations of the Secular: Christianity, Islam and Modernity* (Stanford: Stanford University Press, 2003).

———, 'Thinking About Agency and Pain', in *Formations of the Secular: Christianity, Islam and Modernity* (Stanford: Stanford University Press, 2003), 67–99.

Asan, N. Kumaran, Kumaran Asan's Diary, Microfilm Collection, Nehru Memorial Museum and Library, New Delhi.

———, *Manassakti* (The Power of the Mind; A Malayalam translation of James Allen's *As a Man Thinketh*) (Alwaye: Sarada Book Depot, 1950).

———, *Maitreyi* (Malayalam translation of a Bengali novel by Sitanath Tatvabhushan) (1913; Ernakulam: Sahodaran Press, 1953).

———, *Kumaran Asante Gadyalekhanangal* (Kumaran Asan's Prose Essays), ed. N.K. Damodaran, vol. 1 (1981; Thonnakkal: Kumaran Asan Smaraka Committee, 1984).

———, *Kumaran Asante Sampurna Padya Krtikal* (Complete Poetic Works of Kumaran Asan) (Kottayam: Sahitya Pravarthaka Co-operative Society, 1981).

———, *Kumaran Asante Gadyalekhanangal* (Kumaran Asan's Prose Essays), ed. N.K. Damodaran, vol. 2 (Thonnakkal: Kumaran Asan Smaraka Committee, 1982).

———, 'Mataparivartana Rasavadam' (The Alchemy of Religious Conversion), in *Kumaran Asante Gadyalekhanangal* (Kumaran Asan's Prose Essays), vol. 2, ed. N.K. Damodaran (Thonnakkal: Kumaran Asan Smaraka Committee, 1982), 300–13.

———, *Kumaran Asante Gadyalekhanangal* (Kumaran Asan's Prose Essays), ed. N.K. Damodaran, vol. 3 (Thonnakkal: Kumaran Asan Smaraka Committee, 1987).

Bailey, Benjamin, *Dictionary of High and Colloquial Malayalam and English, Dedicated by Permission to His Highness the Rajah of Travancore by the Rev. B. Bailey of the Church Mission Society* (Cottayam: CMS Press, 1846).

———, *Dictionary, English and Malayalam, Dedicated by Permission to His Highness the Rajah of Travancore by Rev. B. Bailey of the Church Missionary Society* (Cottayam: CMS Press, 1849).

Balakrishnan, P.K., *Chandu Menon: Oru Padanam* (Chandu Menon: A Study), 3rd edn (Kottayam: Sahitya Pravarthaka Co-operative Society, 1971).

———, *Jativyavastayum Keralacharitravum* (The Caste System and Kerala History) (Kottayam: Sahitya Pravarthaka Co-operative Society, 1992).

———, ed., *Sree Narayana Guru* (1954; Trissur: Kerala Sahitya Akademi, 2000).

Basheer, Vaikom Muhammad, *Basheerinte Sampurna Krtikal* (The Complete Works of Basheer) (Kottayam: D.C. Books, 1994), 2 vols.

Bayly, Susan, 'Hindu Kingship and the Origin of Community: Religion, State and Society in Kerala, 1750–1850', *Modern Asian Studies*, 18: 2 (1984), 177–213.

Benjamin, Walter, *The Work of Art in the Age of Its Technological Reproducibility and Other Writings on Media*, ed. Michael W. Jennings, Brigid Doherty, and Thomas Y. Levin (Cambridge, Mass.: Belknap Press, 2008).

Bhaskaran, K.R., *Sreenarayanaguruswamikal* (1935; Pudukad: Kerala Bhanu Book Depot, 1936).

Bhaskaran, T., ed., *Sree Narayana Guru Vaikhari* (Collected Utterances of Sree Narayana Guru) (1994; Perumbavur: SNDP Yogam Kunnathunad Union, 2010).

Bhattatiripad, M.R., *Ritumati* (The Pubescent Girl) (1944; Trissur: Current Books, 1991).

Bhattatiripad, V.T., *V.T.yude Sampurna Krtikal* (The Complete Works of V.T.) (Kottayam: D.C. Books, 1997).

Blackburn, Stuart, 'The Death of the Little Brothers', in *Singing of Birth and Death: Texts in Performance* (Philadelphia: University of Pennsylvania Press, 1988), 89–140.

———, *Print, Folklore and Nationalism in Colonial South India* (Delhi: Permanent Black, 2006).

Bourdieu, Pierre, *Distinction: A Social Critique of the Judgement of Taste*, tr. Richard Nice (Harvard, Mass.: Harvard University Press, 1987).

Brahmashri Thycaud Ayya Swamikal (*Jeevacharitram*) (Brahmashri Thycaud Ayya Swamikal: A Biography) (Trivandrum: Sri Ayya Mission, 1997).

Butler, Judith, *Gender Trouble: Feminism and the Subversion of Identity* (1990; London: Routledge, 1999).

———, *Giving an Account of Oneself: A Critique of Ethical Violence* (Amsterdam: Koninklijke van Gorcum, 2003).

———, 'What is Critique? An Essay on Foucault's Virtue', in Sara Salih with Judith Butler, eds, *The Judith Butler Reader* (Oxford: Blackwell, 2004), 302–22.

Caldwell, Robert, *A Comparative Grammar of the Dravidian and South Indian Family of Languages*, 3rd edn rev. and ed. J.L. Wyatt and T. Ramakrishna Pillai (London: Kegal Paul, Trench, Trubner, and Co., 1913).

Cameron, J.M., 'Autobiography and Philosophical Perplexity', in Eva Schaper, ed., *Pleasure, Preference and Value: Studies in Philosophical Aesthetics* (Cambridge: Cambridge University Press, 1983), 158–90.

Carus, Paul, *The Gospel of Buddha* (Chicago: The Open Court Publishing Company, 1915).

Cavarero, Adrianna, *Relating Narratives: Storytelling and Selfhood*, tr. Paul A. Kottman (London and New York: Routledge, 2000).

———, 'Narrative Against Destruction', tr. Elvina Roncalli, *New Literary History*, 46: 1 (2015), 1–16.

Chandran, K. Vinod, 'The Counter Narratives of Power and Identity in Colonial Keralam: A Reading of C.V. Raman Pillai's Historical Novels', Unpublished PhD thesis, Jawaharlal Nehru University, New Delhi, 2004.

Chatterjee, Partha, 'The Nationalist Resolution of the Women's Question', in *Recasting Women: Essays in Colonial History*, eds. Kumkum Sangari and Sudesh Vaid (Delhi: Kali for Women, 1989), 233–53.

———, 'Critique of Popular Culture', in idem, *Lineages of Political Society: Studies in Postcolonial Democracy* (Ranikhet: Permanent Black, 2011), 165–86.

Cohn, Bernard, 'The Census, Social Structure and Objectification in South Asia', in *An Anthropologist among the Historians and Other Essays* (New Delhi: Oxford University Press, 1987), 224–54.

———, *Colonialism and Its Forms of Knowledge* (Princeton, NJ: Princeton University Press, 1996).

Collins, Mrs Richard, *Ghatakavadham* (Slayer Slain) (1877; Kottayam: D.C. Books, 1976).

Dalmia, Vasudha, 'Merchant Tales and the Emergence of the Novel in Hindi', *Economic and Political Weekly*, 43: 34 (2008), 43–60.

——— and Stuart Blackburn, eds, *India's Literary History: Essays on the Nineteenth Century* (Delhi: Permanent Black, 2004).

Damodaran, K., *Sree Narayana Guru Swamy Jeevacharitram* (A Biography of Sree Narayana Guru Swamy) (Kollam: V.V. Press, 1929).

———, *Ezhavacharitram* (A History of the Ezhavas), vol. 1 (Trivandrum: Keralakesari Press, 1935).

Deleuze, Gilles, *Proust and Signs*, tr. Richard Howard (London: Allen Lane, 1972).

——— and Félix Guattari, *Kafka: Toward a Minor Literature*, tr. Dana Polan (Minneapolis: University of Minnesota Press, 1986).

Derrida, Jacques, *Of Grammatology*, tr. Gayatri Chakravorty Spivak (Baltimore, MA: Johns Hopkins University Press, 1974).

Desai, Manali, 'Indirect British Rule, State Formation and Welfarism in Kerala, India, 1860–1957', *Social Science History*, 29: 3 (2005), 457–88.

Devika, J., 'The Idea of Being Malayali: The *Aikyakeralam* Movement of the Mid-Twentieth Century', Paper presented at the Conference on South Indian History, Madras Institute of Development Studies, December 2004.

———, 'The Aesthetic Woman: Re-forming Female Bodies and Minds in Early Twentieth-Century Keralam', *Modern Asian Studies*, 39: 2 (2005), 478–9.

———, *Engendering Individuals: The Language of Reforming in Twentieth Century Keralam* (Hyderabad: Orient Longman, 2007).

———, ed., *Her-Self: Early Writings on Gender by Malayalee Women 1898–1938* (Kolkata: Stree, 2005).

Dharmanandaji, Swami, *Sree Narayana Gurudevan* (Kottayam: B. Damayanti/National Book Stall, 1965).

Dirks, Nicholas, *Castes of Mind: Colonialism and the Making of Modern India* (Delhi: Permanent Black, 2001).

Eck, Diana L., *Darsan: Seeing the Divine Image in India* (Delhi: Motilal Banarsidass, 2007).

Elaya Nayar, Kannambra Ramanunni, *Bhadraswayambaram* (Bhadra's Wedding) (Calicut: Vidya Vilasam Press, 1891).

Embrantiri, A. Krishnan, 'Antakaranam' (The Inner Sense), *Mangalodayam*, 2: 11 (1910), 481–4.

Fawcett, Fred, *Nayars of Malabar* (Madras: Government Press, 1901).

———, *Nambutiris: Notes on Some of the People of Malabar* (1900; New Delhi: Asian Educational Services, 2001).

Forbes, Geraldine, 'Education for Women', in *Women and Social Reform in Modern India*, eds Sumit Sarkar and Tanika Sarkar (Delhi: Permanent Black, 2007), vol. 1, 83–112.

Foucault, Michel, *The Use of Pleasure: Volume 2 of the History of Sexuality*, tr. Robert Hurley (New York: Vintage Books, 1990).

Freedgood, Elaine, *Ideas in Things: Fugitive Meaning in the Victorian Novel* (Chicago: University of Chicago Press, 2006).

Freeman, Rich, 'Genre and Society: Literary Culture of Premodern Kerala', in Sheldon Pollock, ed., *Literary Cultures in History: Reconstructions from South Asia* (New Delhi: Oxford University Press, 2003), 437–500.

Freeman, Rich, 'Rubies and Coral: The Lapidary Crafting of Language in Kerala', *Journal of Asian Studies*, 57 (1998), 38–65.

Ganapathy, T.N., *The Philosophy of the Tamil Siddhas* (New Delhi: Indian Council of Philosophical Research, 1993).

Gopalakrishnan, Naduvattom, *Atmakathasahityam Malayalathil* (Autobiographical Writing in Malayalam) (Trivandrum: Kerala Bhasha Institute, 1985).

Gopalan, A., *Yesu Daivamayirunnuvo?* (Was Jesus God?), Theist Postal Mission No. 7 (Calicut: Spectator Press, 1910).

Gopalan, A.K., *Ente Jeevitakatha* (The Story of My Life) (1955; Trivandrum: Desabhimani Book House, 2004).

Greenblatt, Stephen, and Catherine Gallagher, 'Counterhistory and the Anecdote', in idem, *Practising New Historicism* (Chicago: University of Chicago Press, 2000), 49–74.

Gundert, Hermann, *A Malayalam and English Dictionary* (Mangalore: C. Stolz, Basel Mission Book and Tract Depository, 1872).

Gupta, Charu, *Sexuality, Obscenity, Community: Women, Muslims, and the Hindu Public in Colonial India* (Delhi: Permanent Black, 2001).

Gutman, Judith Mara, *Through Indian Eyes: Nineteenth and Early Twentieth Century Photography from India* (New York: Oxford University Press, 1982).

Habermas, Jürgen, *The Structural Transformation of the Public Sphere: An Inquiry into a Category of Bourgeois Society*, tr. Thomas Burger with the assistance of Frederick Lawrence (Cambridge, Ma.: Polity Press, 1989, rpt. 1996).

Hansen, Thomas Blom, 'Sovereigns Beyond the State: On Legality and Public Authority in India', in Ravinder Kaur, ed., *Religion, Violence and Political Mobilisation in South Asia* (New Delhi: Sage, 2005), 109–44.

Harisharma, A.D., *Kandathil Varghese Mappila* (Ernakulam: Deepam Press, 1951).

Heehs, Peter, ed., *Indian Religions: A Historical Reader of Spiritual Expression and Experience* (New York: New York University Press).

Heidegger, Martin, *Kant and the Problem of Metaphysics*, tr. Richard Taft (Bloomington: Indiana University Press, 1997).

Heston, Mary Beth, 'Mixed Messages in a New "Public" Travancore: Building the Capital, 1860–1880', *Art History*, 31: 2 (2008), 211–47.

Holden, Philip, 'Other Modernities: National Autobiography and Globalization', *Biography* 28: 1 (2005), 89–103.

———, *Autobiography and Decolonization: Modernity, Masculinity and the Nation-State* (Madison: University of Wisconsin Press, 2008).

Ikkazhinja Kanathur Charitram (The Recent History of Kanathur) (Kannur: Thiyya Samudayoddharana Sangham, 1926).

Irumbayam, George, *Adyakala Malayala Novel* (Early Malayalam Novel) (Kottayam: Current Books, 1982).

———, ed., *Naalu Novelukal* (Four Novels) (Trissur: Kerala Sahitya Akademi, 1985).

———, ed., *Anthappayiyude Novelukal, Chandu Menonte Saradayum* (Anthappayi's Novels and Chandu Menon's *Sarada*) (Kottayam: Current Books, 1991).

Isvara Krsna, *Sankhya Karika of Isvara Krsna*, ed. S.S. Surya Narayana Sastri (Madras: University of Madras, 1973).

Iyer, K.N. Sundara, *Mohanangi* (Palghat: Kamprom Brothers, 1907).

Jeffrey, Robin, *The Decline of Nair Dominance: Society and Politics in Travancore 1847–1908* (1976; Delhi: Manohar, 2014).

Johnson, Samuel, *Rasalesika* (Rasselas), tr. Thatha Kanaran (1898; Madras: Malabar Publishing House, 1941).

Joseph, T.K., 'The Hand Dipping Ordeal', in *Kerala Society Papers*, vol. II, series 2, reprinted in *Kerala Society Papers*, vols I and II (1929; Thiruvananthapuram: Kerala State Gazetteers, 1997), 110.

K.M., 'Antakarana Samskaram' (The Culture of Inner Sense), *Mangalodayam*, 2: 8 (1910), 312–19.

Kalidasa, *Abhijnana Shakuntalam*, tr. Kuttikrishna Marar (Calicut: Mathrubhoomi, 1988).

Kamalamma, P., ed., *Swadeshabhimaniyude Sahitya Sapraya* (Swadeshabhimani's Literary Vocation) (Trivandrum: The Author, 1987).

Kanaran, Thatha, *A Comparative Study of English and Malayalam as a Guide to Reciprocal Translation for the Use of Upper Secondary Schools and Colleges*, ed. Joseph Mooliyil (Mangalore: Basel Mission Book and Tract Depository, 1899).

Kant, Immanuel, *Critique of Pure Reason*, tr. Norman Kemp-Smith (London: Macmillan, 1929).

Kapila, Shruti, 'Race Matters: Orientalism and Religion, India and Beyond', *Modern Asian Studies*, 41: 3 (2007), 471–513.

Kaur, Ravinder, ed., *Religion, Violence and Political Mobilisation in South Asia* (New Delhi: Sage, 2005), 109–44.

Kemper, Stephen, 'Time, Person and Gender in Sinhalese Astrology', *American Ethnologist*, 7: 4 (1980), 744–58.

Kesavan, B.S., *History of Printing and Publishing in India: A Story of Cultural Re-awakening, Vol. II: Origins of Printing and Publishing in Karnataka, Andhra and Kerala* (New Delhi: National Book Trust, 1988).

Kesavan, C., *Jeevitasamaram* (Life Struggle), first published in 2 vols (1953–65; combined volume Kottayam: Sahitya Pravarthaka Co-operative Society, 1990).

Kochu Thampuran, Kochi 12th Koor Ramavarma, *Bhaskara Menon* (Trivandrum: B.V. Book Depot, 1909).

Kodoth, Praveena, 'Courting Legitimacy or Delegitimising Custom?: Sexuality, Sambandham and Marriage in Late Nineteenth Century Malabar', *Modern Asian Studies*, 35: 3 (2001), 349–84.

Kojève, Alexandre, *An Introduction to the Reading of Hegel: Lectures on the Phenomenology of Spirit*, ed. Allan Bloom, tr. James H. Nichols, Jr (Ithaca and London: Cornell University Press, 1969).

Krishnan, C., ed., *Buddhatatvapradeepam* (The Light of Buddhist Thought) (Calicut: Empire Press, 1921).

Kumar, Udaya, 'Seeing and Reading: Some Questions of Visibility in the Early Malayalam Novel', in Meenakshi Mukherjee, ed., *Early Novels in India* (New Delhi: Sahitya Akademi, 2002), 161–92.

——, 'Kazhchayum Vayanayum: *Indulekhayum* Chihnavyaparathe Sambadhikkunna Chila Prasngangalum' (Seeing and Reading: *Indulekha* and Some Problems Related to the Exchange of Signs), published as the Introduction in O. Chandu Menon, *Indulekha* (Kottayam: D.C. Books, 2004), 7–18.

———, 'Literature and Intensity: Deleuze's Stuttering Machine', in *Trajectory of French Thought* (New Delhi: Rupa and FIRC, 2004), 123–35.

———, 'The Public, the State and New Domains of Writing: On Ramakrishna Pillai's Conception of Literary and Political Expression', *Tapasam: A Quarterly Journal of Kerala Studies*, 2: 3 & 4 (2007), 413–41.

———, 'Writing the Life of the Guru: Chattampi Swamikal, Narayana Guru and Modes of Biographical Construction', in Vijaya Ramaswamy and Yogesh Sharma, eds, *Biography as History: Indian Perspectives* (Hyderabad: Orient Blackswan, 2009), 53–87.

———, 'Shaping a Literary Space: Early Literary Histories in Malayalam and Normative Uses of the Past', in Hans Harder, ed., *Literature and Nationalist Ideology: Writing Histories of Modern Indian Languages* (New Delhi: Social Science Press, 2010), 19–50.

———, 'Consciousness, Agency and Humiliation: Reflections on Dalit Life Writing and Subalternity', in Cosimo Zene, ed., *The Political Philosophies of Antonio Gramsci and B.R. Ambedkar* (London: Routledge, 2013), 158–70.

———, 'Dr. Palpu's Petition Writings and Kerala's Pasts', *NMML Occasional Papers, History and Society*, n.s., no. 59 (New Delhi: Nehru Memorial Museum and Library, 2014).

———, 'Ambivalences of Publicity: Transparency and Exposure in K. Ramakrishna Pillai's Thought', in Divya Dwivedi and Sanil V., eds, *The Public Sphere from Outside the West* (London: Bloomsbury Academic, 2015), 79–96.

Kumaran, Kottayi, *Sree Narayana Guru Charitam* (The Story of Sree Narayana Guru) (Tellicherry: Vidyavilasam Press, 1929).

Kumaran, Moorkothu, *Vasumati* (Tellicherry: The Author, 1912).

———, *Oyyarathu Chandu Menon* (Trissur: Kerala Sahitya Akademi, 1996).

———, *Sree Narayanaguruswamikalude Jeevacharitram* (A Biography of Sree Narayana Guru Swamikal) (1930; Varkala: Sree Narayana Dharma Sangham Trust, 2007).

Kunjambu, Potheri, *Saraswativijayam* (The Triumph of Learning), reprinted in George Irumbayam, ed., *Naalu Novelukal* (1892; Trissur: Kerala Sahitya Akademi, 1985), 49–124.

Kunjappa, Moorkothu, *Moorkothu Kumaran: Oru Jeevacharitram* (Moorkothu Kumaran: A Biography) (Kottayam: Sahitya Pravarthaka Co-operative Society, 1975).

Kunjukkuttan, Madambu, *Bhrashtu*, tr. as *Outcaste* by Vasanthi Sankaranarayanan (Delhi: Macmillan India, 1996).

Kunjuraman, C.V., 'Buddhamatavadangal: Oru Samadhanam' (Arguments on Buddhism: A Response), serialized in several issues of *Kerala Kaumudi* in August 1923.

———, 'Adhakrtarkku Buddhamatamanu Nallathu' (Buddhism is Best for the Oppressed), *Kerala Kaumudi Weekly*, 27 February 1925, 1, 4.

———, 'Thiyyarkku Nallatu Buddhamatam Thanneyanu' (Buddhist Faith is Best for the Thiyyas), *Mitavadi Varshikapathippu* (Annual Issue), 1926.

———, 'Njan' ('I'), in Hasheem Rajan, ed., *C.V. Kunjuraman: Smaranika* (C.V. Kunjuraman: Souvenir) (1948; Trivandrum: Kaumudi Public Relations, 2000), 126–44.

Kurukkal, K. Narayana, *Parappuram* (Rockface) (1908; Trivandrum: B.V. Book Depot, 1949).

———, *Udayabhanu* (The Morning Sun), 4 vols (1905; Trivandrum: Kamalalayam Book Depot, 1949).

Lakshmi Amma, Mantaraveettil, 'Ente Jeevacharitravum Grhnidharmavum', 2: 12 (1907), 529–47, tr. as 'My Life and My Home-Making', in J. Devika, ed., *Her-Self: Early Writings on Gender by Malayalee Women 1898–1938* (Kolkata: Stree, 2005), 10–21.

Lal, Vinay, ed., *Political Hinduism: The Religious Imagination in Public Spheres* (New Delhi: Oxford University Press, 2009), 66–7.

Levinas, Emmanuel, *Of Escape / De l'evasion*, tr. Bettina Bergo (Stanford: Stanford University, 2003).

Life of Samuel Hebich, The, By Two of His Fellow-Labourers, translated from the German by Colonel J.G. Halliday (London: Shelley, Jackson, and Halliday, 1876).

Life of Dr. H. Gundert: Gundert Panditharute Jeevacharitram (Mangalore: Basel Mission Book and Tract Depository, 1896).

M.K., 'Streevidyabhyasavum Taravaduswathum' (Women's Education and Family Property), *Lakshmibai*, 1: 6 (1905), 233–5.

Madhavan, Arya, *Kudiyattam: Theatre and the Actor's Consciousness* (Amsterdam: Rodopi, 2010).

Madhavan, P.K., *T.K. Madavante Jeevacharitram* (T.K. Madhavan's Biography) (Kottayam: D.C. Books, 1986).

'Malayalikalum Streevidyabhyasavum' (Malayalis and Women's Education), *Sarada*, 1: 7 (1905), 5–9.

Manalil, Paul, 'Malayalathile Adyathe Atmakatha' (The First Autobiography in Malayalam), in Yakob Ramavarman, *Yakob Ramavarmante Atmakatha*, ed. Paul Manalil (Trichur: Kerala Sahitya Akademi, 2008), 12–25.

Manavalan, Paul, *Kerala Samskaravum Kraistava Missionarimarum* (Kerala Culture and Christian Missionaries) (Kottayam: D.C. Books, 1990).

Mannadiar, V.I., *Kamalam: Oru Samoohya Novel* (Kamalam: A Social Novel) (1924; 3rd reprint Calicut: P.K. Brothers, 1949).

Mascuch, Michael, *Origins of the Individualist Self* (Cambridge: Polity Press, 1997).

Mathen, Rev. George, *Satyavadakhetam: Oru Virutu Prakaranam* (The Shield of Truthfulness: An Honoured Treatise) (Cottayam: C.M. Press, 1863).

Mauss, Marcel, 'Techniques of the Body', tr. Ben Brewster, *Economy and Society*, 2: 1 (1973), 70–88.

Menon, C.P. Achyuta, *C.P. Achyuta Menonte Sahitya Vimarsanam* (The Literary Criticism of C.P. Achyuta Menon), ed. T.P. Sukumaran (Calicut: Mathrubhumi, 1988).

Menon, Dilip M., *Caste, Nationalism and Communism in South India: Malabar 1900–1948* (Cambridge: Cambridge University Press, 1994).

———, *The Blindness of Insight: Essays on Caste in Modern India* (Pondicherry: Navayana, 2006).

Menon, Kizhakkeppatt Raman Kutty, *Parangodi Parinayam* (Parangodi's Wedding), in George Irumbayam, ed., *Nalu Novelukal* (1892; Trissur: Kerala Sahitya Akademi, 1985), 218–69.

Menon, Komattil Padu, *Lakshmikesavam* (1892), in George Irumbayam, ed., *Nalu Novelukal* (1892; Trissur: Kerala Sahitya Akademi, 1985), 125–217.

Menon, Manjapra Ramunni, *Rasakkatta athava Ente Diaryile Chila Bhagangal* (Titbits of Fun, or Selections from My Diary) (Ottappalam: Kamalayalam Press, 1927).

Menon, O. Chandu, Letter to W. Dumergue, 19 December 1889, published in O. Chandu Menon, *Indulekha: A Novel from Malabar*, tr. W. Dumergue (1890; Calicut: Mathrubhumi, 1963), 19–25.

———, *Indulekha, A Novel from Malabar*, tr. W. Dumergue (1890; Calicut: Mathrubhumi Press, 1965).

———, *Sarada* (1892; Kottayam: D.C. Books, 1996).

———, 'Appendix IV: Chandu Menon's Memorandum to the Malabar Marriage Commission', in O. Chandu Menon, *Indulekha*, tr. Anitha Devasia (New Delhi: Oxford University Press, 2005), 248–62.

———, *Indulekha*, tr. Anitha Devasia (New Delhi: Oxford University Press, 2005).

———, *Indulekha* (1889; 20th rev. edn Kottayam: D.C. Books, 2014).

Menon, P. Shungoonny, *A History of Travancore from the Earliest Times* (Madras: Higginbothams, 1878).

Menon, T.C. Sankara, *Makers of Indian Literature: Chandu Menon* (New Delhi: Sahitya Akademi, 1974).

Menon, Vidwan T.K. Raman, *Ente Ayushkala Anubhutikal* (My Experiences of a Life Time) (Madras: Yasoda Ammal, 1989).

Mooliyil, Joseph, 'Sukumari' (1897), in George Irumbayam, ed., *Nalu Novelukal* (1892; Trissur: Kerala Sahitya Akademi, 1985), 271–395.

Moosad, C.K., *Vaikathu Pachu Moothathu* (Thiruvananthapuram: Department of Cultural Publications, 1996).

Moothathu, Vaikathu Pachu, 'Atmakatha' (Autobiography), in Naduvattom Gopalakrishnan, ed., *Atmakathasahityam Malayalathil* (Autobiographical Writing in Malayalam) (Trivandrum: Kerala Bhasha Institute, 1985), 147–55.

———, 'Pachu Moothathinte Atmakatha' (Pachu Moothathu's Autobiography), in *Yakob Ramavarmante Atmakatha* (Yakob Ramavarman's Autobiography), ed. Paul Manalil (Trissur: Kerala Sahitya Akademi, 2008), 55–64.

———, *Tiruvitamkoor Charitram* (1867; A History of Travancore) (Cochin: Pratibha Publications, 1989).

Mukherjee, Meenakshi, *Realism and Reality: The Novel and Society in India* (New Delhi: Oxford University Press, 1985).

———, ed., *Early Novels in India* (New Delhi: Sahitya Akademi, 2002).

Muthulekshmi, K., 'Samskrtapadanam Keralathil: Sangharshavum Samanvayavum' (Sanskrit Education in Kerala: Conflict and Concord), in Malayala Padana Sangham, ed., *Samskarapadanam: Charitram, Siddhantam, Prayogam* (Cultural Studies: History, Theory, Practice) (Kalady: Malayala Padana Sangham, 2007), 306–28.

———, 'Samskrtabhashayude Navodhanasandarbham: Kerala Parisaram' (The Moment of Renaissance of Sanskrit Language: The Kerala Context), Paper presented at the School of Renaissance Studies, Sree Sankaracharya University of Sanskrit, Kalady, 16 June 2011.

Nadar Sangam. Internet. http: //nadarsangam.com/whoswho.html.

Nair, C. Sankaran, *Autobiography of Chettur Sankaran Nair* (1966; Ottappalam: Chettur Sankaran Nair Foundation, 1998).

Nair, Cheruvalathu Chathu, *Meenakshi* (1890; Trissur: Kerala Sahitya Akademi, 1990).

Nair, K. Bhaskaran, *Daivaneetikku Dakshinyamilla* (Divine Justice is Merciless) (Kottayam: Sahitya Pravarthaka Co-operative Society, 1959).

Nair, K. Kannan, 'Keraliya Samudayam' (Keralite Community), *Bhashaposhini*, 5: 6 (1901), 193–201.

———, *Karuthodi Kannan Nayarude Atmakatha* (The Autobiography of Karuthodi Kannan Nair) (Calicut: Mathrubhumi, 1989).

Nair, K. Maheswaran, ed., *Chattampi Swamikal: Jeevitavum Krtikalum* (Chattampi Swamikal: Life and Works) (Trivandrum: Dooma Books, 1995).

Nair, Kannambra Ramanunni, *Kerala Charitram* (A History of Kerala) (Kottakkal: P. Kunhikrishna Menon, 1910).

Nair, N. Balakrishnan, *Sakshal C.V.* (The Real C.V.) (Trivandrum: Kamalalayam Book Depot, 1951).

Nair, P.K. Parameswaran, *C.V. Raman Pillai* (Kottayam: Sahitya Pravarthaka Co-operative Society, 1973).

Nair, Pandit C. Ramakrishnan, 'Chattampi Swamikalum Teerthapadasampradayavum' (Chattampi Swamikal and the Thirthapada Lineage), in *Sree Chattampi Swami Satabdasmarakagrantham* (Sree Chattampi Swamikal Centenary Volume) (Kollam: Sreeramavilasam Press, 1953), 70–1.

Nair R. Raman, and L. Sulochana Devi, *Chattampi Swamikal: An Intellectual Biography* (Trivandrum: Centre for South Indian Studies, 2010).

Nair, S. Guptan, *Gadyam Pinnitta Vazhikal: Pathonpatham Noottandile Malaya Gadyathekkuricchu Oru Avalokanam* (Paths Traversed by Prose: A Survey of Malayalam Prose in the Nineteenth Century) (Kottayam: D.C. Books, 2001).

Nambiar, Ashokan, 'Print, Communities and the Novel in Nineteenth-Century Kerala', Unpublished Doctoral Dissertation, University of Delhi, 2015.

Namboodiripad, E.M.S., *Atmakatha* (Autobiography) (Trivandrum: Deshabhimani, 1970).

———, 'Avatarika' (Foreword), in Cherukad, *Jeevitappata* (The Path of Life) (Pattampi: Shakthi Publishers, 1974), i–viii.

———, *E.M.S.inte Teranjedutha Prasangangal 1935–1995* (Selected Speeches of E.M.S., 1935–1995), ed. C. Bhaskaran (Kottayam: D.C. Books, 1996).

———, *Keralam Malayalikalude Mathrubhumi* (Kerala, the Motherland of the Malayalis), reprinted as vol. 9 in *EMS-inte Sampurna Krtikal* (The Complete Works of E.M.S.) (1947–8; Trivandrum: Chinta Publishers, 2000).

——, *Atmakatha* (Autobiography), rev. edn (Trivandrum: Chinta Publishers, 2005).

Namboodiripad, Kanippayyur Sankaran, *Nayanamrude Purvacharitram* (The Early History of the Nayars), vol. 1 (Kunnamkulam: Panchangam Book Stall, 1962).

———, *Ente Smaranakal* (My Reminiscences), vol. 3 (1964; Kunnakulam: Panchangam Pusthakasala, 1991).

———, *Ente Smaranakal* (My Reminiscences), vol. 2 (1963; Kunnakulam: Panchangam Pustakasala, 1999).

———, *Aryanmarude Kutiyettam Keralathil* (1965–7; The Aryan Immigration in Kerala) (Kunnamkulam: Panchangam Pustakasala, 2000–2), 4 vols.

———, *Ente Smaranakal* (My Reminiscences), vol. 1 (1963; Kunnamkulam: Panchangam Pustakasala, 2004).

Namboodiripad, Venmani Mahan, 'Ambopadesam' (Mother's Advice), in Sivolli Narayanan, ed., *Venmani Krtikal* (Kottayam: CBEBF, 1988), 406–18.

———, 'Poora Prabandham' (Composition on the Pooram Festival), in Sivolli Narayanan, ed., *Venmani Krtikal* (Kottayam: CBEBF, 1988), 59–124.

———, 'Srngara Slokangal' (Amatory Verses), in Sivolli Narayanan, ed., *Venmani Krtikal* (Kottayam: CBEBF, 1988), 458–76.

Narasu, P. Lakshmi, *The Essence of Buddhism* (1907; New Delhi: Asian Educational Services, 1985).

Narayana Guru, *One Hundred Verses of Self-Instruction (Atmopadesa-Satakam)*, tr. Nataraja Guru (Varkala: Gurukula Publishing House, 1967).

Narayana Guru, *Sreenarayanaguruvinte Sampurna Krtikal* (Complete Works of Sree Narayana Guru), ed. T. Bhaskaran (Calicut: Mathrubhumi, 1995).

———, *Sree Narayana Gurudeva Krtikal: Sampurna Vyakhyanam* (Works of Sree Narayana Guru with Complete Interpretation), Interpreted by G. Balakrishnan Nair, Part I and Part II (Thiruvananthapuram: State Institute of Languages, 2003).

Nation Master, Encyclopaedia, Internet. http://www.nationmaster.com/encyclopedia/Pandiya-Kula-Kshatriya-Mara-Nadar

Nayanar, Vengayil Kunjuraman, 'Bhramam', *Kesari Nayanarude Krtikal* (The Works of Kesari Nayanar), ed. K. Gopalakrishnan (Calicut: Mathrubhumi, 1987), 54–6.

Nedumpally, Sunandan Kizhakke, 'Ways of Knowing: Asaris, Nampoothiris and Colonialists in Twentieth Century Malabar in South India', Unpublished PhD Dissertation, Emory University, 2012.

Nedungadi, Appu, *Kundalata* (1887; Calicut: Mathrubhoomi, 1987).

O'Hanlon, Rosalind, *Caste, Conflict and Ideology: Mahatma Jyotirao Phule and Low Caste Protest in Nineteenth Century Western India* (Cambridge: Cambridge University Press, 1985).

Orsini, Francesca, ed., *Love in South Asia: A Cultural History* (Cambridge: Cambridge University Press, 2006).

Ouwerkerk, Louise, *No Elephants for the Maharaja: Social and Political Change in Travancore, 1921–1947*, ed. Dick Kooiman (Delhi: Manohar, 1994).

Oxford English Dictionary, Second Edition on CD-ROM, 2009.

Padmanabhan, Mannathu, *Jeevitasmaranakal* (Life Reminiscences), vol. 1 (Changanassery: N.S.S. Press, 1957).

Palpu, P., Dr Palpu Papers, Nehru Memorial Museum and Library, New Delhi.

———, 'Memorandum: Some Additional Notes on Ancient and Modern History of Kerala', 30 June 1927, Dr Palpu Papers, subject file no. 6, Nehru Memorial Museum and Library, New Delhi.

Pandian, M.S.S., 'Meanings of Colonialism and Nationalism: An Essay on Vaikundaswamy Cult', *Studies in History*, n.s. 8 (1992), 167–85.

Paniker, C. Vasava, *Sarasakavi Muloor S. Padmanabha Paniker* (The Poet of Wit Muloor S. Padmanabha Paniker) (1944; Quilon: M.S. Printers, 1976).

Panikkar, K.K., *Sree Narayana Paramahamsan* (Alleppey: Vidyarambham Press, 1954).

Panikkar, K.N., *Against Lord and State: Religion and Peasant Uprisings in Malabar 1836–1921* (New Delhi: Manohar, 1989).

Panikkar, Muloor S. Padmanabha, *Streedharmam* (The Duties of a Woman) (Kadappakkada: Roby Books, 1961).

Panikkassery, Velayudhan, *Do. Palpu* (Dr Palpu) (Trissur: Current Books, 2002).

Parayil, Sujith Kumar, 'Photography(s) in Twentieth-Century Kerala', Unpublished PhD Thesis Manipal University, Centre for the Study of Culture and Society, Bangalore, 2007.

Patrick, G., *Religion and Subaltern Agency: A Case Study of Ayya Vali—A Subaltern Religious Phenomenon in South Travancore* (Chennai: Department of Christian Studies, University of Madras, 2003).

Pattanathu Pillayar, *Padalukalum Bhashapadyangalum* (Songs and Verse Translations), tr. K.N. Subramania Iyer (Quilon: Manòmohanam Press, 1900/1901).

Phule, Jyotirao, 'Slavery' (1873), tr. Maya Pandit, in *Selected Writings of Jyotirao Phule*, ed. G.P. Deshpande (New Delhi: LeftWord, 2002), 22–99.

Pillai, C.V. Raman, *Videshiyamedhavitvam* (Foreign Rule), ed. N.K. Krishna Pillai (Trivandrum: National Printing and Trading Company Ltd., 1922).

———, *Martandavarma (A Historical Romance)*, tr. B.K. Menon (Trivandrum: Kamalalaya Printing Works, 1936).

———, *Prahasanamala* (Kottayam: Sahitya Pravarthaka Co-operative Society, 1973).

———, *Martandavarma* (1891; Kottayam: D.C. Books, 1992).

———, *Dharmaraja* (1914; Kottayam: D.C. Books, 1997).

———, *Ramaraja Bahadur* (1918–19; Kottayam: D.C. Books, 2001).

———, *Premamrtam* (The Nectar of Love) (1914; Kottayam: D.C. Books, 2004).

Pillai, E.V. Krishna, 'Jeevitasmaranakal' (Life-Memories), in *E.V.yude Teranjedutha Krtikal* (Selected Works of E.V.) (Kottayam: D.C. Books, 1996), 583–878.

Pillai, Elamkulam P.N. Kunjan, *Keralacharitrathile Iruladanja Edukal* (The Dark Pages of Kerala History) (Kottayam: The Author, 1953).

———, *Chila Keralacharitra Prasnangal* (Some Problems Related to Kerala History) (Kottayam: Sahitya Pravarthaka Co-operative Society, 1955).

———, *Keralabhashayude Vikasaparinamangal* (The Development and Transformation of Kerala's Language) (Kottayam: Sahitya Pravarthaka Co-operative Society, 1957).

———, *Janmisampradayam Keralathil* (The System of Land Ownership in Kerala) (Kottayam: Sahitya Pravarthaka Co-operative Society, 1959).

———, *Sahityacharitrasamgraham* (A Short History of Literature) (1962; Kottayam: National Book Stall, 1970).

———, *Lilatilakam: Manipravalalakshanam* (Lilatilakam: Features of Manipravalam Poetry) (1955; Kottayam: Sahitya Pravarthaka Co-operative Society, 1985).

Pillai, K. Bhaskara, *Swadeshabhimani* (1956; Thiruvananthapuram: Department of Cultural Publications, Government of Kerala, 1998).

Pillai, K. Ramakrishna, 'Dharmaraja', *Atmaposhini*, 4: 2 (1910): 83–9.

———, *Karl Marx*, 2nd edn (Trivandrum: K. Gomathi Amma, 1928).

———, 'Onnam Pathippinte Mukhavura' (Preface to the First Edition), in K. Narayana Kurukkal, *Parappuram* (Trivandrum: B.V. Book Depot, 1949), i–iv.

Pillai, Kumbalathu Sanku, *Ente Kazhinjakala Smaranakal* (My Memories of Times Past) (1985; Trivandrum: Prabhat Book House, 2006).

Pillai, N. Krishna, *Pratipatram Bhashanabhedam* (For Each Character a Different Speech) (Kottayam: Sahitya Pravarthaka Co-operative Society, 2011).

Pillai, P. Govinda, *Malayalabhashacharitram* (A History of the Malayalam Language) (1881; Kottayam: Sahitya Pravarthaka Co-operative Society, 1956).

Pillai, P. Sundaram, *Some Early Sovereigns of Travancore: For the First Time brought to Notice with their Dates determined by Inscriptions* (Madras: Addison and Co., 1894).

Pillai, Paravur K. Gopala, *Paramabhattarashri Chattampi Swamikal Jeevacharitram* (The Biography of Paramabhattarashri Chattampi Swamikal) (Trissur: V.K. Ammunni Menon, 1935).

Pillai, Sreekanteswaram Padmanabha, *Sabdataravali* (The Galaxy of Words) (1913; 8th edn Kottayam: Sahitya Pravarthaka Co-operative Society, 1977).

Pillai, T.K. Velu, *The Travancore State Manual, Vol. II: History* (1940; Trivandrum: Government of Kerala, 1996).

Pinney, Christopher, *Camera Indica: The Social Life of Indian Photographs* (Chicago: University of Chicago Press, 1997).

———, *'Photos of the Gods': The Printed Image and Political Struggle in India* (London: Reaktion Books, 2004).

Pinto, Rochelle, *Between Empires: Print and Politics in Goa* (New Delhi: Oxford University Press, 2007).

Prabhakaran, K., *Asante Diarikalilude* (Through Asan's Diaries) (Thonnakkal: Sarada Book Depot, 1988).

Prasad, Ganga, *Jatibhedam* (Caste Distinction), tr. T. Narayanan Nambiar (Calicut: Arya Samajam, 1923).

Prasad, M. Madhava, *Ideology of the Hindi Film: A Historical Construction* (Delhi: Oxford University Press, 1998).

Priyadarshan, G., 'Alpam Charitram' (A Little History), in *Keralathile Navoddhanam: Kandathil Varghese Mappilayude Mukhaprasangangal*

(The Renaissance in Kerala: Kandathil Varghese Mappila's Editorials) (Kottayam: Malayala Manorama, 1997), 15–23.

———, *Kerala Patrapravarthanam: Suvarnadhyangal* (Journalism in Kerala: The Golden Chapters) (Trissur: Current Books, 1999).

———, *Adyakala Masikakal* (Early Magazines) (Trissur: Kerala Sahitya Akademi, 2007).

Raja, Padinjare Kovilakathu Ammaman, *Indumatiswayamvaram* (Indumati's Wedding) (1890; Kottayam: D.C. Books, 1979).

Rajadhyaksha, Ashish, 'The Phalke Era', in Tejaswini Niranjana, P. Sudhir, and Vivek Dhareswar, eds, *Interrogating Modernity: Culture and Colonialism in India* (Calcutta: Seagull, 1993), 47–82.

Rajagopalan, E.P., *Indulekha: Vayanayude Dishakal* (Indulekha: Directions of Reading) (Trissur: Kerala Sahitya Akademi, 2001).

Rajan, Roby, and J. Reghu, 'Backwater Universalism: An Intercommunal Tale of Being and Becoming', in Vinay Lal, ed., *Political Hinduism: The Religious Imagination in Public Spheres* (New Delhi: Oxford University Press, 2009), 66–7.

Rajeevan, B., 'Sree Narayanante Rashtriyam' (Sree Narayanan's Politics), in *Vakkukalum Vasthukkalum* (Words and Things) (Kottayam: D.C. Books, 2011), 241–347.

———, 'Sreenarayanaguruvum Vedantathinte Nyunapakshavatkaranavum' (Sree Narayana Guru and the Minorization of Vedanta), in *Vakkukalum Vasthukkalum* (Words and Things) (Kottayam: D.C. Books, 2011), 249–53.

———, *Vakkukalum Vasthukkalum* (Words and Things) (Kottayam: D.C. Books, 2011).

Raju, S., 'Politics and Culture in Kerala: A Study of Travancore State', Unpublished PhD thesis, Jawaharlal Nehru University, 1999.

Ramadas, Cherayi, *Ayyankalikku Adarattode* (For Ayyankali, Respectfully), revised and enlarged edition (Ernakulam: Uparodham Books, 2009).

Ramakrishnan, E.V., 'Vartamanappatrangaludeyum Achadiyantrangaludeyum Vyapanathode Malayaliyude Sahityasamkalpangalilum Bhashavyavaharangalilum Sambhaviccha Mattangal' (Transformations in the Conception of Literature and Uses of Language among Malayalis Occasioned by the Spread of Newspapers and the Printing Press), in M.N. Vijayan, ed., *Nammude Sahityam, Nammude Samuham 1901–2000* (Our Literature, Our Society), vol. 2 (Trissur: Kerala Sahitya Akademi, 2000), 480–504.

Ramaswamy, Vijaya, and Yogesh Sharma, eds, *Biography as History: Indian Perspectives* (Hyderabad: Orient Blackswan, 2009).

Ramavarman, Yakob, 'Yakob Ramavarman Enna Swadesabodhakante Jeevacharitram' (1874; The Biography of Yakob Ramavarman, the Native Preacher), *Bhashaposhini*, 28: 7 (December 2004), 5–10.

———, *Yakob Ramavarmante Atmakatha* (1874; Yakob Ramavarman's Autobiography), ed. Paul Manalil (Trissur: Kerala Sahitya Akademi, 2008).

Ranciere, Jacques, *Dissensus: On Politics and Aesthetics*, ed. and tr. Steven Corcoran (London: Continuum, 2010).

Rao, T. Madhava, *The History of Travancore from 904 to 973 M.E., translated by the Travancore Government Book Committee from the English Original written by Sir T. Madhava Row, K.C.S.I.* (Cochin: Printed at the Western Star Office by B. Fernandez, 1873).

Rao, Velcheru Narayana, David Shulman, and Sanjay Subrahmanyam, *Textures of Time: Writing History in South India* (Delhi: Oxford University Press, 2001).

Reed-Danahay, Deborah E., ed., *Auto/Ethnography: Rewriting the Self and the Social* (Oxford: Berg, 1997).

Reghu, J., 'Sree Narayana Prasthanam Keralattinte Yuvatvamanu' (The Sree Narayana Movement is Kerala's Youthfulness), serialized in *Madhyamam Weekly* (21 November 2003–19 March 2004).

Roy, Arundhati, *Public Power in the Age of Empire* (New York: Seven Stories Press, 2004).

Samarendra, Padmanabh, 'Anthropological Knowledge and Statistical Frame: Caste in the Census in Colonial India', in Sumit Sarkar and Tanika Sarkar, eds, *Caste in Modern India: A Reader* (Ranikhet: Permanent Black, 2014), vol. 1, 255–96.

Sanu, M.K., *Narayanaguruswamy* (1976; Kottayam: Sahitya Pravarthaka Cooperative Society, 1986).

Sarkar, Sumit, and Tanika Sarkar, eds, *Caste in Modern India: A Reader*, 2 vols (Ranikhet: Permanent Black, 2014).

Sarkar, Tanika, *Hindu Wife, Hindu Nation: Community, Religion and Cultural Nationalism* (Delhi: Permanent Black, 2001).

———, '*Strishiksha* and its Terrors: Re-reading Nineteenth Century Debates on Reform', in *Literature and Gender: Essays for Jasodhara Baghchi*, eds Supriya Chaudhuri and Sajni Mukherjee (Hyderabad: Orient Longman, 2002), 153–84.

Scharfe, Hartmut, *Education in Ancient India* (Leiden: Brill, 2002).

Shaji, K.N., ed., *Narayanaguru: Jeevitam, Krtikal, Darsanam* (Narayanaguru: Life, Works, and Philosophy) (Trissur: Current Books, 2002).

Sivayogi, Brahmananda, *Mokshapradeepam* (The Light of Liberation) (Alathur: Mookambika Press, 1905).

'Streevidyabhyasam: Chila Yogyanmarude Abhiprayangal' (Women's Education: The Opinions of Some Experts', *Lakshmibai*, 5: 2 (1909), 49–52.

Surendran, K., *Guru* (Kottayam: D.C. Books, 1992).

Swami Brahmavratan, *Maharshi Vagbhatananda Gurudevar* (Thottappali: The Institute of Vagbhatananda Memorial Research, 1971).

Swamikal, Chattampi, *Chattampi Swamikal: Jeevitavum Krtikalum* (Chattampi Swamikal: Life and Works), ed. K. Maheswaran Nair (Trivandrum: Dooma Books, 1995).

———, 'Jivakarunya Nirupanam (On Compassion Towards Living Beings)', in K. Maheswaran Nair, ed., *Chattampi Swamikal: Jeevitavum Krtikalum* (1903; Trivandrum: Dooma Books, 1995), 747–71.

———, *Pracheena Malayalam* (Ancient Kerala) in K. Maheswaran Nair, ed., *Chattampi Swamikal: Jeevitavum Krtikalum* (1903; Trivandrum: Dooma Books, 1995), 303–460.

Swamikal, P. Sundaram and K. Ponnumani, *Ayya Vaikuntanathar* (Kanyakumari: Ayya Vaikuntanathar Siddhasramam, 2001).

Tagore, Rabindranath, *Veettilum Purathum* (Home and Outside), tr. B. Kalyani Amma (1921; Kottayam: Sahitya Pravarthaka Co-operative Society, 1956).

Tharakan, K.M., *Malayala Novel Sahitya Charitram* (A History of the Malayalam Novel) (Trissur: Sahitya Akademi, 1978).

Tharakan, P.K. Kocheepan, *Balikasadanam* (A Home for Girls) (1922; Trissur: Kerala Sahitya Akademi, 1993).

Tharu, Susie, 'The Impossible Subject: Caste in the Scene of Desire', in Meenakshi Thapan, ed., *Embodiment: Essays on Gender and Identity* (Delhi: Oxford University Press, 1997), 256–70.

Therenjedutha Rajakiya Vilambarangal (Selected Royal Proclamations—From 1811 to 1936 AD) (1937; Thiruvananthapuram: Kerala State Archives, 2005).

Thomas, P.J., *Malayalasahityavum Kristianikalum* (Malayalam Literature and Christians), revised and enlarged by Scaria Zacharia (1935; Kottayam: D.C. Books, 1989).

Thomssen, George N., *Samuel Hebich of India: The Master Fisher of Men* (Cuttack: Orissa Mission Press, 1905).

Thurston, Edgar, *Castes and Tribes of Southern India* (Madras: Government Press, 1907), 7 vols.

Tirumular, *Tirumantiram: A Tamil Spiritual Classic*, tr. B. Natarajan (Madras: Sree Ramakrishna Math, 1991).

Unni, P. Bhaskaran, *Pathonpatham Noottandile Keralam* (Kerala in the Nineteenth Century) (Trissur: Kerala Sahitya Akademi, 1988).

Vaidyan, P.M. Govindan, *Sootikamrtam* (Nectar for Lying-in Women) (Trivandrum: Ananda, 1909).

Vaidyan, Perunelli P.K. Krishnan, *Kachacharitam Ammanappattu* (The Story of Kacha in Ammanappattu Song Form) (Trivandrum: Travancore Printing Co., 1897).

———, *Subhadraharanam Bhashanatakam* (The Abduction of Subhadra, A Vernacular Play) (Trivandrum: Travancore Printing Co., 1897).

Vaidyar, C.R. Kesavan, *Sree Narayana Guruvum Kumaran Asanum* (Sree Narayana Guru and Kumaran Asan) (Kottayam: Current Books, 1993).

Varghese Mappila, Kandathil, *Kandathil Varghese Mappilayude Krtikal* (Works of Kandathil Varghese Mappilai) (Kottayam: Manorama Publishing House, 1977).

———, *Kerala Navothhanam: Kandathil Varghese Mappilayude Mukhaprasangangal* (The Kerala Renaissance: The Editorials of Kandathil Varghese Mappila), ed. G. Priyadarshan (Kottayam: Malayala Manorama, 1997).

Variar, M.R. Raghava, *Madhyakala Keralam: Sampattu, Samuham, Samskaram* (Medieval Kerala: Resources, Society, and Culture) (Trivandrum: Chinta Publishers, 1997).

Variar, P.S., *Varianmarude Purvacharitra Samkshepam* (A Summary of the Early History of the Variars) (Kottakkal: P. Gopala Menon, 1921).

Venkatachalapathy, A.R., *The Province of the Book: Scholars, Scribes, and Scribblers in Colonial Tamilnadu* (Ranikhet: Permanent Black, 2012).

Venugopalan, P., '"Martandavarma": Srshtiyum Swarupavum' (Martandavarma: Creation and Form), in C.V. Raman Pillai, *Martandavarma* (Kottayam: D.C. Books, 1992), 11–50.

'Veettuvela' (Household Work), *Sarada*, 1: 7 (1905), 5.

Vijayan, M.N., ed. *Nammude Sahityam, Nammude Samooham 1901–2000* (Our Literature, Our Society, 1901–2000), vol. 2 (Trissur: Kerala Sahitya Akademi, 2000).

Walsh, Judith E., *Domesticity in Colonial India: What Women Learned When Men Gave Them Advice* (Oxford: Rowman and Littlefield, 2004).

White, David Gordon, *The Alchemical Body: Siddha Traditions in Medieval India* (Chicago: University of Chicago Press, 1996).

Wood, Ananda, *Knowledge Before Printing and After: The Indian Tradition in Changing Kerala* (New Delhi: Oxford University Press, 1985).

Yesudasan, T.M., *Baliyadukalude Vamshavali: Separate Administration Movementinte Vamshavum Avirbhavavum* (A Genealogy of Sacrificial Lambs: The Lineage and Origins of the Separate Administration

Movement) (Thiruvananthapuram: Prabhatam Printing and Publishing Co., 2010).

Zene, Cosimo, ed., *The Political Philosophies of Antonio Gramsci and B.R. Ambedkar* (London: Routledge, 2013).

Zvelebil, Kamil, *The Smile of Murugan: On Tamil Literature of South India* (Leiden: E.J. Brill, 1973).

Periodicals

Atmaposhini
Bhashaposhini
Desabhimani
Dharmam
Kerala Kaumudi
Keralapanchika
Lakshmibai
Mahila
Malayala Manorama
Mathrubhumi
Mitavadi
Sarada
Swadeshabhimani
Unninambuthiri
Vidyavinodini
Vivekodayam

Index